The Blueprint for
Business Objects

Pages #

① outputs of BPR, OO, etc. ⟶ 26, 27

② object fundamentals ⟶ 15

③ BPR requires reeng. of IS ⟶ 12

④ 3 difficult challenges for BPR ⟶ 10

⑤ EM as a jump start for new ⟶ ix (Foreward)
(Enterprise modeling) | learning

(i.e. to inform, motivate, & guide)
to use EM + BPR + OO

Managing Object Technology Series

Charles F. Bowman
Series Editor

Editor
The X Journal
SIGS Publications, Inc.
New York, New York

and

President
SoftWright Solutions,
Suffern, New York

Additional Volumes in Preparation

The Blueprint for Business Objects

Peter Fingar
The Technical Resource Connection, Inc.

SIGS
BOOKS & MULTIMEDIA

New York • London • Paris • Munich • Cologne

Library of Congress Cataloging-in-Publication Data

Fingar, Peter, 1946–
    The blueprint for business objects / Peter Fingar.
        p.   cm — (Managing object technology series; 6)
    Includes bibliographical references and index.
    ISBN 1-884842-20-8 (pbk. : alk. paper)
    1. Object-oriented programming (Computer science)   2. Management
information systems.   3. Business—Data processing.   I. Title.
II. Series.
QA76.64.F54   1996
658.4'063—dc20   96-625
                                                                      CIP

PUBLISHED BY
SIGS Books & Multimedia
71 W. 23rd Street, Third Floor
New York, New York 10010

Composition by Barbara Crawford. Set in Palatino.
Cover design by Bob Potter, McShane & Moore Communications, Tampa, FL.
Printed on acid-free paper.

SIGS Books ISBN 1-884842-15-1
Prentice-Hall ISBN 0-13-242009-0

Printed in the United States of America
00 99 98 97 96   10 9 8 7 6 5 4 3 2 1
First Printing

*Dedicated to those who would excel
in the 2nd era of the information age.*

ABOUT THE AUTHOR

Peter Fingar has a unique blend of technical, management, and teaching experience. He is an expert in information technology education. He has led information technology curriculum teams in both business and academe, and has focused on object technology since the early 1980s. Peter taught computing studies in universities and the private sector both in the United States and abroad. He has held technical and management positions with GTE Data Services and the Arabian American Oil Company, and served as CIO for the University of Tampa.

Peter explains complex technical subjects in plain language. He has authored three books on computing, published numerous professional articles, and presented professional papers in the United States, Austria, United Arab Emirates, and Saudi Arabia. His most recent article related to business strategy and object technology appears in *CIO Magazine*. Peter is co-editor of another new book, *Next Generation Computing*, which was introduced at OOPSLA '95. Peter can be reached at PFingar@ACM.ORG.

FOREWORD

As the business world rushes to take advantage of the Information Revolution, we are going to be facing new challenges along the way. Just as the Industrial Revolution of the eighteenth and nineteenth centuries forced us to rethink the way that we organized ourselves, so, too, is the Information Revolution forcing the same kind of introspection.

As with all revolutions, we will undergo a period of chaos while we straighten out our priorities. Eventually, a discipline, a set of principles, and an entirely new organizational paradigm will emerge to help us manage, monitor, and control the new universe that has been created.

Although some might argue that it is still too early to tell, it is clear that the discipline known as object orientation and its related organizing concepts are going to form the paradigm that leads our charge into the brave new world of computer information systems.

Of course, when trying to solve problems and make changes by using techniques that require completely new ways of looking at problems, organizing problems, and developing solutions, it is difficult to get started. That's because there is just so much unlearning and relearning to do to make the new approach work, for in the world of paradigm changing, one can't really go halfway.

It is precisely this reason that Peter's book is so important. Because of the depth, breadth, and diversity of the challenges that we must face in our movement to an object-oriented world, a work of this nature is essential. By striving to provide us with a framework for understanding exactly what is involved when we discuss object orientation and a road map for understanding what needs to happen in order to internalize it as individuals and organizations, this book will contribute much to making the transition as painless and natural as possible.

Rob Mattison
Author of The Object-Oriented Enterprise

PREFACE

The Blueprint for Business Objects was developed to provide a model of or guide to what must be learned to make informed decisions about emerging object technology and to master the skills needed to use the technology effectively in business. The book's model curriculum was inspired by the workplace experiences of several major corporations and researching the work of leading thinkers. The curriculum, in whole or part, may be implemented in business training programs or in graduate and undergraduate business schools.

The curriculum provides a taxonomy or road map of the fields of object-oriented technology and business reengineering as they apply in the context of business. This book provides insight into the education and training issues facing businesses engaged in reengineering through information technology.

The book develops a model curriculum designed for business and information systems professionals. In addition, it can serve as a guide for self-study. It provides the reader with a road map from initial concepts to mastery-level skills.

The curriculum is explained in detail and accompanied by course descriptions. The reader will gain an in-depth understanding of what skills must be mastered. Trainers and mentors are provided with teaching and learning strategies.

The book includes useful information to help select and find learning resources. Books and other resources are listed by subject. Contact information for companies referenced in the book is provided for convenient reference.

The book concludes with profiles of the object-oriented training masters. These leading providers of object-oriented tools, methods, training, and consulting tell their stories: what they do and why they do what they do. These brief vignettes provide useful insight as they share experience and knowledge gained by the early adopters of object technology.

WHO THIS BOOK IS FOR

Practitioners and academics alike will find material here to inform, motivate, and guide. Many readers will find the book to be a useful desk reference. Professionals in business and government who are charged with reengineering using information technology will benefit from this book.

Object orientation may be viewed from two perspectives: "in the large," where it relates to enterprise domains, and "in the small," where it is applied to user interfaces and programming on single machines or simple networks. The book addresses both domains and thus provides the education and training information needed by a broad audience. Anyone wanting to learn how to learn the new way of competing with the new technology will benefit from the information and insights contained in the book.

The Blueprint for Business Objects speaks to CEOs, business managers, CIOs, IS managers, project managers, team leaders, systems analysts/designers, and programmers. It is a useful guide for corporate trainers, technology trainers, mentors, and curriculum developers.

In academia, the book can provide ideas for the many curriculum development efforts underway in schools of business and computing. Business management and information systems programs are being affected by the changes outlined and discussed in the book. Business schools are beginning to offer management courses in business process reengineering, and their curriculums will no doubt expand to include many of the subject areas presented in the book. Libraries will find it popular with their faculty and their business communities.

ACKNOWLEDGMENTS

Colleagues Bob Ettl of Salomon Brothers, Inc. and Dennis Read of the Technical Resource Connection, Inc. contributed ideas, concepts, essence, and encouragement for this work. Bob's work in developing "infobuilder" and team design concepts gave practical insight into effective organization models. Dennis developed his art of napkin drawing (the art used for most good curriculum designs) while influencing this work over lunch (the only way to get him away from his object development workbench or an advanced object technology book). Ron Aronica, founder of the Greystone Group, provided valuable review and comment. And then there is Jim Stikeleather, a virtuoso of object technology and next-generation business. Jim's insight into this new paradigm of business and his deep understanding of cognitive science and object technology are matched only by his dedication and hard work. Jim significantly influenced this curriculum work.

Some of the companies that are leading the way in the use of object-oriented technology shared their experiences and lessons learned by developing the profiles that appear in Chapter 4. These companies have made and continue to make major contributions to the field of object-oriented technology. They include the Hewlett-Packard Company, IBM, Iconix, Knowledge Systems Corporation, and Object International. Individuals from these companies who made contributions to the book are cited in Chapter 4. In addition, with the vital importance of designing useable human interfaces for object-oriented information systems, a special review of this topic and a practical guide are included in Appendix B, which was prepared with Richard Chimera of the Carm Group.

TABLE OF CONTENTS

CHAPTER 1

THE NEW BUSINESS KNOW-HOW

This chapter examines the business challenges of the coming decade and argues the need to learn the new object-oriented approaches to business reengineering and information systems development. Unlike traditional approaches to information systems development, object-oriented development can be business-centric. It can align business and technology. However, the object-oriented approach requires new systems development roles and new relationships between end-users and systems developers.

The new business know-how is not just about business and not just about technology: it's inseparably about both. This chapter develops a rationale for expanded knowledge and skills and encourages the reader to learn more about the new way of competing in business.

INTRODUCTION

Profound changes are taking place in the world of business. Driven by rapidly advancing technology and the globalization of markets and competition, companies are using information technology to make radical changes in the fundamental ways they organize work and conduct business. The new way of competing demands a sharper focus on customers, cost-cutting, quality, and constant adaptability. At stake is survival in the business world during the coming decades.

As companies recognize the need to change, they refocus on key business processes that ultimately provide benefit and value to customers. This shift results in management taking a business process view of the company rather than a traditional functional view. To undertake this change, organizations need support from two vital disciplines. First, *business process reengineering* enables companies to see themselves as a group of value-adding processes. Second, *object-oriented technology* provides the foundation for the initial and subsequent changes to the underlying information systems.

To take hold, these two disciplines require a third ingredient, the learning discipline. A corporate education and training curriculum is needed to link business reengineering and object-oriented technology together, letting business people and technologists share a set of common principles (education) and then excel in their respective skills (training). Learning new ways of doing business and continually adapting to a changing business environment requires that an organization commit to continuous learning.

Identifying and maintaining process-focused business knowledge is critical. Studying the issues and challenges of business reengineering and object-oriented technology helps to discover the key elements of the expanded corporate know-how for the future. Our investigation begins with an overview of the changing business world and proceeds to a brief overview of business reengineering and object-oriented technology. While the discussion does not go into detail, the reader is led to the key work in these fields.

NEW WORLD ORDER OF BUSINESS

What if something can be done that has never before been possible? What if that something fundamentally alters what is being done? The result would be a paradigm shift.

The capability of the emerging generation of information technology makes it possible to do things that were never before possible. Some businesses have already learned to harness these capabilities as competitive weapons. Competing against these transformed companies will become increasingly difficult.

Companies will seek to dominate their industries by using information technology to streamline management structure and internal operations. They will become the lean and aggressive businesses of the future. Shifts in the paradigms of business competition have already greatly impacted several industries, creating big risks, big challenges, big-name consultants, and significant hype.

In the mid-1990s paradigm shifts are occurring on many business fronts. Businesses are rushing about trying to reinvent their futures through information technology. The issues they face are not just about business and not just about technology. They are about both. Technology enables, business changes.

Appendix A describes the work of leading thinkers and writers who are exploring the nature of business in the twenty-first century. These works are required reading for today's business and technology leaders.

Following are some key concepts that describe the changes taking place in the business world. They are listed here in no particular order but indicate the forces underlying the need for the expanded business know-how described in this book. The list is meant to convey main ideas and is not intended to be exhaustive.

- **Next-generation computing.** The next generation of computing is emerging and has radical consequences for business. It can change the way companies do business by making it possible to radically reengineer fundamental business processes.

- **The network has become the computer.** Computing no longer centers on computers; it centers on networks. Distributed-object computing architectures tie network computing resources into an intelligible, cohesive whole.

- **Global economy and commerce.** Advanced information technology has enabled a global economy. Commerce increasingly takes place on global information networks.

- **Mass customization.** Mass production is giving way to mass customization. Manufacturing industries will be greatly impacted.

- **Time-to-market.** Time-to-market is approaching zero with mass customization. To meet such tight time demands, information systems must be adaptive and support rapid applications development.

- **Long-range planning.** Traditional long-range planning for information systems is increasingly difficult since the technology is advancing so rapidly. Technology infrastructures that support continuous change are required.

- **Workflow technology.** Intelligent workflow technology based on distributed object computing will become a competitive necessity.

- **Business process reengineering.** A new era in business has dawned. It requires companies to focus on core business processes that directly affect customers. Lessons from early business reengineering efforts reveal negative side effects. Confronted with major change, people experience anxiety levels sufficient to lead to dysfunctional organizations. To many in today's workforce, *reengineering* is a dirty word synonymous with *downsizing,* but business reengineering is here to stay; companies, industries, and whole markets cannot turn back.

- **Team structures.** Business process orientation requires multifunctional team structures. Teams are replacing individuals as basic work entities. Enterprises that want to shift to multifunctional team structures require new team skills, workgroup technologies, and motivations.

- **Object orientation manages complexity.** The complexity of emerging information technology and of business reengineering is driving new interest in object-oriented technology, an approach to problem-solving that helps to manage complexity. As a way of thinking, object orientation applies to business problem solving equally as well as technology. Companies are learning to model their core business processes and their information systems together with object-oriented thinking, methods, and tools. Human-centered design is essential to next-generation computing, and object technology can make a significant contribution to human-centered design.

- **New skills.** Current information systems professionals by and large lack the experience, skills, and mental models of the new object-oriented technology.

Much prior knowledge and skill no longer apply due to the paradigm shift of object orientation.

- **General systems thinking.** "Systems thinking" is emerging as a basic business discipline required of both technology and business professionals. Innovative business processes must be tested and tuned through what-if analyses. Through simulation, process teams can learn and continually improve business and technology processes. Simulations continue into production and mirror business operations. When new business problems arise, the live simulator is used for problem solving.

- **Interdisciplinary systems development teams.** The expertise of cognitive scientists; human factors engineers; and simulation, learning, and general systems specialists is now required by information-systems development teams.

- **Learning organizations.** Successful competitors in the emerging world of business will be learning organizations that grasp the business value of knowledge and deploy powerful learning systems. These organizations view learning as a key business process. They design corporate curriculums and implement and nurture processes that deliver continuous learning.

- **Interenterprise corporations.** As business processes continue to be emphasized, "departments" are being deemphasized. Organizations that see themselves as a series of connected processes will soon realize that they are uniquely qualified to deliver some of these processes. Others, they will "outsource." This will lead to an increasing number of virtual or inter-enterprise corporations whose organizational boundaries blur and where each participant provides excellence for a specific set of processes. Customers interact electronically and directly with the information systems of these extended enterprises.

In summary, *economical, better,* and *faster* are the bywords of successful business: economical, better, and faster products and services and economical, better, and faster software. New organizations, technologies, and business processes are needed. Companies require new ways of thinking about business and core business processes, and they need the disciplines, methods, and techniques for making adaptability and change first-class business concepts. Business processes and their underlying information systems must be designed for continuous change.

Not exempt from the challenges of the business world, information systems and computing disciplines are being propelled into a new era by powerful storms of change. The foremost challenge to business today is developing the know-how to deploy innovative business processes through next-generation information technology.

BUSINESS REENGINEERING

Businesses traditionally organized themselves by pooling skills and knowledge into departments that perform specialized functions. The origins of specialization and functional management go back over two hundred years and were first articulated in Adam Smith's classic, *The Wealth of Nations* (Smith, 1776). The principles Smith used to organize work are with us today. The focus has been on maximizing the efficiency of the functions performed by departments, not on the cross-functional processes that deliver benefit or value to customers.

Today the focus is changing. Businesses that want to succeed have sharpened their focus on customers, and the reengineering of customer-facing processes is well under way. When Dr. W. Edwards Deming, father of total quality management, pronounced that the improvement of quality is 90% centered on the system, on processes, the bell tolled for the business world. Those who heard the tolling are now heavily engaged in business process reengineering and the transformation from functional management to process management.

Corporate hierarchies are being flattened. Cross-functional work teams are being charged with the complete management of customer-facing processes (business processes that provide value to customers). This new way of organizing work is impossible without a fundamental change in the underlying information systems.

The enabling technologies needed for process management are far more extensive and complex than the technologies underlying traditional data processing. The new automation does not speed up what we currently do; it fundamentally alters what we do and provides an infrastructure for ongoing change. The domain of automation is being expanded both quantitatively and qualitatively. New disciplines and new players are needed to design and construct the dynamic information systems of the future. The systems development team composition will forever change.

Business process reengineering teams must be experienced in general systems thinking. Systems thinking provides a new perspective to business process analysis and redesign. For example, can you imagine holding up your hand a foot before your face and blocking your view of the earth, the entire earth? Astronauts have been able to do that. The world looks drastically different from their perspective. They see the whole earth. Unfortunately, we only see bits and pieces of our company and industry in our day-to-day work.

Today's businesses need an astronaut's perspective of whole, end-to-end business processes. Systems thinking is a formal discipline of management science that deals with whole systems and with the interconnections and interactions of the individual parts.

Why has work been so specialized and fragmented? Scientific management instructs us to break large organizations down into smaller, specialized units that are more easily managed. This divide-and-conquer approach to organizational design has greatly influenced the ways businesses organize work. Specialized skills and activities are grouped into functional departments. Each department strives to optimize its specialty. However, such specialization has powerful side effects.

Within individual specialties, we lose sight of the overall business. We are deprived of knowing the results of our individual actions on the customer. We do not get to see outcomes in cause and effect relationships. In many of today's corporations, we are locked up in our own departmental worlds.

Unfortunately, when we do not see the effects of our actions, we stop learning. Feedback, specifically knowledge of results of our actions, is absolutely required for learning.

The tough part of corporate reengineering is understanding the interconnections and the interactions of the business processes and subprocesses, the variables affecting processes, and the overall effects of decisions made by the team members. Systems thinking provides the basis for modeling the environment under study, and the long-term effects are revealed by running simulations of the models.

Business simulations have been termed *management flight simulators* and *management practice fields*. Mistakes and erroneous team assumptions can be observed in the laboratory instead of the marketplace. If reengineered business processes are tested in the real world, the very real results can be disastrous. What avionics engineer would introduce a new airplane without first testing it in a wind tunnel?

Software makers that support business process reengineering have introduced tools to build process models and management simulators (Spurr et al., 1994). These include:

- iThink from High Performance Systems, Inc.

- Business Design Facility from Texas Instruments

- Object Management Workbench from Intellicorp

- Architect from LBMS and James Martin and Company

- PTech, Inc.'s Process and Modeling environment

- Proforma's Pro Vision Workbench

- Interfacing Technologies' FirstStep

- Action Workflow Analyst from Action Technologies, Inc.

Systems thinking is also a learning method. Team members can make assumptions about improved business processes and test those assumptions with the systems model. Feedback closes the loop and causes learning.

Peter Senge is Director of the Systems Thinking and Organizational Learning Program at MIT's Sloan School of Management. Senge calls systems thinking the "fifth discipline" and the cornerstone of the learning organization (discussed further in Chapter 3). In the opening of his book, *The Fifth Discipline: The Art and Practice of the Learning Organization*, he quotes Arie DeGeus of Royal Dutch/Shell, "The ability to learn faster than your competitors may be the only sustainable competitive advantage" (Senge, 1990).

Are the new approaches, tools, and techniques of business reengineering too much to learn, especially since we have so little time? Business reengineering, business process reengineering, or whatever one wishes to call it, is here to stay but not in its present ill-understood, ill-practiced form that has so far produced dismal results. Business process reengineering must include the following seven activities:

1. Form and empower cross-functional business teams whose members have a stake in a customer-facing business process.

2. Research and analyze customer needs.

3. Analyze core business processes that serve customer needs.

4. Reinvent core processes using modeling and simulation methods and tools. Radical redesign is characteristic of business reengineering.

5. Develop reengineered information systems to implement the reengineered business processes.

6. Train the business users of the new processes and underlying technologies.

7. Establish a program of continuous quality improvement for key processes.

Before taking a mechanistic approach to these steps, before plunging into reengineering, and before searching for methods and techniques, successful businesses should first become very familiar with the work of Strassmann, Wheatley, and Kelly. Strassmann explains that, "like democracy and religion, reengineering is theoretically a sensible and rational concept. But . . ." (Strassmann, 1994). Wheatley's work explains that "reengineering is the supernova of our old approaches to organizational change, the last gasp efforts that have consistently failed. What is reengineering but another attempt, usually by people at the top, to impose new structure over old—to take one set of rigid guidelines and impose them on the rest of the organization?" (Wheatley, 1994). Meanwhile, Kelly's contributions delve into the basic laws of nature to suggest the self-organizing structures that embody true adaptability in the globally distributed, interconnected worlds of business in the coming century (Kelly, 1994).

The works of these writers should be front loaded in any corporate curriculum targeted at business reengineering. They go below the surface of the seven steps to reveal the real human, organizational, and political challenges that can make or break the entire process reengineering effort.

OBSTACLES TO BUILDING THE TWENTY-FIRST-CENTURY ENTERPRISE

The transformation from function to process-driven enterprises makes good sense and many companies have made significant progress. But studies reveal a reengineering failure rate of about 70%! Business reengineering is much, much more difficult than initially thought.

Three reasons for failure provide an understanding of the degree of difficulty. First, business reengineering is a cultural problem. Second, many information systems professionals currently do not know the object-oriented technology and development methods. Third, although a company is a very complex system, systems thinking is not a basic business skill. These are simple but significant reasons behind the difficulty of business reengineering.

Business Reengineering Is a Cultural Problem

The challenges of the emerging high-tech business world are not only technical, but cultural and political as well. Reinvention and reengineering are threatening notions to the people that operate our businesses. These terms imply radical change, and people do not like radical change in any area of their lives. Perhaps the most significant lesson learned in the early efforts is that business reengineering is fundamentally a cultural issue, a people issue.

A discussion of the emerging information technology in *Computerworld* pointed out that "executives don't understand it. Programmers don't want it. Learning it takes more time and money than anyone wants to commit" ("Getting to 'Aha'," 1994). Though the article was not backed by scientific study, these observations should not be surprising. People naturally react negatively to major change.

Transforming the cultural and the political world of an organization is usually doomed to failure. Paradigm shifts destroy existing power systems within organizations. True business reinvention is not the stuff people willingly adopt. Denial, anger, and resistance are relevant terms here. In the work *The Cultural Dimensions of Technology Enabled Corporate Transformations*, Marietta Baba and her colleagues suggest that successful reengineering of basic business processes requires application of the science of culture. These researchers maintain that "many American corporations tend to view information technology as a solution to their business process integration problems without recognizing that processes are fundamentally human phenomena" (Baba et al., 1994). Companies can safely be advised not to touch reengineering without first reviewing Baba's work and gaining insight into what is really going on here.

Traditionally, work is centered on the individual. But what happens when the team, not the individual, is the primary unit of work? In general, businesses do not know how to empower, reward, manage, or participate in the work of teams.

Cross-functional work teams may have been appointed by top management, and the teams may have been given some training. Team members know they are supposed to be open and creative and that their charge is to redesign current work flows into world-class business processes enabled by advanced information technology. Unfortunately, building effective work teams is not a trivial task. Newly formed work teams are made up of individual members who have deeply ingrained attitudes, habits, world views, and a particular status within the corporation. Inter- and intra-team dynamics tend to pattern after the functional department dynamics that they were supposed to overcome. Turf battles and power struggles ensue.

The job descriptions of many top managers have been recast as a result of business reinvention. The new job description contains language about feeding and caring for teams, shaping shared visions, mentoring, nurturing learning organizations, and applying general systems theory to maintain the interconnections that make up virtual corporations.

The transformed role also means hands-off implementation. In the emerging business order, operating the enterprise is the business of the self-directed work teams—the people who do the work, not top management. To make a difference, corporate work teams must be empowered, and a corresponding corporate culture must be established.

If the prerequisite cultural transformations cannot be made, the likelihood of success with business reinvention is marginal—and the business stakes are high.

Mainstream Information Systems Professionals Are Not Trained in Object Technology

Business process reengineering requires reengineering the information systems function, which in turn requires reengineering the education and training provided in the workplace and in university information systems curriculums. The inertia caused by having to maintain existing "legacy systems" and "legacy curriculums" while trying to make the paradigm shift presents significant challenges.

Technology transitions are neither cheap nor painless whether in the corporation or in the university environment where tomorrow's professionals are being trained. Heavy investments in education and training are needed. The methods and tools of information systems development have changed to a new level of abstraction. Unfortunately, few working professionals have had the time, directive, or resources to make the transition to object-oriented information systems. For example, the design of dynamic user interfaces is a realm where few commercial systems developers have ventured. User interfaces for traditional commercial information systems were generally simple menus served up by the system to guide the user to a data entry or report screen. Essentially, the user interface was a static view of the information system. Object-oriented information systems emphasize dynamic interaction between the user and the system, where the user starts with a goal and, based on a conceptual model of the problem domain, formulates strategies to reach the goal.

Such dynamic human interfaces require multidisciplinary knowledge if they are to be designed successfully. These disciplines include human factors engineering, cognitive science, human-computer interaction, graphics and media design, and object-oriented software engineering. Developers new to the world of object technology are usually new to these disciplines as well. Further, some of these disciplines have not yet adopted object-oriented notions, and thus the literature is sparse. David Collins' book, *Designing Object-Oriented User Interfaces*, is one of the first in this growing field. Richard Chimera's *Guide to Useable Interface Design for Object-Oriented Systems* in Appendix B has been included to highlight the importance of dynamic user interfaces in the design of successful object-oriented systems and to provide a useful description of the development process.

The transition to object orientation involves a steep learning curve. Professionals must learn to "object think," must be retrained in object-oriented systems analysis and design methods and tools, and must learn new programming languages such as C++ or Smalltalk. And the learning curves are not limited to software developers. For example, the changes in the software development life cycle require a new approach to project management. The stages, the increased involvement of business users, and the deliverables in object-oriented projects are substantively different from those of traditional projects. All business and technical parties involved face new learning curves.

The lack of time and resources are not the only barriers to making the leap to the new technologies. How many professionals are eager to set aside familiar approaches and learn different ways of problem solving? How many professors are ready to throw out their class notes, to disregard what they have been teaching for many years, and to become beginners at the foot of an enormous learning curve? Learning anxiety is an obstacle to retraining professionals in both business and the university.

Evolutionary, nondestructive approaches to adopting the technology are needed. Information systems professionals in business and academic communities need incentives, support, resources, and recognition if they are to raise the discipline to the next level of abstraction.

Systems Thinking Not Done Here

As Deming pointed out, it is "the system" that is the problem. Cross-functional business processes are dynamic systems. Yet, today's business professionals are not trained in general systems thinking. From their departmental perspective, few professionals have experience dealing with end-to-end, business processes that deliver value to the customer. Furthermore, the tools of general systems thinking require moderate to advanced skills in quantitative methods, and this is an obstacle for many.

The technological challenges alone can be overwhelming. Mix in the cultural variables, shift the problem-solving approach to systems thinking, raise levels of abstraction, and the true scope and complexity of the emerging world of business comes into focus.

Today, the worlds of business and technology are growing more complex. Managing complexity is the goal of systems thinking, the science of culture, and object technology. Each of these disciplines focuses on the whole, as opposed to the parts, of complex systems. These disciplines concentrate on the interfaces and boundaries of the components, their connections and arrangements, and their capabilities for creating results that are greater than the sum of the component parts.

Mastering these disciplines is to overcome the major obstacles to building the twenty-first century enterprise.

OBJECT ORIENTATION

Immense challenges face business and computing professionals who are grappling with business reengineering. The overwhelming complexity of advanced information technologies and the reengineered business processes that they can implement has rekindled interest in a quarter-century-old software technology: object technology.

Object orientation is a set of organizing principles that provides a comprehensible structure or framework for modeling and constructing complex systems. Computer programs are complex systems, and object-oriented programming principles help tame the complexity. Companies are complex systems, and object notions help simplify modeling complex business processes. Thus object orientation has wide application: programming, software analysis and design, computer operating systems, graphical user interfaces, database management systems, computer networks, and business process reengineering.

As a means of addressing complexity, the object-oriented approach adds useful levels of abstraction for problem-solving. Problems are partitioned into layers. At each layer, the prevalent vocabulary and concepts are used to describe that part of the domain. At the highest level, concepts center on overall enterprise procedures and workflows. Next are the business processes that support the enterprise-level procedures and workflows. Finally, there are the technical implementation details.

These layers of abstraction provide several benefits. First, their interfaces provide stability. Changes made in one layer do not disrupt other layers. Second, once the interfaces are established, parallel work can be performed at all levels. Such parallel work is essential to the development of large-scale systems and programming in-the-large. Third, business models can be constructed using business vocabulary, concepts, and notions expressed as familiar, real business objects. Examples of business objects include: people and the roles they play (stock clerk, head cashier), places (store, warehouse, shelf), things (cash drawer, check out lane, delivery van), and business events (sale, delivery, payment). With object orientation, technology-based details can be suppressed, allowing more focus on the problem to be solved and on the business process to be reengineered.

What are the fundamental concepts of object orientation? Object orientation is a way of modeling real systems in the real world. Within object orientation are several fundamental concepts that contribute to the modeling process. Since people regard the world around them in terms of objects, business and software models based on real-world objects will reflect reality more naturally. Thus business object models can be easier to understand and communicate than traditional computer-centered models. Business people think in terms of people, places, things, and events.

What is an object? An object is a self-contained software package consisting of its own private information (data), its own private procedures (private methods) that manipulate the object's private data, and a public interface (public methods) for communicating with other objects. An object contains both data and procedures in a single software entity or package. Objects provide properties representing a coherent concept and a set of operations to manage these properties. The fusion of process logic with data is the distinguishing characteristic of objects.

Each object is capable of acting in much the same way that the real object behaves in the real world. Objects are assigned roles and responsibilities, and they contain all of the information they need to carry out their actions. The only way to use an object is to send it a message that requests a service be performed.

When a service is requested of an object, the object is sent a message, much like a traditional function call. However, the difference is that the rest of the system does not know how the object is implemented and cannot suffer integration problems if the object's internal implementation is changed.

Object-oriented developers surround themselves with objects relevant to the tasks to be automated. If an office-related application is being developed, objects in the mind's eye of the developer may include pencils, file folders, word processors, spelling checkers, in-baskets, and documents. The developer's task is to create new objects that use messaging to communicate dynamically with the other objects in the application setting.

Objects are grouped into classes of specialization and subclasses inherit the properties of their parents as well as adding their own unique characteristics and capabilities. Object-oriented systems are easy to maintain and expand by changing existing objects or adding new objects to the application. Because the appearance and behavior of software objects mimic objects in the real world, an object-oriented application looks and feels natural—both to the developers and to the business users of the system.

What is the impact of object technology? Business and technology must be tightly integrated if the dynamic information systems needed in the next decade are to be constructed. Because of its focus on modeling real-world business objects, object technology can close the gap between technology and business by bringing technology in line with business concepts, perceptions, and semantics.

Since object orientation can be applied to both business engineering and information systems, developers can work with a single model. This "one model" approach allows business models to be linked directly to the information system models. Business users and technologists communicate better if they work with a single model that can be expressed in business, rather than computer, terms and notions. The results can be significantly higher-quality information systems capable of rapid change.

In the first era of the information age, businesses that had not successfully automated clerical functions and procedures could not compete and are no longer among us. Although this form of information automation—data processing—is still necessary today, it is no longer sufficient. According to Jim Stikeleather of The Technical Resource Connection, "The systems we need to build in the future are real-time, event-driven simulations of the business, not the transaction processing, record-keeping, and reporting systems we built during the past 30 years" (An Open Letter to Vendors, 1994). Simulation concepts are important because they accept ambiguity and multiple perceptions of the same concept.

The seed for object-oriented technology was planted in the 1960s in Norway. Kristen Nygaard and Ole-Johan Dhal of the Norwegian Computer Center developed a programming language called Simula-67 to support the modeling of discrete event simulations of scientific and industrial processes with direct representation of real-world objects. Why, a quarter of a century later, has the business world begun to express great interest in object-oriented technology? The goal of economical, faster, and more powerful software is the driving force behind the paradigm shift to a new kind of software (simulation of real-world objects) developed with a new problem-solving approach (object orientation).

Information systems developers not only need new approaches such as simulation, they also need to develop computer applications much faster than ever before. Since time-to-market for new process ideas is short, it is crucial to be able to develop the underlying software as rapidly as possible. Meeting such complex and rapid software development demands is a monumental challenge.

Reuse and extendibility for rapid software development are basic goals of object technology. Even with the object approach, program code reuse is important, but coding is a small percentage of the total development effort. We need to reuse our requirements models, our testing, our design patterns, and the lessons learned from our prior efforts. This is a principal reason the popular prototype-to-production philosophy is difficult to accept. It neither takes advantage of prior work nor provides benefit to later work. In object-oriented development, "prototypes" are not thrown away; they are reused.

Historically, advances in software development have paled in comparison to those of hardware. The "structured" methods of the past contributed significantly to the development of reliable data processing applications. However, when applied to the application portfolios needed in today's competitive organization, structured methods are strained and object-oriented extensions are increasingly used.

Business process reengineering requires a very tight coupling to information systems engineering. Object orientation can help align the two activities. Business processes and their underlying information systems can be designed together, iteratively and dynamically, over time.

Business processes are expected to change in response to changing business dynamics—so, too, the software. Accommodating change is a key benefit of object technology. For example, we may know some objects will be a part of a given problem domain. However, all of the roles these objects will play are unknown. Object classification systems—schemes used to classify types of objects—need to be flexible to provide an evolutionary approach to business change. The notion of having to write "conversion programs" for each business process change is not practical. The concept of change must become a first-class concept if information systems are to be truly adaptive.

Systems in use today and those being built today are not flexible enough to survive normal business changes, let alone the changes introduced by reengineering. They do not "bend" easily. They do not scale-up. The object approach helps prepare for, even plan for, change through explicit techniques like abstraction and interface–implementation separation. Further, the object-oriented approach partitions information systems in a way that minimizes disruptions from change in any one partition.

An object-oriented infrastructure requires roles and responsibilities that need fresh job descriptions. In their book, *The Object-Oriented Enterprise*, Mattison and Sipolt identify some of the new job titles: object manager, object architect, object administrator, object designer, and object builder (Mattison and Siopolt, 1994). These job titles reflect the roles and responsibilities needed to support an object-oriented information system infrastructure.

Object orientation can make a significant contribution to business reengineering and information systems development. To be successful with the object approach, companies must redesign the software development process and align it with business process engineering. For developers and managers alike, new work structures, roles, responsibilities, knowledge, and skills are needed for the transition to object orientation. Since the pace of business change is not likely to slow, object orientation will become increasingly important to businesses of the future and to the future of business.

SUMMARY

Modern business is growing increasingly competitive and complex. As companies redesign the way they operate using information technology, additional knowledge and skills are needed to master business reengineering and the advanced information systems that make reengineering possible. Essential corporate knowledge must be expanded to include the science of culture, human-centered design, learning disciplines, general systems thinking, self-directed team management, and object-oriented frameworks for business process modeling and information systems development.

The object-oriented approach contributes to problem solving by building on established disciplines and raising them to new levels of abstraction. These new levels of abstraction help deal with the tremendous complexity of business processes and distributed information technology. Weaving these disciplines into a corporate curriculum, a corporate knowledge base, is the subject of the next chapter.

REFERENCES

"An open letter to vendors" (1994, February). *Computerworld: Client/Server Journal*, p. 87.

Getting to "Aha!"(1994, March 21). *Computerworld*, p. 99.

Baba, Marietta, D. Falkenberg, and D. Hill. (1994). The cultural dimensions of technology-enabled corporate transformations. In M. Josefa Santos and R. Diaz

Cruz (Eds.), *Technological Innovations and Cultural Processes: New Theoretical Perspectives*. Mexico, D.F.: National University of Mexico.

Kelly, K. (1994). *Out of Control: The Rise of Neo-Biological Civilization*. Reading, MA: Addison-Wesley.

Mattison, R., and M. J. Sipolt. (1994). *The Object-Oriented Enterprise: Making Corporate Information Systems Work*. New York: McGraw-Hill.

Senge, P. M. (1990). *The Fifth Discipline: The Art and Practice of the Learning Organization*. New York: Doubleday/Currency.

Smith, A. (1776). *An Inquiry into the Nature and Causes of the Wealth of Nations*. London: W. Strahan and T. Cadell in the Strand.

Spurr, K., P. Layzell, L. Jennison, and N. Richards (Eds.). (1994). *Software Assistance for Business Reengineering*. New York: Wiley.

Strassmann, P. A. (1994). *The Politics of Information Management*. New Canaan, CT: Information Economics Press.

Wheatley, M. (1994). *Leadership and the New Science: Learning about Organization from an Orderly Universe*. Berrett-Koehler Publishers.

CHAPTER 2

A CURRICULUM MODEL FOR OBJECT-ORIENTED INFORMATION SYSTEMS DEVELOPMENT

This chapter provides an overview of the teaching and learning challenges presented by the object-oriented paradigm. It presents the structure of a model object-oriented curriculum for business, followed by model course descriptions. The curriculum is a taxonomy, or road map, of the knowledge and skills needed by twenty-first-century business and computing professionals. Businesses and universities can benefit from the model by using it as a framework to design specific curricula that meet their unique requirements.

CAN WE RETOOL? THE LEARNING CHALLENGE

A key influence on the design of the business object curriculum is the learning challenge presented by the paradigm shift of object technology. While well codified in computer science, current business literature lacks the vocabulary and constructs of the technology. Yet both business and computing professionals must learn to "object think" to gain the knowledge and skills needed for business reengineering with next-generation technology.

Learning challenges include:

- A paradigm shift for commercial systems developers

- The lack of a mature vocabulary

- The need to learn new programming languages and tools

Paradigm Shift

It has been suggested that the convertibility ratio of commercial programmers to object-oriented developers is as low as 13%. This may be accurate if it is a measure of how many commercial programmers could get through Stroustrup's *The C++ Programming Language* as an introduction to object-oriented systems.

One mainframe programmer who made the transition to objects described the essence of the new way of thinking: "In any kind of procedural language you are breaking down work flow and coding it. In object-oriented design, you're breaking down events and assigning responsibilities to objects and not really dealing with work flow anymore." ("Mainframers' Transition," 1994) Once the new way of thinking is instilled, the syntax, grammar, and complexities of object-oriented tools and techniques become manageable.

Vocabulary

If object technology is to become mainstream in the business world, its proponents and users need to develop a vocabulary that conveys its basic concepts to potential users. Progress is being made with the publication of the object technology dictionaries such as *The Dictionary of Object Technology*, developed by Don Firesmith and Edward Eykholt for SIGS Books (Firesmith and Eykholt, 1995). The nonprofit Object Management Group, founded in 1989, has also contributed much in this area, but much remains to be done if object-oriented terminology is to become common business terminology.

New Programming Languages and Tools

Some predict that both C++ and Smalltalk will one day become the "machine languages" of the object world as fully developed graphical, object-oriented CASE (computer-assisted software engineering) tools make visual programming and development the tools of choice. Developers will then focus totally on the problem domain, not the technical domain. The object world will be business-centric, not technology-centric. Someday we may be able to work at the requirements and design levels and let vendors handle construction through their tool sets. This is the promise of object-oriented CASE. But today, users of object technology need to address construction issues and gain substantive language and tool skills.

New concepts explained with new words are obvious learning barriers. The approach to learning reflected in this curriculum strives to respond to the needs of most people who are trying to learn a totally unfamiliar subject. The following might be representative of most people's thoughts:

> *Please don't explain new concepts with new words I don't understand when I have no mental models to attach the words to. Please don't overwhelm me with general concepts—show me concrete examples. Please don't teach me the syntax of an object-oriented programming language throughout a course, then ask me to design an object-oriented system.*
>
> *Please do map the field for me. Teach me the details after I have a conceptual map to place the many details I am learning. Please put my hands on the stuff right up front, day one, even while learning concepts. Please teach me to "object-think" before giving me drill and practice in programming techniques. Please give me small evenly paced chunks to consume and some time to sleep on them before moving on.*

The whole-to-the-parts, hands-on approach to teaching and learning is the key to the learning process.

In the discussion of obstacles to building the twenty-first-century enterprise in Chapter 1, a number of additional learning challenges were explained. Chapter 4, "Profiles of the Object Training Masters" describes obstacles experienced by the object training pioneers. These learning challenges and obstacles must be recognized and incorporated into the design of this or any curriculum aimed at mastery of the object-oriented technologies.

DESIGN OVERVIEW OF THE CURRICULUM

The business object curriculum mirrors the emerging state of business and computing practice. Subjects in the curriculum map the business issues to the technology issues. The road map progresses from object literacy to specialized knowledge and skills.

The curriculum carefully addresses the learning process associated with learning fundamentally new concepts and new ways of thinking. For example, the object-oriented programming text by Coad and Nicola is suggested within the curriculum because it is based on notions such as "having fun" and "just-in-time concepts" as it instills "object think" in the learner (Coad and Nicola, 1993). It adopts a holistic approach to teaching and learning. It requires teaching from the whole-to-the-parts in manageable bites. It is designed to teach completely *by example*. It provides immediate, hands-on application of concepts and thus provides the feedback so essential to adult learning.

The curriculum structures the field of object technology for both business professionals and business computing specialists. Although both groups will not participate in all modules, specifically specialized training, the core content of the curriculum is required by both. They should participate in learning activities together since they will be developing information systems together. Nontechnical business users play an expanded role and have direct involvement in object-oriented systems development.

The curriculum model, or parts of it, may be implemented in business training programs or in graduate and undergraduate university programs. The curriculum maps the structure and content. Business organizations and faculty will need to slice, dice, and otherwise package the components to conform to the constraints of time and available technological resources.

Both business and computing professionals must share in a common foundation, a common understanding of the business impact of the technology. Then they can pursue individual tracks to develop the specialized competencies needed to excel at their work. The business object curriculum develops the big picture for both groups of learners and then proceeds with in-depth skill building along more specialized tracks.

The structure of the curriculum mirrors the new approach to object systems development. The curriculum is incremental and iterative. Step-wise refinements in concepts and techniques are implemented as the learner progresses from beginner to mastery levels. Object-oriented systems design concepts and practice are intertwined with implementation (programming) concepts and practice: object-oriented analysis, then object-oriented design, then object-oriented programming and testing, then object-oriented design, then object-oriented programming and testing.

Just-in-time concepts should flow between object-oriented analysis, object-oriented design, and object-oriented programming as the level of complexity is increased. Pioneer Grady Booch describes the process as "analyze a little, design a little, code a little" (Booch, 1991). The unifying concepts of objects in these development activities should be stressed.

The business object curriculum is not a quick-fix solution. The course descriptions suggest that there is an overwhelming amount of material to master, which is exactly why a *curriculum* is needed instead of a one-shot, how-to course.

The curriculum incorporates many how-to books written by experienced practitioners and adds educational principles to optimize the learning process. Time, resources, and hard work are its key ingredients. Theory, practice, and experience are needed in small, manageable packages for the learner to master the object technologies.

Principles and hands-on practice must be broken down into small, evenly paced packages. Learners will need time to "sleep on it," to let it incubate. Moreover, the technology and the curriculum are works-in-progress: the next release of the curriculum will reflect the next release of the state of the art. Business process reengineering is the driving force; object-oriented technology, the enabler. Although object technology can be learned as an entity unto itself, both disciplines should be learned together to assure relevance to business.

STRUCTURE OF THE CURRICULUM

The business object curriculum is a high-level learning requirements specification. The overall curriculum goal is to build journeyman-level knowledge and skills needed to develop nontrivial, human-centered, object-oriented information systems that support reengineered business processes. Three different views of the structure of the curriculum are shown in Tables 2.1–2.3.

Table 2.1 shows modules and indicates the course goals in performance or behavioral terms. The goals are stated in such a way that they answer the question,

Table 2.1 Components, Goals, and Outcomes

Curriculum Component	Goals	Desired Outcomes
The New World Order of Business	Understanding the nature of paradigm shifts. General overview of twenty-first-century business. Long-term implications of technology.	Aware and motivated.
Business Reengineering and Object Technology	Business process reengineering and object technology concepts. Object information systems life cycle and hands-on examination of an object-oriented information system.	BPR and OT mental models.
Learning to Object Think and Program (I and II)	Analyze, design, and implement simple object-oriented programs. Beginning programming skills with object-oriented CASE, Simple C++, or Smalltalk in a nonthreatening, fun setting.	Object-oriented mental models and beginning programming skills.
Business Process Reengineering	Process innovation framework. Understanding the enablers of process change: technology and human resources. Design and implement new processes and organizations.	BPR mental models and skills.
Human Cognition and Work	Understanding how people think while accomplishing work. Role of cognitive sci-	Human-centered design mental models and skills.

Table 2.1 (Continued)

Curriculum Component	Goals	Desired Outcomes
	ence in object-oriented information systems. Design of human-centered, multimedia user interfaces. Influence of mental models and artifacts.	
Object-Oriented Systems Development (I and II)	Problem classification and method selection. Journeyman skills in object-oriented analysis and design. Develop heuristics for implementing a design in an object-oriented language or using an object-oriented CASE environment.	Journeyman-level skills in object-oriented information systems development.
The Endless Skills Pursuit	Develop advanced and specific knowledge and skills. Team learning and mentoring. Developing a learning organization.	Advanced and specialized knowledge and skills.

What can the learner do after completing the module? In addition, the table provides a brief statement of the overall learning outcomes. These outcomes answer the question, What is the state of the learner's knowledge and competencies after successfully mastering the materials at each step?

Table 2.2 shows the roles and competencies required by a typical object-oriented development team. This table is a corporate curriculum derived from the curriculum model. Notice it is somewhat more specific than the model shown in the previous table. This table shows who needs to know what. The competencies are listed in the leftmost column, and roles requiring the competencies are listed in the column headings. A core concepts and principles component strives to develop an in-depth understanding of object-oriented technology and business process reengineering. *Core* means that both business and technology professionals must gain these competencies through shared learning experiences—they are the core competencies of the business. As competencies become more specialized, skills training becomes

Table 2.2 An Example of the Business Object Curriculum

Core Concepts and Principles

An example of a curriculum matrix for business	Business Manager	Business Process Analyst	System Architect	Information Modeler	Developer
New World Order of Business	CORE	CORE	CORE	CORE	CORE
BPR and Object Technology Fundamentals	CORE	CORE	CORE	CORE	CORE
Learning to Object Think	CORE	CORE	CORE	CORE	CORE
Business Process Reengineering	Required	Required	Required	Required	Concepts
Human Cognition and Work	Concepts	Required	Required	Required	Concepts

Object-Oriented Information Systems Development

	Business Manager	Business Process Analyst	System Architect	Information Modeler	Developer
Object-Oriented Systems Development Methods	Concepts	Concepts	Required	Required	Concepts
Object-Oriented Analysis and Design	Concepts	Concepts	Required	Required	Required
Introductory Object-Oriented Language			Required	Required	Required
Advanced Object-Oriented Language/Testing				Concepts	Required
Tool Sets	As Appropriate	As Appropriate	As Appropriate	As Appropriate	As Appropriate

The Endless Skills Pursuit

	Business Manager	Business Process Analyst	System Architect	Information Modeler	Developer
Software Quality Assurance	Concepts	Concepts	Required	Concepts	Concepts
Human-Computer Interaction			Concepts	Required	Required
Object-Oriented Database Management			Concepts	Required	Required
Distributed Object Computing	Concepts	Concepts	Required	Required	
Modeling and Simulation	Concepts	Concepts	Required	Required	Concepts
Systems Architecture			Required	Required	
Object-Oriented Project Management	Concepts	Concepts	Required	Required	Concepts

more specialized. Hence the notations of "Required," "Concepts," and "As Appropriate" are useful in assessing who needs to master what.

Throughout a well-designed corporate curriculum, hands-on learning is needed—at the educational core as well as in the specialized training components.

Learning the concepts and the first principles of new disciplines requires hands-on exploration and reinforcement.

Table 2.3 provides a kind of shorthand description of the level and content of the curriculum. Readers familiar with these books will immediately understand the scope and depth of the course of study. These books are the works of the leading thinkers and developers in the fields of object-oriented technology and business reengineering and are the substance of the curriculum. However, the brief list in the table is not meant to be exhaustive. The titles are simply examples, and new titles are appearing with increasing frequency.

Together the three tables map the breadth and depth of knowledge and skill needed to develop nontrivial, user-centered, object-oriented information systems.

The following pages outline model course descriptions for each module of study in the curriculum. In addition to the usual elements of course descriptions, these include reference to Benjamin S. Bloom's taxonomies of educational objectives (Bloom et al., 1964). Bloom is a key contributor to modern curriculum design, and his cognitive and affective taxonomies of educational objectives have made a major impact on teaching and learning. Bloom gives us a framework to develop realistic, achievable learning goals.

In the course descriptions, overall learning objectives are classified according to Bloom's taxonomy of cognitive domains, which include the following:

- **Knowledge.** Remembering or recognizing something previously encountered without necessarily understanding, using, or changing it.

- **Comprehension.** Understanding the material being communicated without necessarily relating it to anything else.

- **Application.** Using a general concept to solve a specific problem.

- **Evaluation.** Judging the value of the materials or methods as they might be applied to a particular situation.

A large part of the systems designer's competency includes judgment and the ability to make engineering trade-off decisions. The understanding and application of Bloom's learning objectives is essential to our ability to design education and training programs that really work.

Table 2.3 Syllabus for the Curriculum

Subject	Recommended Reading
The New World Order of Business	Barker, *Future Edge* Tapscott, *Paradigm Shift* Martin, *The Great Transition* Gelernter, *Mirror Worlds*
Business Reengineering and Object Technology	Hammer, *Reengineering the Corporation* Mattison and Sipolt, *The Object-Oriented Enterprise* Taylor, *Object-Oriented Technology: A Manager's Guide* Taylor, *Business Engineering with Object Technology* Firesmith and Eykholt, *The Object Technology Dictionary*
Learning to Object Think and Program	Ambler, *Objects Primer* Coad and Mayfield, *Object Models: Strategies, Patterns* Coad, *The Object Game* Coad and Nichola, *Object-Oriented Programming* Korienek, *A Quick Trip to Objectland with Smalltalk/V* Cogswell, *Simple C++* Hands on: Relevant software manuals

Business Process Reengineering	Davenport, *Process Innovation: Reengineering Work Through Information Technology*
	Rummler and Brasche, *Improving Performance*
	With one of the following object-oriented approaches
	   Shelton, *Understanding Business Objects*
	   Jacobson, *The Object Advantage: BPR with Object Technology*
	   Taylor, *Business Engineering with Object Technology*

Human Cognition and Work	Norman, *Design of Everyday Things* Norman, *Things That Make Us Smart* Laurel, *Art of Human Computer Interface Design* Shneiderman, *Designing the User Interface* Preece, *Human-Computer Interaction* Collins, *Designing Object-Oriented Interfaces*
Object-Oriented Systems Development Methods	Graham, *Object-Oriented Methods* Carmichael, *Object Development Methods* Coleman, *Object-Oriented Development* Embley et al., *Object-Oriented Systems Analysis: A Model-Driven Approach*

Table 2.3 (Continued)

Subject	Recommended Reading
	Firesmith, *Software Engineering Object-Oriented Requirements Analysis and Logical Design: A Software Engineering Approach*
	Rumbaugh, *Object-Oriented Modeling and Design*
	Wirfs-Brock, *Designing Object-Oriented Software*
	Henderson-Sellers and Edwards, Book Two of *Object-Oriented Knowledge*
	Shlaer, *Object-Oriented Systems Analysis and Object Lifecycles*
	Martin and Odell, *Object-Oriented Analysis and Design* (3 books)
	Booch, *Object-Oriented Analysis and Design with Applications*
	Jacobson, *Object-Oriented Software Engineering*
	Shelton, *Understanding Business Objects*
	Object-oriented programming books are listed in Appendix A

The course descriptions also contain samples of relevant, exemplary texts that may be considered for adoption. The lists of books are not exhaustive, and additional texts and references are provided in Appendix A. The books have been reviewed for their readability as well as technical content.

The demonstration method of instruction is recommended for the skills development modules found throughout the curriculum. Predeveloped programs and systems should be demonstrated and explained using the following sequence: instructor says, instructor does; instructor says, learner does; learner says, learner does. This method allows an instructor or tutor to shape the behavior of learners in a natural, step-by-step process.

Case studies and stereotypical examples should be the basis of instruction, laboratory exercises, and projects. Partially complete information systems should be provided for hands-on work. Common patterns and strategies must be discovered and internalized to gain journeyman knowledge and skills. Hands-on experience is essential for learning, but facing a blank computer screen is intimidating. Working within the bounds of partially complete examples accelerates learning and is preferable to starting from scratch.

THE COURSES

The following pages present the course descriptions for the model curriculum. Like the model curriculum itself, the course descriptions are models. They serve as templates or guides for educators, mentors, and trainers to develop specific courses to meet specific needs.

Course: The New World Order of Business

Audience: Information systems developers
Business professionals

Relevant Texts: Barker, *Future Edge*
Martin, *The Great Transition*
Tapscott, *Paradigm Shift*
Gelernter, *Mirror Worlds*
Other books are listed in Appendix A.

Laboratory Tools: Discussion and debate.

Duration: Business Course: 8–24 contact hours, ideally broken into workshops, presentations, reading assignments, and discussions over several weeks. **University Course:** This material may be included in introductory computer or business management courses.

Bloom's Taxonomy: Comprehension. Transitioning the existing value sets of experienced professionals is very difficult. Change is never painless, old ways die hard, and real change requires significant motivation.

Desired Learning Outcome: Awareness and comprehension of the nature of mission-critical success factors of the enterprise in the coming century. Motivation to learn more—much more—is a complimentary outcome.

Learning Objectives: Upon successful completion, the learner will be able to describe the general nature of paradigm shifts and the paradigm shifts now occurring that are reshaping the business world.

As businesses reinvent themselves to compete successfully in the coming century, business processes will be the focus. Formal methods of business process engineering are emerging and maturing. Redesigned processes allow businesses to give suppliers and customers direct access to their information base, their computers, and their workflows. Extended enterprises will conduct business on the information superhighway, they are global, and the technology they use erases time and place.

The success of this course may be measured by the number of "ahas" experienced by the participants as they explore the new world of business and relate it to their organization and their jobs.

In addition to gaining a working knowledge of the new business environment, the new enterprise, and the emerging information technology, the course focuses the learner's attention on the long term implications of the technology. For participants interested in the technological underpinnings, David Gelernter's book *Mirror Worlds* (Gelernter, 1991) provokes thought as readers explore the world in the object era. Really new terms such as *ensembles, orbs,* and *trellises* become a meaningful part of the learner's vocabulary as the second era of the information age unfolds in this book.

In addition to the technological environment, the impact on the human condition must be understood. Dr. Tom Milazzo, a Fellow with AT&T Bell Labs, reminds us that companies making radical changes like reengineering tamper with human identity. Moreover, once transitions are made, there is no turning back.

This course must provide insight into the new technology and its impact on business. The big picture must be related to the participants' own business plans and strategies. For the course to succeed, it must bring change home to the participants.

Sample Topic Flow: The nature of paradigm shifts. The new business environment. Business process reengineering. High-performance business teams. Work reengineering. The extended business enterprise. The new object paradigm. Network computing. Critical technology and application shifts. The future business environment. Leadership for the transition.

Key Terms: Paradigm shift, work reengineering, workgroup computing, workflow computing, interenterprise computing, open systems, object-oriented information systems.

Course: Business Reengineering and Object Technology

Audience: Information systems developers
Business professionals
Relevant Texts: Hammer, *Reengineering the Corporation*
Mattison and Sipolt, *The Object-Oriented Enterprise*
Taylor, *Object-Oriented Technology: A Manager's Guide*
Taylor, *Business Engineering with Object Technology*
Firesmith and Eykholt, *The Dictionary of Object Technology*
Other relevant books are listed in Appendix A.

Sample Laboratory Tools: Smalltalk working example and graphical object tool (e.g. PartsWorkbench, Visual Age). Videos: Borland, *The World of Objects;* AT&T, *Connections;* Apple Computer, *Knowledge Navigator* and *Business Navigator.*

Duration: **Business Course:** 24 hours, ideally broken into workshops, presentations, and discussions over a few weeks. **Undergraduate Course:** One semester. This material may be given less in-depth treatment by incorporating it into introductory computer courses.

Bloom's Taxonomy: Comprehension.

Desired Learning Outcome: Business reengineering and object technology mental models.

Learning Objectives: Upon successful completion, the learner will be able to describe the concepts and practice of business process reengineering and will be able to explain the essential concepts of object technology and the object systems development life cycle.

Concepts are reinforced through hands-on use and examination of a previously developed object-oriented information system. Participants will interact with the system and use graphical tools to explore object classes and modify object behavior.

Sample Topic Flow: Rethinking business processes. Reengineering strategies. Case study reviews. The enabling role of information technology. Beating the software crisis. Nature's building blocks. The promise of object technology. Fundamental Concepts of object orientation. Network computing. Enterprise modeling. Methods for object development. Object-oriented languages, databases, and supporting tools.

Key Terms: Process reengineering, workgroup computing, workflow computing, interenterprise computing, open systems, classification, enterprise modeling, OO methods and OO CASE, OO business process reengineering.

Course: Learning to Object Think and Program (I & II)

Audience: Information systems developers
Business professionals with basic computing skills

Relevant Texts: Ambler, *Objects Primer*
Coad and Mayfield, *Object Models: Strategies, Patterns . . .*
Coad, *The Object Game*
Coad and Nicola, *Object-Oriented Programming*
Korienek, *A Quick Trip to Objectland with Smalltalk/V*

Cogswell, *Simple C++*

Microsoft, *C++ Tutorial*

Hands on: Parts Workbench, or Visual Age manuals.

Other relevant books are listed in Appendix A.

Sample Laboratory Tools: Hands-on Smalltalk or C++ workshop with lower object-oriented CASE tools such as Parts Workbench or VisualAge. The problem domain should consist of a real application of the business or a very similar sample application.

One or Two Course Strategy (I & II):   This course may be broken into two courses. The first course can be designed so that business and computing professionals participate together. The second course can provide more advanced programming and tools training for computing professionals in preparation for the systems development course. For example, study of C++, Smalltalk, or an object-oriented CASE tool set can make up the second course.

Duration: Business Course: 24 hours, preferably spread over several weeks with homework. **University Course:** One semester. Note that the programming languages and tools should be the same as those that will be used in the object-oriented systems development course.

Bloom's Taxonomy: Application.

Desired Learning Outcome: Object-oriented programming mental models and novice skills.

Course Strategy: Many suggest that learning to "object think" is best done with Smalltalk, Eiffel, or a high-level CASE tool, even if the target platform will be C++ ("Mainframers Transition," 1994). Because the goal is to develop a new way of thinking, this course must be learner-friendly; in other words, fun, interactive, easy, challenging, and engaging. Let's take a quick trip to "objectland" before getting too serious.

Learning Objectives: Upon successful completion, the learner will be able to use and modify an existing object-oriented information system.

If a second course is implemented, learners are expected to analyze, design, and implement simple object-oriented programs in C++, Smalltalk, or related object-oriented CASE tools. These skills will be expanded in the object-oriented systems development course.

Sample Topic Flow: Modeling and modifying business processes in an object-oriented development environment. Overview of the Smalltalk language: encapsulation, polymorphism, inheritance, debugging and testing. Collections classes. Booleans and blocks. Programming strategies: metaphors, visualization, animation, anthropomorphism, and perspective. Continuous hands-on assignments are required throughout the course.

Course: Business Process Reengineering

Audience: Information systems developers
Business professionals
Relevant Texts: Davenport, *Process Innovation*
Rummler and Brasche, *Improving Performance*
Shelton, *Understanding Business Objects*
Jacobson, *Object Advantage: BPR with Object Technology*
Taylor, *Business Engineering with Object Technology*
Other relevant books are listed in Appendix A.

Reference Book: Spurr et al., *Software Assistance for Business Reengineering.* This book provides an excellent survey of automated tools for business process reengineering.

Sample Laboratory Tools: Examples of computer-based tools: Object Management Workbench, Intellicorp; Apache, EDS Corporation; Business Design Facility, Texas Instruments; Business Development Facility, Virtual Software Factory; CADDIE, Logica Cambridge Ltd.; iThink, High Performance systems; Processwise Workbench, Business Process Management Unit of I.C.L.; RADitor, Co-ordination Systems Ltd.; SES Workbench, Scientific and Engineering Software; and TOP-IX, TOP-IX Ltd; Pro Vision Workbench, Proforma; FirstStep, Interfacing Technologies; and Architect, LBMS.

If business modeling tools and object-oriented systems development tools and methods are the same, business modelers are always working with the same model. This one-model approach has a dramatic impact on productivity and quality of both software and business processes.

A growing number of companies are providing integrated BPR and object-oriented development methods and tools. Some methods and tools support an entire life cycle. Some do simulation only. Some are very expensive. Some were developed by workflow companies, some by companies that specialize in general systems theory and simulation, and others by CASE tools companies.

The tools for BPR and process reengineering are emerging so rapidly that a UK-based company, Enix Limited, offers a business research service that tests and evaluates the tools. *Process Product Watch* reports the results and bills itself as "providing subscribers with practical advice and guidance on the selection and use of technology and tools to support the reengineering, redesign, and management of business processes" (Derek Miers, miers@enix.co.uk, personal communication, October 31, 1994).

Duration: Business Course: 20–80 hours, preferably spread over several weeks with homework and team assignments. **University Course:** One or two semesters.

Bloom's Taxonomy: Application.

Desired Learning Outcome: Business process reengineering mental models and beginning skills.

Learning Objectives: Upon successful completion, the learner will be able to describe a framework for process innovation: selection of processes for innovation; technological, organizational, and human resource enablers; visioning; analysis of existing processes; and designing and implementing new processes and organizations. Processes include customer-facing processes and management processes.

The course investigates the relationships between process engineering and the information systems function. Transformation strategies, the leadership crisis, and the learning challenges are examined and discussed.

Object-oriented technology is an approach to problem solving that strives to tame the complexity of both business process reengineering and development of the underlying information systems. This course should provide an in-depth treatment of object-oriented business process reengineering as developed by Shelton, Taylor, or Jacobson (see Appendix A).

Since reengineered business processes fundamentally change our way of doing business, creativity among developers and business users must be unlocked. In his book, *A Kick in the Seat of the Pants,* Roger Van Oech (1986) describes four roles in creative thinking that can lend some structure to the creative process:

> *Explorer:* Searches for new ideas in new places
> *Artist:* Configures ideas in creative ways
> *Judge:* Evaluates ideas for their applicability
> *Warrior:* Fights for the ideas you believe in.

As learners move through these roles, they can foster creativity while balancing it with sound judgment, neither at the expense of the other. Guy Kawasaki (1994) of Apple Computer recommends another book for releasing creativity, *Uncommon Genius—How Great Ideas Are Born* by Denise Shekerjian (1990). Readings from the book *Intelligent Offices: Object-Oriented, Multi-Media Information Management in*

Client/Server Architectures (Khoshafian et al., 1992) present the learner with a wide variety of notions of the state of the possible as process visioning is developed.

Sample Topic Flow: The human, technological, and organizational framework for process innovation. The three levels of performance. Object-oriented business engineering overview. Process and business area analysis. Visioning and process innovations. Designing and implementing new processes. Walk-through and evaluation of case study results.

Key Terms: Business process reengineering, organizational, process, and individual performance, process innovation, continuous process improvement.

Course: Human Cognition and Work

Audience: Information systems developers
              Business professionals

Relevant Texts: Norman, *Design of Everyday Things*
                    Norman, *Things That Make Us Smart*
                    Shneiderman, *Designing the User Interface*
                    Preece, *Human-Computer Interaction*

Useful readings: Norman, *Turn Signals are the Facial Expressions of Automobiles*
                     Laurel, *The Art of Human-Computer Interface Design*
                     Laurel, *Computers as Theatre*
                     Collins, *Designing Object-Oriented User Interfaces*

Laboratory Tools: Object-oriented development tools.

Duration: Business Course: 20–80 hours, preferably spread over several weeks with homework and team assignments. **University Course:** One or two semesters.

Bloom's Taxonomy: Application.

Desired Learning Outcome: Human-centered design mental models and skills.

Learning Objectives: Upon successful completion, the learner will be able to explain the critical role of cognitive science in object-oriented information systems. Cognitive science models the people system, whereas computer systems developers have been shaped to think of the world in terms of hardware and software systems.

Human-centered design is indivisible from the object paradigm. Winning businesses in the coming century will work smart, very smart. What makes humans so smart is not a simple matter of gray matter between the ears. A big part of what makes people smart is the information artifacts they surround themselves with as they go about their work, solve business problems, and seize business opportunities.

Knowledge of human cognition is a basic competency required of the object-oriented developer. After all, the developer is charged with building affordances to the information highway and on-ramps to the minds of the twenty-first-century workforce. The new world of distributed computing is very complex, and the need for human-centered design has never been so pressing.

Sample Topic Flow: Overview of human computer interaction disciplines and practice. Conceptual models for human computer interaction. Methods and techniques of user-centered design. How people work. Forming the goal. Execution: forming the intention, specifying the action, executing the action. Evaluation: perceiving the state of the world, interpreting the state of the world, evaluating the outcome. Principles for transforming difficult tasks into simple ones. Human-centered design strategies.

Course: Object-Oriented Systems Development: I & II

Audience: Information systems developers

Relevant Texts: A library, not a book, is needed for this course of study. Since most of the second-generation methods incorporate tools and techniques from other first-generation contributors, several key works are needed.

Once a method has been selected for instruction, the cornerstone text should be supplemented with the books referenced by the cornerstone. For example, the Fusion method is so named for fusing Rumbaugh, Booch, Wirfs-Brocks, Jacobson, and formal methods of the mathematics. (See also the following discussion of course strategy.)

Sample of books and videos for study of object-oriented methods:

Love, *Design Masters* and *Choosing Object-Oriented Methods* (videos)
Hutt, *Object Analysis and Design: Description of Methods*
Carmichael, *Object Development Methods*
Graham, *Object-Oriented Methods*

Sample of object-oriented methods to use as a cornerstone text:

Coleman et al., *Object-Oriented Systems Development: the Fusion Method* (with Protosoft's Paradigm+)
Martin and Odell, *Object-Oriented Analysis and Design, Principles of Object-*

Oriented Systems Analysis and Design, and *Object-Oriented Methods* (with Intellicorp's Object Management Workbench or Intersolv's Excellerator II)

Sample of books to supplement the cornerstone text:

de Champeaux et al., *Object-Oriented Systems Development*
Wirfs-Brock et al., *Designing Object-Oriented Software*
Booch, *Object-Oriented Design With Applications* (2nd Ed.)
Embley et al., *Object-Oriented Systems Analysis: A Model-Driven Approach*
Firesmith, *Software Engineering Object-Oriented Requirements Analysis and Logical Design: A Software Engineering Approach*
Henderson-Sellers and Edwards, *Book Two of Object-Oriented Knowledge*
Jacobson, *Object-Oriented Software Engineering*
Jacobson et al., *The Object Advantage: Business Process Reengineering with Object Technology*
Rumbaugh et al., *Object-Oriented Modeling and Design*
Berard, *Essays on Object-Oriented Software Engineering*

Some business-friendly Smalltalk texts:

Lalonde, *Discovering Smalltalk*
Lalonde and Pugh, *Smalltalk Practice and Experience*
Shafer and Ritz, *Practical Smalltalk*
Coad and Nicola, *Object-Oriented Programming*
Shafer, *Smalltalk Programming with Windows*
Savic, *Object Oriented Programming with Smalltalk/V*

Some introductory C++ texts:

Coad and Nicola, *Object-Oriented Programming*
Cogswell, *Simple C++*
Lafore, *Object Oriented Programming With C++*
Mark, *Learn C++ on the PC*
Mark, *Learn C++ on the Macintosh*
Microsoft, *C++ Tutorial*
A C++ reference set for experienced programmers:

Ellis and Stroustrup, *The Annotated C++ Reference Manual*
Coplien, *Advanced C++ Styles and Idioms*
Coplien and Schmidt (editors), *Pattern Languages of Program Design*
Stroustrup, *The C++ Programming Language*

Beyond this short list of books, Appendix A and the *Classified Bibliography* list many intermediate and advanced programming books. Several books should be reviewed for study based on the individual preference and taste of the reader.

Laboratory Tools: See CASE tools listed under the business process reengineering course description. The methods and tools that will be used for development should be one and the same as those in the systems development course.

Duration: Business Course: 80 to 160 contact hours, preferably with study and workplace application intermixed over several months. **University Course:** One semester.

Course Strategy: The design and implementation of this course should vary with the goals selected. Three skill sets must be acquired: Problem domain classification and method selection; creation of object-oriented analysis and design artifacts; and construction using object-oriented implementation tools and testing techniques.

1. Problem classification and method selection. Object-oriented analysis and design methods have strengths and weaknesses relative to different problem classes. For example, real-time systems are driven by the arrival of events; transaction processing systems repeatedly perform low-complexity, high-volume operations; and decision-support systems provide navigation through complex relationships.

The overall goals of a method are to

   a. Perform an object-oriented analysis that describes the structure and content of the domain as well as how it changes. In structured methods these two areas are addressed separately. Object-oriented methods attempt to study them together.
   b. Propose an object-oriented design that meets the needs defined during analysis and is achievable with the available computing resources.
   c. Provide heuristics for implementing the design in an object-oriented programming language.

Most methods use some form of object model to describe the structure and content of the domain. The exceptions, known as *responsibility-driven methods,* use scenarios and contracts to describe the domain. In either case, a list of classes representing the major abstraction in the domain is produced.

There are several options for describing the dynamic part of a domain. Depending on the method chosen, the focus will be on the notable conditions (states) through which the domain moves, the events that cause the movement, or the interaction between classes/objects that causes these movements.

The ability to classify the problem domain and evaluate a method's suitability to the domain is an essential skill and is the first component of the course.

A cornerstone of object technology is the concept of inheritance as a technique to achieve reuse in a dynamic environment. This feature of the technology is often misused and overused. The addition of a powerful concept such as dynamic classification (classification at run-time) confuses matters further. Before introducing language features supporting inheritance, training should be provided in the general area of classification (see the book, *Women, Fire, and Dangerous Things* by George Lakoff).

2. Creation of object-oriented analysis and design artifacts. Artifacts are created as analysis findings and design decisions are made. Artifacts are the deliverables from analysis and design, that is, an object-interaction graph. These artifacts are not a goal in themselves but rather the means to communicate and facilitate system construction.

   The domain used for instruction should exercise both the strengths and weaknesses of the selected method. Several iterations though object-oriented analysis, design, and programming should be made.

   Programming language features can be introduced just-in-time as each iteration is made. On the first pass, a minimal subset of a language can be used, and expanded during subsequent iterations.

3. Construction using object-oriented implementation tools: Like the selection of

object-oriented analysis and design methods, the selection of an object-oriented programming environment should take into consideration the type of problem being solved. The features and limitations of each language or CASE tool should be evaluated with respect to the proposed design.

Issues to consider include memory management and garbage collection, support for concurrency, and the availability of class libraries. The general goal is an environment that maximizes ease of use and productivity while still providing for more technical needs.

Learning Objectives: Upon successful completion, the learner will be able to evaluate and select an appropriate object-oriented development method and develop a simple, but complete object-oriented system.

Bloom's Taxonomy: Application, Evaluation.

Desired Learning Outcome: Object-oriented systems development mental models and journeyman skills upon successful completion of courses I and II.

Sample Topic Flow: Comparative study of several major object-oriented systems development methods (the following sample flow reflects the Fusion method. The flow may vary with other methods): Object-oriented analysis: the object model. The system object model. Object-oriented design: object interaction graphs. Visibility graphs. Class descriptions. Inheritance graphs. Principles of good design. Implementation: implementation life cycle using object-oriented programming or CASE tools. Review and extend programming skills in C++ or Smalltalk. Translation of class descriptions. Method bodies. Data dictionary. Error handling. Performance. Object lifetime.

Course: Object-Oriented Systems Development-II

Audience: Information systems developers

Learning Objectives: This course is a second iteration of Object-Oriented Systems Development-I. Boundaries of the problem domain and levels of complexity are expanded. The issues of scale and architecture can be introduced so that learners will gain experience in team approaches to systems development and programming in-the-large.

As a university course, this is the second semester continuation. As a business course, the duration will depend on the skills requirements for planned systems development projects.

Bloom's Taxonomy: Application, Evaluation.

Course: The Endless Skills Pursuit

Audience: Information systems developers and business professionals who would excel in the information age

Duration: Lifelong learning.

Laboratory Tools: Mentors; Internet discussion groups; attendance at OOP-SLA, Object EXPO, Object World, PLoP (Pattern Languages of Programs; http://c2.com/ppr/about/plop.html), and TOOLS conferences.

Relevant Publications: *Journal of Object-Oriented Programming*

Object Magazine

The C++ Report

The Smalltalk Report

Report on Object Analysis and Design

Wired Magazine

ACM's interactions

Journal of Business Change and Reengineering

OOPSLA Proceedings

See Appendix A for additional information on these publications.

ADVANCED AND PLATFORM-DETERMINED STUDIES

Much of what has been presented in the previous course descriptions may be summarized as "development in-the-small." However, the potential of object technology is realized in business when it is applied in-the-large to an entire enterprise. Enterprise-wide computing introduces a quantum leap in complexity. To scale up to enterprise object computing, the subjects outlined in Table 2.4 must be mastered. Although it is beyond the scope of this book to provide complete course descriptions, the table maps the subjects to key works on each topic.

Table 2.4 Enterprise Object Computing Reference Works

Subject	Book
Software Quality Assurance	Humphrey, *Managing the Software Process* and *A Discipline for Software Engineering* Jones and Caper, *Applied Software Measurement: Assuring Productivity and Quality*
Human-Computer Interaction	Collins, *Designing Object-Oriented User Interfaces*
Object-Oriented Database Management	Loomis, *Object Databases: The Essentials*
Distributed Object Computing	Orfali, Harkey, and Edwards, *The Essential Distributed Objects Survival Guide*
Modeling and Simulation	Fishwick, *Simulation Model Design and Execution: Building Digital Worlds*
Systems Architecture	Mowbray and Zahavi, *The Essential CORBA: System Integration Using Distributed Objects* Shaw and Garlan, *Software Architecture Perspectives on an Emerging Discipline*
Object-Oriented Project Management	Berard, *Project Management Handbook for Object-Oriented Software Development* Goldberg and Rubin, *Succeeding with Objects: Decision Frameworks for Project Management*

Client/server and other distributed computing architectures require specialized and superspecialized knowledge and competencies. While it would not be productive to describe these specialties here, a useful road map was developed by Jeffrey Tash of Database Decisions, Inc. A summarized version of Tash's Client/ Server Infrastructure Road Map appears in Figure 2.1.* The complete version shows hundreds of options for the technology components shown in the figure.

The competencies associated with each of the options shown in Tash's road map represent training and learning requirements. The road map represents a curriculum structure within a curriculum. Nothing less than a systematic learning organization is needed to gain and maintain the breadth of skills needed. Creating a learning organization is taken up in the next chapter.

---

* The complete Client/Server Infrastructure Road Map is available from Database Decisions, 41 Marcellus Drive, Newton, MA 02159. Phone: 617.332.3101; fax: 617.891.0935.

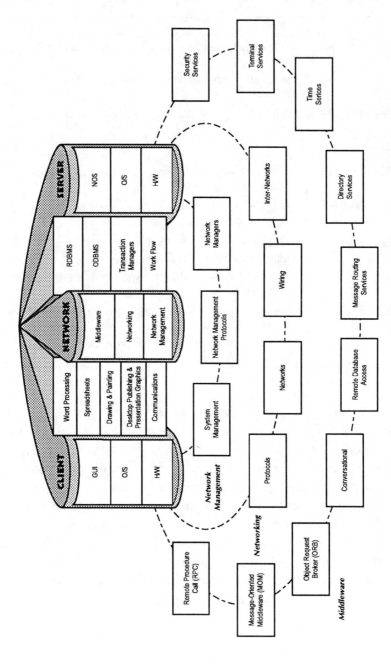

Figure 2.1 Client/server infrastructure road map. Copyright © 1994 by Jeffrey B. Tash, Database Decisions, (617) 332-3101.

REFERENCES

Bloom, B. (1956). *Taxonomy of Educational Objectives. Handbook I: Cognitive Domain.* New York: David McKay Pubs.

Bloom, B., D. R. Krathwohl, and D. B. Masia. (1964). *Taxonomy of Educational Objectives. Handbook II: Affective Domain.* New York: David McKay Pubs.

Booch, G. (1991). *Object-Oriented Design with Applications.* Reading, MA: Addison-Wesley.

Coad, P., and J. Nicola (1993). *Object-Oriented Programming.* Englewood Cliffs, NJ: Prentice Hall.

Firesmith, D. G., and E. M. Eykholt. (1995). *Dictionary of Object Technology.* New York: SIGS Books.

Gelernter, D. (1991). *Mirror Worlds, or the Day Software Puts the Universe in a Shoebox . . . How it Will Happen and What it Will Mean.* New York: Oxford University Press.

Kawasaki, G. (1994, August). Wise guy, *Macworld.*

Khoshafian, S., B. Baker, R. Abnous, and K. Sheperd. (1992). *Intelligent Offices: Object-Oriented, Multi-Media Information Management in Client/Server Architectures.* New York: Wiley.

Mainframers transition. (1994, March 14). *Computerworld,* p. 103.

Shekerjian, D. (1990). *Uncommon Genius—How Great Ideas are Born.* New York: Penguin Books.

Van Oeech, R. (1986). *A Kick in the Seat of the Pants: Using Your Explorer, Artist, Judge, and Warrior to be More Creative.* New York: Perennial Library.

CHAPTER 3

A PLAN OF ACTION FOR LEARNING

T his chapter focuses on practical approaches to building and maintaining learning organizations. What are the issues, strategies, and tactics associated with transforming learning in the corporation? What is a practical approach for reengineering the corporate learning process? How does a company build a learning organization in times of very limited resources? How can unified training and learning programs be designed and developed?

The links between business planning, technology planning, and training are explained. A systematic approach to identifying training needs of both business and technology professionals is presented. Strategies to sustain learning and to keep abreast of the fast-changing technology are outlined.

IN BUSINESS AND IN THE UNIVERSITY, GET STARTED NOW

Object-oriented knowledge and skills will be fundamental in twenty-first-century business. The standards organization, the Object Management Group (OMG), gives us insight into how rapidly object orientation is becoming mainstream. OMG began independent operations as a nonprofit corporation in October 1989, with headquarters located in Framingham, Massachusetts. The organization was founded by eight companies: 3Com Corporation, American Airlines, Canon, Inc., Data General, Hewlett-Packard, Philips Telecommunications N.V., Sun Microsystems, and Unisys Corporation. The original eight firms united to foster the development and growth of object-oriented software development.

Through the OMG's commitment to developing technically excellent, commercially viable, vendor-independent specifications for the software industry, the consortium now includes over 500 members. More information about the OMG can be obtained on the Internet at the web site http://www.omg.org.

An OMG survey in January 1994 indicated that the percentage of commercial object adopters would grow to approximately 40% by 1997 and 80% by 2001. Those surveyed who are already using object technology are planning to spend increasing amounts on the technology (Yourdon et al., 1995). Object technology is rapidly becoming mainstream. Whether considering transformations to object-oriented disciplines in business or in the university, now is the time to develop and implement a plan of action.

A plan of action for adopting object technology must take into account that object-oriented disciplines are works-in-progress. The object-oriented paradigm involves a rapidly emerging, multifaceted body of knowledge and techniques. Thus the goal of learning faster than the competition demands aggressive learning strategies. It requires building a learning organization, making time to learn, making learning an integral part of job descriptions, encouraging multidisciplinary studies and rewarding people for learning. Even in times of scarcity, major resources must be committed for these goals to be reached.

University business schools can make business reengineering and business modeling a part of the undergraduate and graduate curriculums. A number of schools have already embarked on the path. Universities can introduce clean-slate curriculums in business management and information systems. In a less ambitious approach, students may be provided options in existing curricula that would allow them to take a one-semester course on learning to object think and program and a one-semester course on object-oriented systems development. This approach will not disturb the legacy curriculum, and demand for these courses will be high.

Universities can benefit greatly by establishing partnerships with the object-oriented methods developers and object-oriented CASE tool makers. These companies generally place a high value on education and training for their employees and their customers. They know that knowledgeable and skilled users of their methods and tools are the keys to their success. Through educational discounts or creative joint ventures, partnership opportunities abound and offer much potential for universities that want to excel in the new disciplines. This is an opportunity to provide more value to students and the CASE companies benefit by exposing their future customers to their products.

The business object curriculum specifies learning requirements that can be useful in developing a plan of action. The model curriculum is intended to be used as a guide or template to help in designing programs for specific needs, methods, tools, and business requirements, but no cookie-cutter approach will work. The problem domain of the business will determine the appropriate path. For example, development methods that target the various problem domains—decision support, transaction processing, workflow, or office automation—must be evaluated and selected. Much homework is required, but the goal is to adopt appropriate process development life cycle methods and to deploy the right hardware and software tools. Computer-assisted tools are essential as process reengineering is no pencil-and-paper exercise.

Corporations and universities that recognize the emerging patterns of business competition are acting now to build their futures. Time will probably not be kind to those who hesitate. On the other hand, organizations must proceed into new territory with caution. Paradigm shifts are not easy.

THE UGLY REAL WORLD

While researching this book, the author visited several pioneering companies to exchange views and information. In a meeting with one technology training manager who had read an early draft of the curriculum, he said, "Although we are in the middle of one of the largest conversions to client/server computing any company has attempted, our management has one overriding concern: Wall Street. The short-term cost and productivity pressures are so great in this company, why, I couldn't begin to even read the books suggested in the curriculum." Holding an audio cassette containing a summary of a popular business book, he said, "What I need are tapes to listen to while commuting to work."

Corporate education and training strategy must be rooted in the harried, ugly real world of business in the 1990s. This world is characterized by downsizings, layoffs, firings, contract workers, temporary workers, and outsourcing.

In the *Object-Oriented Enterprise* Mattison and Sipolt point out that computing professionals are already being assaulted by concurrent technological and business revolutions: network revolution, client-server revolution, graphical user interface revolution, PC revolution, open systems revolution, flattened organization revolution, work team revolution, and the business reengineering revolution. They explain, "Obviously, with so many other pressures and prerogatives at the same time that object technology is beginning to make its presence felt in the marketplace, it is naive to think that it can have any impact whatsoever without responding to and adjusting to all of these other pressures simultaneously" (Mattison and Sipolt, 1994).

However, the onslaught of new business pressures does not change the requirement to develop the knowledge and analytical skill prescribed by the curriculum. Robust object-oriented information systems, the type needed for the competitive edge, cannot be designed and developed with the traditional data processing skill set. There are no short-cuts and no one-week programmer classes that bring about corporate transformations. The challenge is to develop an effective learning strategy within the constraints of the 1990s.

Enterprises that adopt object-oriented problem-solving will have a different view of doing business that permeates from the board room to the new employee. As corporate transformations are begun, an education and training program must be designed to reach the entire workforce. Herein lies the real challenge to an effective plan of action: How do we reeducate and retrain an entire workforce in times of chaos, business and economic uncertainty, and increasing pressure to produce more with less?

While it would be fabulous to establish a corporate Object-Oriented University and formally teach the entire object curriculum to all employees, the chances of doing so are minimal. Training budgets have always been one the first to be cut in trying times. Now is not the time to propose grandiose training schemes. However, now is the time to take a significant first step: to study the entire curriculum and then tailor it to fit the time and resource constraints.

Perhaps surviving and learning in a particular organization means buying or borrowing books and working with hands-on tools on a personal computer. Not many businesses are willing to make the huge training investment it can take to make the paradigm shift to objects in one major step. Yet most computing professionals know they must learn the new approach, and they can.

Learning on Your Own

Is it possible to learn without an instructor? How about self-study? Sure it is possible, but because we are talking about a new way of thinking, a paradigm shift, the road will be tough to navigate without a guide. Self-study with a practicing object developer serving as a mentor will likely be a practical strategy. Having a mentor, however, is essential. The learning process will be more productive if small teams of interested people work together, sharing information, providing feedback, and assisting each other over hurdles along the way.

Even if classroom training is available, the knowledge and skill levels contained in this curriculum require doing, and doing in the live business world, for real, over time. Along the way, mistakes are to be expected. The mentor's role is not to prevent mistakes but to use the experience to shape learning.

Read a Lot

Use the "Essential Object-Oriented Library for Business" provided in Appendix A as a guide. Find relevant courses at a local university or community college. Buy David Marks' books on learning C++ or Gene Korienek's *Quick Trip to Objectland*. Buy Smalltalk and C++ software for a personal computer (college students can get significant discounts). Join special interest groups. Read more. Get on the Internet immediately (see tactic 8 later in this chapter). Take that new object developer friend to lunch, and do not forget to get his or her e-mail address. Take that next vacation at the OOPSLA conference. Just do it.

Corporate Learning

Large organizations, on the other hand, require the development of formal processes of education and training to achieve organization-wide understanding and cohesion. Large organizations are complex cultural systems, and the science of culture must be mastered if effective learning organizations are to be created. The following section describes a more formal approach to developing and delivering information, education, and training across an enterprise. This systematic approach to curriculum definition, program design, delivery, and ownership of training responsibility is needed if companies are to gain maximum return on their education and training investment.

A UNIFIED APPROACH TO EDUCATION AND TRAINING

Informed and competent people are the key to information systems that can be deployed as strategic business weapons. Although business users of information systems need not know the internals of the technology, they require sufficient knowledge of the business potential and impact of technology, and need to continually gain new hands-on information skills. Business people must maintain a working knowledge of how the emerging technology can be harnessed for competitive advantage. This knowledge and these skills provide the foundation of the enterprise of the future.

Today's competitive enterprises are *learning organizations*. They must be. At heart of a learning organization is an education and training process that enables the continued growth and development of both information systems professionals and business users of information systems. That means an entire workforce must develop new skills and acquire new knowledge continuously. This is no small order.

As shown in Figure 3.1, the business plans of an enterprise drive the information systems, corporate work group, and individual work plans. The work requirements derived from these plans determine the competency requirements, which, in turn, determine the education and training requirements. This systematic approach to developing training plans is essential if scarce resources are to be maximized.

The traditional approach to information systems training has centered on specific technical skills. What is the common scenario? Crash courses in programming, job control languages, systems development methods, and CASE tools have been implemented in response to the acquisition of new software, hardware, or applications. Companies that provided hardware and software, the vendors, were the source of much training. The training was often limited to specialists and technicians on a need-to-know basis. Much training has been restricted to the information

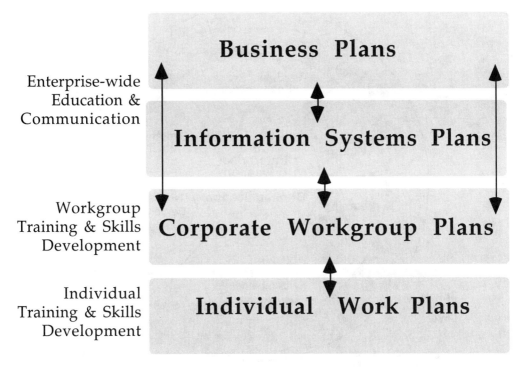

Figure 3.1. Relationships of planning, training, and skills development.

systems department and thus separated from an organization's mainstream career paths and training programs.

This limited approach to training is no longer sufficient. Every employee should be provided both continuing education and training related to technology and the specific business plans of the company. A unified approach to curriculum and training development is necessary. Guidelines for a unified approach appear in Figure 3.2. The model shows a layered approach to education and training.

The purpose of the core education and communication layer is to provide enterprise-wide understanding about the capabilities and impact of information technology and its planned deployment in the enterprise. Where are we going? Why? How do we get there? What is my role? Education and ongoing communications provided by a business keeps all employees abreast of the technology, its potential impact, and company business and technology plans. This common pool of understanding is needed to increase utilization of technology and foster the

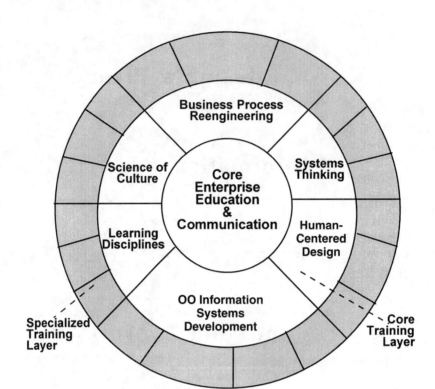

Figure 3.2 A unified approach to education and training.

working relationships needed among business users, systems developers, and management. It keeps the entire workforce in-the-know. Informed business decisions require an in-depth understanding of the emerging technologies.

Regular briefings, seminars, telecasts, newsletters, electronic discussion groups, and other means of company education and communications can accomplish the following:

- Provide all employees with a working knowledge of technology and how it is being deployed in the business

- Foster a better understanding of the cross-functional work groups that are developing and supporting the technology infrastructure and the new object-oriented applications

- Explain the roles and responsibilities of work groups and their relationships to other work groups

- Provide all employees with the opportunity to keep abreast of emerging technology and business practice

- Keep all employees informed about changes and new plans for technology resources within the enterprise.

Both business and technology workers should participate in these activities together. Communication, understanding, and other essentials of solid working relationships are fostered by joint participation. Interaction and exchange can lead to common attitudes of mind. Teams that learn together excel together.

Programs developed and offered by universities, educational broadcasters, and technology firms such as the Computer Channel, Inc. can go a long way toward keeping an entire workforce current with business technology developments.

Forty years ago in his paper "The Impact of Communications on Productivity," William Oncken told the story of sagging productivity aboard a submarine (Oncken, 1954). It seems that even in times of war, productivity can sag.

When people are not necessarily doing what they are supposed to do, the boilers do not produce quite enough steam. The problem aboard the sub was that the folks in the bowels of the ship were not kept informed of their position, where the enemy was, or where they were going. The solution was simply to turn on the microphone of the guy with the periscope. The public address system gave the entire ship a view of what was on the horizon and the plan of attack. Suddenly, the boilers were at full steam.

People want to know. We are "explaining" creatures. The need for explanations is a fundamental part of the human condition. In the battles for the twenty-first-century marketplace, people need to be constantly in-the-know.

Education and communication programs must be interesting and motivating. The goal is to have all workers pulling together in well-defined directions. Building shared vision is also achieved when technology and business professionals participate together in learning experiences. This is one way to keep business and technology from drifting apart.

If education and communication programs inform and clarify what must be done, the goal of training is to learn how to do what must be done. Learning progresses from knowing to doing, from understanding to skills competencies.

While the education and communication center of this model keeps people in-the-know, the training layers provide the know-how, the analytical competencies and skills. Specialized skills training layers shown in the model reach more segmented groups than the education and communication program. Skills quickly become specialized and superspecialized, and the half-life for technology skills is short. For these reasons, careful skills needs analyses must be conducted continually to determine which employees need what training to do what job.

From the needs tabulation, cost effective selection of training courses can be made available from many sources. Object-oriented training and consulting firms, object-oriented methods providers, video-based learning, computer-based training, in-house courses, and on-the-job training are some of the many alternatives. The appropriate mix can be determined by the cost/benefit in relation to the number of people needing specific training.

KEY STEPS TO ESTABLISHING A LEARNING ORGANIZATION

Peter Senge asserts it is possible to create learning organizations. In addition to the cornerstone, systems thinking, he describes four other core disciplines required to build such an organization (Senge, 1990). The core disciplines include personal mastery, working with mental models, building shared vision, and team learning. These disciplines are not necessarily in the policy manuals of personnel departments of today's corporations nor in the realm of our individual thinking.

The entities of teams and organizations can learn, but the learning structures are complex. Individual learning and personal mastery are prerequisite to team learning. Team learning is prerequisite to organizational learning, and learning disabilities abound in all three domains.

Learning is often a painful experience as it disturbs existing, deeply ingrained assumptions, beliefs, and generalizations (mental models) we use to get through the work day, through life. The pain level can be so significant that adults practice defensive procedures in learning situations that threaten their existing mental models.

The discipline of working with mental models is a vital enabler of change, the kind of change needed for corporate transformations. Paradigm shifts require direct manipulation of underlying mental models. Why? Learners are not simply updating or adding to their current knowledge. Instead, they are fundamentally altering the way they think, creating new mental attitudes and altering the way they view their world. Successful corporations of the twenty-first century will systematically manage their mental models.

Team learning, in contrast to individual learning, must be given special attention. Like individuals, teams must also learn. Teams often have built-in learning dysfunctions as a result of the individual behavior of team members. Senge asks, "How can a team of committed managers with individual IQs above 120 have a collective IQ of 63?" On the other hand, successful teams know how to do team learning, and the collective intelligence of the team exceeds the sum of the individual IQs.

Whether we speak of departments or cross-functional work teams, the team, not individuals, is the locus of activity and learning. Sports teams exemplify team learning where total team performance is greater than the sum of the performances of the individual players. That is why teams gel during the season to create something extraordinary. But when the all-star teams are formed at the end of the season, the collections of individual stars produce less than optimal teams. All-star teams are often clumsy. They have had too little time for team learning.

A picture of the future is required if we are to know where we are going and what we are trying to build. Corporations cannot possibly arrive at their destinations if they do not have a clear vision of where that is. Few concepts are more mysterious than corporate vision: shared visions are not pearls of wisdom handed down from an enlightened CEO. Shared vision boils up from individual vision. Shared vision brings about common directions, focus, and the motivation for personal, team, and organizational learning. With genuine shared vision, not imposed corporate vision statements, all workers are able to keep their eyes on the prize. Senge provides insight into how such a vague concept as shared vision can be developed.

When corporations react to threats from global competition by forming high-performance work teams to reengineer business processes, failure can be expected unless the five disciplines of a learning organization are understood and mastered. The often-quoted 70% failure rate of early reengineering efforts clearly indicates this is no trivial undertaking.

Empowered, self-directed work teams are clearly at odds with the traditional manager who does the thinking, makes the key decisions, and directs others. Heros are at odds with the learning organization. True learning organizations need designers, stewards, and teachers in leadership roles. These concepts may disturb the mental models of traditional leaders but are at the core of successful corporate transformations.

What is the bottom line? Systemic business reinvention is nearly impossible. If the deep cultural transformations cannot be made, starting at the top, process reengineering will likely be a waste of time, and corporations that do not make real transformations should not plan to be around in the coming century. The agent for change is continuous learning.

A LEARNING ARCHITECTURE

Because the agent for change is continuous learning, an architecture for learning is required if meaningful change is to be sustained. The corporate goal is the insertion of object-oriented technologies into an already complex environment. This means that successful transition strategies must start small, build proof-of-concept prototypes, increment the scope of the problem domain, and iterate. The key to successful transitions is to take small, incremental steps. Each step requires three fundamental learning actions: inform, educate, and train. As shown in Figure 3.3, these three fundamental activities provide a blueprint or architecture for learning that can be applied throughout the process of developing next-generation know-how.

Inform

Object-oriented technology and business reengineering knowledge is evolving very rapidly. People working with the technology must keep abreast of both the fast-changing technology and the company's plans and projects that involve the technology.

Educate

While training is key to acquiring the skills needed, concepts and theory are prerequisite to training. Exploration and discovery are key goals of educating. Learners should be provided with a nonthreatening, nonpressured opportunity to learn new concepts. As the goal is to develop a new way of thinking, educational activities must be learner-friendly; that is, fun, interactive, easy, challenging, and engaging. Let's develop the big picture before facing the many details and techniques of the technology. Since we are reshaping existing mental models, we must be careful to meet the learners where they are as they participate in educational experiences.

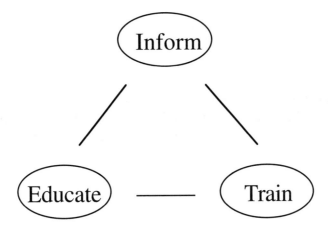

Figure 3.3 A learning architecture.

Education means formulating concepts and learning first principles in the new paradigm. Conceptual learning is prerequisite to learning new skills.

Train

Being informed helps us understand the "why." Being educated in the basic theories helps us to learn "what." Training provides the "how-to." Training should be centered in doing. The most effective means of learning a task is to perform that task. To be effective, the performance of the stated task must be based on actual project deliverables.

Once a learning step has been completed, the scope can be expanded, and the next iteration can proceed with additional information, education, training, and experience. The transition requires heuristics as there are no cookbook or silver bullet solutions. Learn a little, apply a little; learn a little, apply a little. Each iteration increases the overall understanding of the object paradigm and the deepening understanding fosters better decision-making for the next iteration.

ACTION STRATEGIES AND 26 TACTICS FOR LEARNING

Within the context of applying a learning architecture, any of a number of tactics may be deployed. Which ones will depend on the state of the organization. The "architecting" of a learning organization requires the same rigorous analysis and planning as any major human endeavor. Planning and implementation of learning programs are straightforward, common-sense activities:

1. Determine the business and technology environment. Review the long-range goals of the business and information systems plans and analyze the near-term operating plans associated with each key business process.

2. Determine the human resources, roles, and responsibilities needed to empower the business process and technology environment.

3. Document jobs in terms of skills required, activities performed, and standards that define performance.

4. Conduct skills needs assessments that tabulate existing skills against needed skills to yield discrepancies.

5. Count discrepancies to determine training needs.

6. Match and prioritize training needs to financial and other business constraints.

7. Determine the curriculum and course strategies.

8. Make or buy training programs or modules.

9. Deliver or avail the training.

10. Evaluate the effectiveness of the training.

11. Repeat steps 1–10 since there is no sign of business technology slowing its pace of advancement.

These common-sense steps have long been in practice in training departments of large organizations. Annual training needs analyses and annual training schedules are common. Though the planning and implementation steps are much the same for a traditional training department and a "learning organization," the context is radically different. Here is what's different:

- Training needs analyses must be continuous to keep pace with dynamic training needs.

- Training must be on demand, just-in-time, not on an annual training schedule. Learning occurs everywhere, all the time, and in many different ways.

- Training must go beyond the walls of training classes and onto the electronic desktop.

- Learning must include surrounding workers with information artifacts, not just provide training classes.

- Ownership of training must be with business process work teams, not traditional training departments. This approach is needed to make learning an integral part of the reengineering process rather than an after-the-fact turnover to a corporate training department. Traditional training departments transform into new support and facilitation roles.

To architect a learning organization that can meet the enormous, diverse, and widespread needs of corporations in the next century, the process of corporate learning must be reengineered. In his book, *Re-Educating the Corporation*, Dan Tobin provides the rationale, the principles, prerequisites, and foundations for the learning organization (Tobin, 1993). He describes how a corporation can breathe life into a learning organization, how to embrace new ways of learning, and how to create a virtual training organization.

Education and training plans and processes are required on three levels:

1. The overall organization or enterprise

2. The cross-functional work teams

3. The individual members of these teams.

In their work *Improving Performance,* Rummler and Brache use these three levels in addressing performance improvement (Rummler and Brache, 1990). Education and training are the enablers of performance improvement and are integral parts of their three-level management strategy.

The collective knowledge and skills developed and maintained at these three levels are the knowledge base of a corporation. The process of developing and nurturing this knowledge base is so critical that it is a mission-critical business process. A corporate knowledge base process can be formed to develop innovative processes for knowledge acquisition, maintenance, and availability. This knowledge base can be viewed as a strategic competitive weapon.

Much of the knowledge base can be codified into a computer-based repository of the methods, business models, tools, software, information-systems models, and skills inventories of the workforce. Associated computer-based training, discussion groups, FAQS (frequently asked questions), process models, simulators, and other artifacts would be available to all workers from their desktops. Additionally, the online knowledge base would have links to the outside world through the Internet.

With this overall picture in mind, several tactics may be considered to provide continuous learning. These tactics are not sequential steps in a checklist but individual tactics that can prove useful for learning organizations seeking the ability to learn faster than the competition.

A first review of the tactics may seem overwhelming. However, the intent is not to overwhelm but to stimulate thinking about learning challenges in business. Some tactics will be immediately relevant. For example, a company wanting to learn more about object orientation may want to upgrade its corporate library. Team members can consume some of the selected titles and provide summaries to those who do not need the full text. As teams develop learning plans and processes, the tactics can help by providing ideas and guidance.

1. Commit to Building a Learning Organization

Training and learning can no longer be perceived as expenses: they must be viewed as investments. Years ago the computer training company Deltak used the slogan, "If you think training is expensive, consider the cost of ignorance," to make a point with their corporate clients. Without the commitment of adequate resources, corporate learning simply will not happen.

Creating a learning organization requires a leap of faith. Dan Tobin describes the leap of faith as breathing life into the learning organization: "Bringing life into the learning organization is in many ways similar to bringing life to a child. The newborn first needs a shock to its system to get it started. Then, it needs constant care and nurturing as it learns about its new world." (Tobin, 1993) Tobin's approach for breathing life into a learning organization begins with the need for a well-considered decision to have the child in the first place. The decision is not to be taken lightly.

2. Integrate Business, Technology, and Learning

Integration of business, technology, and learning activities keeps projects in context and unified. Business reengineering and systems development methods should be one and the same and tightly linked to training and learning. Some approaches to business process reengineering use traditional input-process-output ideas to define and understand business processes. This is a functional view that runs counter to object-oriented conventions. By using objects to model business processes reengineering teams can work with a single, integrated approach to business modeling that more naturally reflects the true semantics of the business. More meaningful models can be achieved, and learning can be more focused.

3. Place the Locus of Training in the Corporate Work Team

Responsibility for education and training should reside with the cross-functional work groups. This is where the discipline knowledge and competency is based. Decisions regarding who needs to learn what must be with the corporate work teams. Furthermore, these decisions should be driven by the learning requirements uncovered during the reengineering process. Corporate work teams should identify the learning requirements of new business processes throughout the process of reengineering.

Although work groups are responsible for the content and effectiveness of training, they cannot be expected to do the development and delivery of training, at least not all of it. Instead, work groups act in a consumer role demanding the best they can get from training departments, outside training and consulting companies, hardware and software vendors, and the on-job-training skills of the work group. Teams will need to carefully consider how they can make sure the resources are available so that workers and teams can train themselves as much as possible.

4. Reengineer the Corporate Learning Process

As discussed earlier, Rummler and Brasche approach performance improvement by using a three-level framework where organization, team, and individual performance objectives are identified. These performance objectives can be used as the basis of conducting learning needs assessments.

Learning needs assessments reveal the learning impact on individuals, teams, and the overall enterprise as the result of reengineered business processes. Often, such assessments can reveal overwhelming training needs that could not possibly be met with traditional classroom training. Education specialists are needed to provide the expertise to make cost/benefit assessments of alternative learning solutions and optimize the learning processes. Existing corporate learning processes are ripe for reengineering through information technology.

5. Distribute Learning Everywhere

With technology education and training requirements no longer isolated to the information systems department, the audience for technology training programs increases manyfold. Education and training are needed throughout the workforce: customized mass training is needed to meet a massive need. Training must be just-in-time and available everywhere it is needed.

The most practiced form of training for technology and business professionals has been the classroom, often a vendor's classroom. To meet today's needs for enterprise-wide education and training, traditional classroom methods are totally inadequate. There is simply too much to learn, by too many people, with too little time, with too few qualified instructors, and the incredibly high cost of classroom training is prohibitive.

The search for effective and financially reasonable education and training solutions is on. Educational technology is a fast-growing segment of the information industry due to the cost-effectiveness and richness of interactive multimedia. The learner can be in full control, and soon interactive courses will be readily available on the Internet where many useful training and discussion groups already exist.

Distance learning technologies and the community of universities and businesses who provide distance learning are currently in the midst of a renaissance. The ubiquitous Internet makes something new start to happen. With the deployment of multimedia-strength bandwidth, the locus of much of the world's education and training enterprise will likely be the Internet. The Internet will become the school yard for life long education and training.

Technology training companies such as Ireland-based CBT Systems, Ltd., NETG of Naperville, and Learn PC of Minneapolis offer interactive courses that are delivered over local area networks. Microsoft and others have introduced video servers that allow video-on-demand. Technologies such as these tear down the walls of the classroom.

Video teleconferencing provides full, face-to-face communication, and interactive multimedia courseware can be available from virtually any desktop. Video-enhanced e-mail can open powerful means of communications, bringing new dimensions to the flat memo-like mail of today. At this year's national Computer Training and Support conference, one firm displayed its online books system, which can implement a corporate electronic library on a company's existing networks.

Using what Ross Bott of Silicon Graphics, Inc. calls a "file server on steroids," the Vanguard Group, Inc. trains 400 advisors with existing PC-based local area networks and Starlight Networks, Inc. video server products ("Video server big picture," 1994). Vanguard is deploying digitized video technology as a strategic learning weapon in a knowledge-based service industry. They clearly intend that their advisors learn faster than the competitors' advisors. Vanguard performance measurements of their educational technology showed significant cuts in required training time and major improvements in retention of the knowledge acquired.

Wherever workers have access to such networks, they have access not only to information but to learning. They are in control of their individual exploring and learning processes. Interactive, digital learning platforms can accelerate learning and can be implemented geographically across the globe through advanced networks.

Once confined to training departments, technical specialists, specific business units, and classrooms, training in the coming century will be distributed everywhere there is a worker. Computer-mediated learning, distance learning, mentors, electronic references, electronic discussion groups, digital libraries, and much more will be available from the desktop. Embedded performance support systems can help navigate these diverse learning resources. To go beyond the walls of traditional classroom training, Tobin provides principles for building a virtual training organization, the kind of training organization needed for the future.

6. Do Technology Transfer

Making a change of the magnitude of shifting to a new paradigm has one obvious problem. If a company wishes to adopt new ways of thinking about business and technology and new ways of doing business, the "new" part means it does not now have experience in the new paradigm.

Two solutions to this problem are to hire new employees who do have the appropriate knowledge and experience or outsource to consulting and training firms. Such firms offer blends of apprenticeships, mentoring, coaching, contract systems development, and project management.

Over the years, the concept of twinning has been used in technology transfer projects involving developed and developing nations. Twinning involves matching experienced professionals from the developed nation to the learner in the developing country in what is essentially an apprenticeship program. Mentoring and coaching are used in context of day-to-day business operations in this model. Many of the lessons of nation-to-nation technology transfer apply to corporations wanting to accomplish transformations that require outside help from those who have already mastered the new paradigm.

The consequences of business reengineering are so great that corporations should carefully devise a complete program of technology transfer and very carefully build partnerships with providers of object-oriented technology, methods, training, and tools. When evaluating and purchasing automated tools, the training, consulting, and contract systems development experience that goes with the provider's software should be bundled into the purchase.

A typical arrangement may include the following steps and components:

1. The consulting firm provides initial concepts education.

2. With assistance, the corporation develops a plan of action for a pilot project.

3. The consulting firm provides training for the work team, and the pilot is used in the training so that immediate application of the training is assured.

4. The consulting firm provides mentoring and coaching throughout development of the pilot project.

5. Pilot projects are expanded in scope, and steps 1–4 repeated. Each iteration reduces the need for outside assistance.

Successful technology transfer requires initial help from outside masters who have gone before. Smart business people learn from smart scientists and climb on the shoulders of others. As technology transfer progresses, in-house team members can evolve into consultants to other corporate projects.

7. Outsource, Insource

The goal of successful technology transfer is self-sufficiency in the new paradigm. Self-sufficiency will have been achieved when the consulting firm is no longer needed and the expertise is entrenched in the business. In other words, technology transfer has been successfully completed and new approaches are mainstream. Actually, it probably will not work quite this way.

If one studies the vast amounts of specialized and superspecialized knowledge that are needed to run a global corporation, the requirements can be overwhelming. Hence, corporations will continue to outsource superspecialized knowledge requirements to the superspecialists.

Long-term relationships will likely emerge, especially between corporations and business object providers, companies that develop industry specific class libraries for object-oriented information systems. In the future, corporations will forge long-term relationships that blend the right mix of software acquisition, training, consulting, systems development, and contract programming.

Depending on cost/benefit analysis, any or all of these resources may be insourced or outsourced, or this way today and that way tomorrow. Successful corporations recognize the need to bundle training investments into technology justifications and acquisitions. Outsourcers typically provide train-the-trainer services to migrate training in-house if the cost/benefit warrants.

8. Get on the Internet, Now

Distance learning on the information highway will soon become a vital education and training resource, a vital business resource. Education is likely to emerge as the killer application of the Internet. The knowledge and skills needed by the workforce of the coming century will demand it.

Today, the world can be at our fingertips. The Internet is the net, yet it does not even really exist. It has no headquarters. It has no bosses, no top-down control. However, it does have 20,000,000-plus users from all over the globe who can work in a virtual world full of active discussions, libraries, customized news, online courses, company catalogs, electronic mail, university courses, and software. Just about whatever the mind can conceive is or will be on the Internet.

Even without direct access to the Internet, professionals can gain access to discussion groups through e-mail. Current topics are discussed, users tender questions, and dialogue flows. Archives typically contain FAQS (frequently asked questions), bibliographies, and other useful research information, all available by sending an e-mail message. Discussion groups can be accessed from Compuserve, Prodigy, America On Line, MCI Mail, ATT Mail, and other network providers. Following, some of the Internet's useful resources for building a learning organization are briefly described.

BPR-L is the business process reengineering list homed in the Delft University of Technology, the Netherlands. To obtain information about BPR-L send the following e-mail message:

LISTSERV@IS.TWI.TUDELFT.NL
(leave subject blank)
INFO BPR-L (put this line in the body of the message)

The Learning Organization list is moderated by some staff members at Peter Senge's consulting company. Professionals engaged in business reengineering and who follow Senge's "Fifth Discipline" provide dialogue on this list. To obtain information about the Learning Organization, send the following e-mail message:

majordomo@world.std.com
info learning-org (in text body)
END

Usenet news groups such as comp.object, comp.cog, and comp.lang.C++ are available through news readers. Not all Internet providers offer news readers, and users should check with their systems administrator.

Then there is the Web, or the World Wide Web to be more precise. With a good Web browser such as Mosaic or Netscape, the world of business and object technology can be surfed with the click of a mouse button. Some interesting Web sites are listed in Table 3.1. Visiting these sites will result in pointers to many additional interesting places on Web.

Table 3.1 Business and Object Technology Web Sites

Subject	Address
The Object Management Group	http://www.omg.org/
The Object-Oriented Page	http://www.einet.net/galaxy/Engineering-and-Technology/Computer-Technology/Object-Oriented-Systems/ricardo-devis/oo.html
Pointers to Object-Oriented Information	http://swss00.isbe.ch/~bach/oo.html
Object-Orientation FAQ	http://iamwww.unibe.ch/~scg/OOinfo/FAQ/
Object-Oriented Internet Resource Page	http://www.cera.com/object.htm
Distributed Object Environment	http://www.sun.com/sunsoft/doe/
Learning Organization	http://world.std.com/~lo
Object-Oriented Information Sources	http://cuiwww.unige.ch/ooinfo?teaching
OOPSLA Workshop on "Use Cases"	http://www.unantes.univ-nantes.fr/use-case/index.html
Object-Oriented Bibliography	http://cuiwww.unige.ch./bibrefs
Other Object-Oriented Bibliography Sites	http://liinwww.ira.uka.de/bibliography/Object/others.html
GTE:Distributed Object Computing	http://info.gte.com/ftp/doc/doc.html
Is Schroedinger's Cat Object-Oriented?	http://www.taligent.com/quantum-oo.html
Smalltalk, Tokyo	http://web.yl.is.s.u-tokyo.ac.jp/members/jeff/smalltalk. html
PLoP—Annual Conference on the Pattern Languages of Programs	http://c2.com/ppr/about/plop.html
CASE Tool Home Page	http://osiris.sunderland.ac.uk/sst/case-home.html
Yahoo Search OO Page-	http://www.yahoo.com/Business_and_Economy/Companies/Computers/Software/Object_Oriented

Software and consulting companies already provide Internet discussion groups as a means of support. These groups interlock the vendor and the users into a common dialogue and shared base of information resources. They are the beginnings of interenterprise learning nets of the future. As network bandwidth grows, the content will become rich with multiple media. Having direct access to such electronic communities and information resources is having direct access to continuous, just-in-time learning.

Many courses are already available on the Internet. Road Map, a course on the Internet itself, was announced in 1994. Enrollment in its first offering came in at 62,000! It is an excellent course.

What is really going on here? One teacher is teaching a Fall 1994 college course to a class of 62,000 students from 75 countries, broken down to three sections for manageability! The course is produced out of the University of Alabama and is free. Companies can load it on their in-house systems if they wish. This is but a single point of light to indicate what is coming on the Internet.

The application of the Internet to learning organizations has unlimited potential. Learning organizations provide their workers with easy and free access to the net. Most importantly, they do so now.

9. Internal Mentor Network of Subject Matter Experts

The follow-on to initial technology transfer is developing a visible network of internal subject-matter experts whose job it is to push the envelop of knowledge, technology, and technique. Mentors, provocateurs, top guns, and champions are in constant demand in a learning organization. The process of deploying professionals in these or similar roles can be formalized and made a structural part of a virtual training organization.

Masters and apprentices are discussed below (see point 12). They play key roles that can be used to structure a corporate work team. Furthermore, masters are needed by other process teams to mentor and inject fresh concepts and perspectives. Call them top guns, champions, or provocateurs, call them what you like, but make sure that such ilk are visible and available. They are essential catalysts needed to stir team chemistry and trigger team actions.

10. Embedded Performance Support Systems and Artificial Intelligence

Artificial intelligence is not dead. Although predicted to be at the core of modern business in the 1990s, artificial intelligence faded as the eighties came to a close. Or did it? Although artificial intelligence is no longer a front-page icon of the computing and business press, object technology can provide a framework and messaging standards that could increase the use of intelligent software in information systems.

Technology exists which makes it possible to construct intelligent, embedded performance support systems. The technology can surround workers with Donald Norman's "things that make us smart" (Norman, 1993). An embedded performance support system works with users as they work, knows where users are in a process, and knows the kind of help they will need to solve a particular problem. These systems can present information in the form needed for the task at hand.

Embedded performance support systems can play a teaching role as revealing of the rules contained in their expert systems can explain the steps and logic used to solve a problem. Expert systems thus "shape" the behavior of their users. That is called *learning*—and feedback and knowledge of results is immediate. That is called *real-time learning*.

Well-designed performance support systems place the user in control and the content is designed for handling the many seldom-encountered exceptions that occur in a normal work day. Being able to handle exceptions on-the-spot with access to a broad knowledge base is a boon to productivity.

11. Multimedia Courseware and the LAN

Since local area networks are common in the workplace, it does not take a completely new infrastructure to put learning on the network. By using existing local area network infrastructures, multimedia courseware and other digital learning resources can be available on the desktop. Companies such as the Network Connection sell video servers for a local area network and many computer training companies provide network-ready courses on a wide range of technology and business subjects.

Multimedia resources on a corporate network means that company catalogs, books, policy manuals, business process models, and much more can be captured as digital information and made available while we work. Interactive courses, video conferences with experts, expert systems, and traditional print materials can be at the fingertips of an entire workforce. By deploying this technology on existing local area networks, all workers have access to a common, active, and intelligent knowledge base.

Never before has a company been able to completely surround a person with virtually unlimited information resources, in all conceivable media, while they work. These information artifacts fit neatly on a fourteen-inch computer screen.

Without increasing the size of the desktop by even as much as one inch, paradigm shifts can happen.

Aggressive businesses in the twenty-first century will certainly surround their employees with powerful digital artifacts. And, they will gladly wage economic wars with them.

12. Masters and Apprentices

Although the need for master-level knowledge and skill is obvious in the technology transfer phase of corporate transformations, the masters-apprenticeship approach offers benefit over the long haul. Those who were apprentices during a technology-transfer endeavor will grow into master roles as transitions spread throughout the corporation. Corporate work teams, charged with ongoing process innovation and learning, will benefit from sustaining this working and learning model over time.

A common mistake that is made in transitioning an organization to any new technology is that training is perceived as a binary proposition: people are either trained or they are not. Experience indicates that this is a mistaken assumption.

Meilir Page-Jones, President of Wayland Systems, developed a seven-stage model of what software developers actually experience as they learn and develop skills associated with a new technology (Page-Jones, 1990). Developing an environment and a process to move people through those seven stages should be high on the CIO's priority list. In his consulting practice, Jim Stikeleather, Chief Technology Officer of the Technical Resource Connection, adapted Page-Jones' stages to the disciplines of object technology.

Stage 1: Innocent—Never Heard of the Technology

Most developers have heard of object technology but their awareness is actually very low. Someone may be considered innocent if they have not learned enough about the technology to be aware of some of the engineering trade-offs associated with it, some of its costs, some of its benefits, or where and when it might be appropriately applied.

Moving someone from the innocent stage to the next stage is a process of providing gentle introductions to the technology through articles, presentations, and seminars. The goal is to inform and educate. Management-level introductory presentations place the more global issues of the technology into perspective.

Stage 2: Aware—Has Read Something about the Technology

At stage two the person has become aware of the benefits and costs of the technology, as well as when and where it might be successfully applied. The person can generally describe what is involved with the technology, and at a high level can compare and contrast the technology with older approaches. The person has a talking knowledge of the technology.

A person at this stage has not yet achieved the paradigm shift. Their intellectual framework for the technology is still based upon drawing analogies to the old ways of doing things, and probably still draws upon erroneous assumptions when thinking or making decisions about the technology.

Moving a person from this stage to the next involves establishing and executing an initial training program of classes, readings, seminars, and workshops in the higher-level concepts of the technology. With object technology, this training is in the areas of analysis, design, and methodologies.

Stage 3: Apprentice—Has Studied the Technology

At this stage the person is well aware of the high-level concepts of the technology; however, they may or may not have experienced the paradigm shift. This person cannot effectively apply the technology on their own, but can begin to contribute to the use of the technology.

Moving the person from this stage to the next involves establishing and executing a training program that focuses on the details of the technology. In the case of object technology, it is now appropriate to introduce language and tool training.

At this stage and its transition to the next, hands-on training becomes very important. To this end, an apprentice should be teamed up with a mentor, someone who uses the technology naturally and automatically, and who can explain the internal process involved with the technology. For the apprentice, it is sink or swim at this stage. It is time to throw the apprentice into a development project using the new technology.

The mentor expects that the apprentice will swallow a little water and, at times, gasp for breath. Fortunately, the mentor serves as a lifeguard. The mentor has to closely monitor the apprentice to ascertain progress, capitalize on the lessons that are learned from mistakes, and to adjust the detailed goals of the development process.

Stage 4: Practitioner—Ready to Use the Technology

At this stage the person is ready to make engineering decisions on their own. There should be a continuing education program in place to increase their breadth of understanding of the technology and its applications. This is generally a self-managed process.

This stage still needs the presence of a mentor to make assignments and observe results. However, detailed supervision should no longer be required. Mistakes are a significant contributor to the learning process at this level, and the practitioner should be allowed to make them. At this stage the practitioner is given full-responsibility assignments and is an active participant in project review activities.

Movement to the next stage is a function of time, experience, an increasing knowledge base, and specific mentoring.

Stage 5: Journeyman—Uses the Technology Naturally and Automatically

This is the stage that development staff should achieve by the end of the transitioning process. At this stage, participants are able to apply the technology in normal situations and do not require the presence of a mentor to accomplish quality work.

This stage also requires a self-managed learning program to increase the understanding of the technology. In this stage, the journeyman still calls upon a mentor when new or especially complex problems appear.

Movement to the next stage is a function of experience, increasing depth of knowledge, and the evolution of the generic, problem-solving framework. This problem-solving framework is developed through interacting with a master-level person on new or complex situations. In this stage, the solution process is more important than the solution details.

Stage 6: Master—Has Internalized the Technology and Knows When to Break the Rules

This stage is self-explanatory, with continued learning a matter of keeping up with progress being made with the technology.

Every organization needs access to a master either on staff or on retainer. The master can handle new or complex applications of the technology, review journeyman-level work, show alternative or creative solutions to problems, point out subtleties in the engineering decisions, and help keep the organization up to date.

Movement to the next stage is strictly up to the individual. It is based on the individual's thought process and experiences. Moving up to the expert stage generally requires the individual to be actively engaged in a broad range of applications of the technology in new and or unusual situations.

Stage 7: Expert—Writes Books, Articles, Gives Lectures, and Develops Ways to Extend the Technology

Experts are at the pinnacle of the technology. They are generally recognized for their contributions to the industry and are often asked to lecture or give presentations at national meetings for their peers.

Mentoring, in context of the seven-step process for knowledge transfer, can be an effective approach to building a continuous learning process. Since individuals will be at differing stages in their development, mentoring should be formalized through individual development plans (IDPs). Each IDP should include concrete milestones for each component in the learning architecture: inform, educate, and train. Learning goals also must be synchronized with work plans and schedules. For example, training for a new task should be just before the execution of the task.

13. Quiet Time, Learning Time

How many companies require 25% reflective learning time in their jobs? That would be the equivalent of three months training each year. Although few companies even approach that amount of time for learning, the rapid advances in business technology require such expenditures of time to keep up.

Unfortunately, modern life in corporations is hectic. Time is a resource lost, gone the way of simpler times, gone the way of downsizing. Reacting and responding time dominates. We respond on our feet, but do we learn for tomorrow while on our feet? On-the-job training is a classic example of learning by doing and experience teaches us along the way. But most of this type of learning is confined within a given approach, a given way of doing things. We add little bits and pieces.

Learning new ways of thinking, shifting paradigms, requires more than learning by experience. Without calling a time-out and rethinking what we are doing and why, we could be learning more and more about the wrong things.

People do not consciously know what they are doing when they work. They do not have to think about it; they just do it. Likewise, children do not consciously know how to ride a bicycle; they just do it. If we had to be conscious of what we are doing, we would never get through a working day as the dynamics and complexity of what we go through every day would drive us insane.

Entrenched responses to the world around us, responses that require little or no conscious thinking, help us survive. However, such responses can be definite learning disabilities. We need reflective time if were are to learn and use new rules of the game and new ways of problem-solving.

We need this time to reflect on and examine those mental models that we use but do not think about. We need to have time to read quietly about new ideas and ways, and to think about them by comparing and adapting them to our own mental models.

When a new concept sinks in, we have reached "aha." We have adapted our inner mental models, but now we have to test our new understanding with application. Our first few attempts at application will produce mistakes. The feedback from those mistakes will in turn continue to reshape our understanding. By the time we reach mastery, we no longer consciously know what we are doing, we just do it.

With this description of learning in mind, it is easy to conclude that to shift to a new paradigm, a person must become two people. One continues to get today's hectic job done. The other learns the new way of doing business. Work teams in a learning organization must continually grapple with these facts. A wish will not bring about learning. Because reflective time is a scarce resource, work teams must manage it very carefully.

14. Carefully Partner with Universities

University professors are paid by society to specialize in reflective time. They are society's learning engines. University computer scientists have pioneered object-oriented technology and management science is driving process-oriented management. These are major topics in academe, and academe is a resource corporations can consult in times of major transitions.

While partnerships with universities can be a breakthrough strategy for change, they can be disappointing endeavors if not handled with care. Professors are people, too. There are good ones, bad ones, creative ones, and those counting the days to retirement. Some are resistant to change and do not accept the new approaches of management and object orientation. Moreover, some excellent thinkers are too theoretical to make a practical business contribution.

A successful partnership with academe will be one well thought out, planned, and executed. Goals, objectives, and deliverables must be clearly defined as academic and practical perceptions of the same field of endeavor can be quite different.

Federal Express Corporation provides a successful model. FedEx partnered with Christian Brothers University to develop a graduate program that combines the MBA core curriculum with study of object-oriented and distributed technologies. FedEx assisted the university in procuring the required technology, and participants are given company time to attend classes and to learn. The venture is in addition to the continuing college reimbursement program. FedEx is otherwise building a learning organization at its Center for Excellence in Information Technology directed by James C. Wetherbe.

15. Corporate Sabbaticals

One source of masters in the game of technology transfer is the professor on sabbatical. Why not make it reciprocal? Professionals in the corporation can take their workplace experience back to campus with them, do a sabbatical, and return to the workplace refreshed with new ideas and information.

16. The Corporate Library

In the age of electronics, the old-fashioned book does not receive a lot of media attention. While distributed, interactive, multimedia information systems have a role, so, too, does the ordinary medium, the book. To this day, it is through books that the pioneers of object-oriented technologies and business reengineering have asserted their theories, explained their methods, and prescribed their techniques.

The Essential Object-Oriented Library for Business in Appendix A is designed to assist corporations in establishing or updating their libraries. Books remain one of the most cost-effective means of learning; therefore, a good corporate library can be a cost-effective investment in learning.

Personal libraries of individual professionals should not be overlooked. Although books have become more costly, they remain one of the most inexpensive resources for learning. Individual copies of key books and desk references should be made available throughout the workforce. For example, every computer specialist doing object-oriented systems development should have his or her own copy of Booch, Coleman, Odell, Brian Henderson-Sellers, Firesmith, Berard,

Graham, Schlaer/Mellor, Jacobson, Meyer, Goleberg and Rubin, Wirfs-Brock, and Rumbaugh. By having personal copies, each person can mark up, dog ear, and refer to them at any time.

Libraries of the future are emerging today. Electronic books systems and other multimedia products offer the capability to access electronic materials that were traditionally bound to corporate library shelves and filing cabinets. In addition, virtual libraries are beginning to appear on the Internet. Successful organizations will invest heavily in both traditional and electronic corporate libraries.

17. The Corporate Book Report and Other Keep-Abreast Strategies

In the rapidly advancing worlds of business and technology, there is too much to read and too little time. But the dreaded event in high school, the book report, can be an effective means of keeping teams current. Corporate work teams can divide up the key works on a business reengineering or object technology method and facilitate team learning by doing book reports.

Abstracting and indexing companies offer book summaries, another form of book report. Although an eight-to-ten page book summary is not the book, good summaries will convey the key ideas, the gist.

While book reviews and summaries get across main points very well, and many main points are needed during paradigm shifts, books covering details of complex methods and techniques are not appropriate for summary treatment. Thus books reports and summaries have limits.

Work teams can be creative with information dissemination. They can create "brown bag theaters" where workers can bring lunch and gather in a relaxed atmosphere to hear a lecture or watch a video and follow-up with lively discussion. Companies such as the Computer Channel, Inc. and many technology vendors provide excellent materials via satellite down-links.

18. Know the Myths and Pitfalls of Training

Common misconceptions can produce bad training. Dean Spitzer of High Impact Training, Inc. once described several misconceptions in an article in *Training* magazine (Spitzer, 1985). His misconceptions include the following:

- Training is the same as education.

- Training is a program that begins one day and ends on another.

- Trainers should be responsible for training.

- Employees want to learn new skills.

- Trainers are the best people to do the training.

- Quality training should be attractive and impressive.

- The best training departments run the most courses.

- Participation in training should be voluntary.

Spitzer declares that these misconceptions can devastate the most well-intentioned training efforts. Corporate work teams must get beyond these misconceptions if they are to be effective. Corporate training as usual is not up to the challenge of the paradigm shifts in today's business world.

19. Continual Needs Assessment

The annual training needs assessments and the annual training schedule are corporate fixtures. But now the business world is moving far too fast in far too many new directions to rely on the traditional means of training needs assessment. A training need can surface in a telephone call or a process team meeting. The newly revealed need may require a near-zero development time for the solution.

Electronic training administration tools can assist in developing far more frequent learning needs analyses. In addition, corporate help desks gather mountains of learning needs data in their day to day operation. Additionally, training needs assessments should be an integral part of business process reengineering activities and projects. An effective approach to training needs assessment encompasses these many sources of data and is a continuous process.

20. Pay for Certified Skills

At the annual Computer Training and Support Conference in Atlanta in 1994, Mircosoft handed out lapel pins with the slogan

Smart?

Prove It!

The PC revolution was an occurrence in history that gave rise to millions upon millions of self-proclaimed computer experts. Confusion now reigns.

Skills and knowledge have become so diverse, specialized, and superspecialized that it is difficult to go beyond what people can say in job interviews to learn what they really can do and how well they can do it. De facto certification has emerged in response.

Novell, a leading provider of network operating systems and software, launched a certification program that has given a new momentum to widespread certification efforts. Today, computer professionals can become Novell-certified network engineers, certified network administrators, or certified networking instructors. Other companies, including Microsoft, have since established certification programs for their software products.

Teams may use certification as an incentive for workers to develop recognized knowledge and skill. Records of certified skills can be a useful means of tracking and understanding state of the corporation's knowledge base. Pay for skills systems can be designed to include the certification variable. Mastery certification, especially at the superspecialized skill levels, is here to stay.

Certification is not limited to individuals. Software development organizations can attain certification through process improvement programs developed at the Software Engineering Institute at Carnegie Mellon University (the Capability Maturity Model or CMM) and the International Organization for Standardization (ISO 9000 standards). Certification is not a one-shot affair as both of the CMM and ISO process models focus on continuous process improvement.

21. Participate in Professional Conferences

Professional conferences can be little more than perks in times of slow change. In times of rapid change, huddling with colleagues from around the world, doing reality checks with them, and catching up on new developments make professional conferences essential. Some professionals have forgone vacation or taken absence without pay because they just had to go to ACM's OOPSLA conference. They know that it is essential to their growth and development. That is how important that conference is to the object industry and to the professionals who work in the land of object-oriented systems development.

In times of radical change, professional conferences are high payback investments. Learning organizations fully participate, and most conferences are front-loaded with very high quality tutorials conducted by noted experts. Conference tutorials can offer great value.

22. Learn about Learning

Adult teaching and learning disciplines are required if corporations are to design and implement effective learning programs. Adults have been sufficiently trapped in the boxes of life so that their capacity for learning "for learning's sake" is limited by time and energy constraints of real-life.

The adults who run our businesses can be pesky learners. They demand a lot from learning services and experiences. Their expectations include:

- Available just before the knowledge and skill are needed for the job (i.e., just-in-time learning)

- Hands-on, from the beginning

- Preferably skill building training delivered in the privacy of their own office or workspace (sometimes to overcome any anxiety produced while learning with subordinates)

- On demand, when and where it is needed

- Learner controlled instruction

- Readily available at any company location

- Immediately applicable, customized to the immediate need

- Most assuredly, they want a mentor

In the beginning, we are all superlearners. Adult learning, on the other hand, is a different matter. Adults, the people who are our corporations, are very special kinds of learners. They are tough.

Learning and schooling have been modeled after the paradigms of industrial-age thinking. Schools are factories, learning is dispensed in conformance with scientific management, and, like other industrial-age systems, the educational system is under great stress.

Learning and schooling are being increasingly decoupled. In fact, business is the rising institution of learning with a training enrollment growth rate that is the envy of many institutions of higher education.

To build an effective learning organization, the learning process itself must become a core business process. For this to happen, corporations will innovate learning processes through the use of technology. The book list in the Classified Bibliography contains some classics and some of the latest thinking on learning and training. Although there are many dimensions to successful adult learning, interactive, multimedia, computer networks meet many of the criteria discussed earlier. Such learning systems provide time- and space-independent communications with the knowledge base and the learner's mentor.

23. Get Out of the Way

The nature of major transitions is that they are conceived in chaos. Nevertheless, the environment will eventually stabilize. The structure of an enterprise will change many times during transitions, but it will eventually self-organize into a stable form.

People are controlling in nature. People want to make plans, work their plans, and get on with an agenda. All along the way they want to have control of the process. That control involves controlling internal and external influences that affect our place in the enterprise structure.

In times of chaos, we try to exert greater control so that we can keep our world stable. With the coming generation of information technology and the emerging stage of business competition, those who would attempt to control the future will experience great frustration. The external influences are far too powerful to be controlled.

In a nonhierarchical world, control must be tempered with systems thinking and understanding of the interconnections that are shaping business in the coming century. For example, the Internet is out of control. That is, it has no control structure. Instead, it is self-organizing and evolves by the natural laws of systems. The Internet will self-reorganize many times as it continues to thrive well into the coming century.

The imperative for business is: Do not get in the way and do not attempt to control the evolving interconnections in tomorrow's business structures and systems. Instead, successful companies roll with the flow of change with both eyes open. Successful business transitions require extraordinary adaptability.

24. Select Development Methods and Buy the Tools

Golf cannot be played without golf balls, clubs, and tees. No golf clubs, no golf. The object-oriented business reengineering game cannot be played without development methods, modeling and simulation tools, and object-oriented tools.

The necessary tools include enterprise modeling and simulation tools, enterprise object repositories, business process reengineering tools, systems development tools, integrated project support environments, and computer-mediated learning systems.

Companies should obtain qualified assistance to study and select the appropriate systems architectures, then development life cycle methods, and, only then select appropriate tools. The endeavors of object-oriented business reengineering are far too complex to attempt without appropriate, automated tools.

25. Get Whacked on the Side of the Head

Creativity is needed to shape a corporation's future. Specialization and control hierarchies have done much to foster standardization over creativity. Newly formed process teams, made up of members from the existing hierarchical world, may find it very difficult to sit around a table and be creative. The work of Van Oreck, *A Whack on the Side of the Head,* or others can be used to help unlock the needed creativity.

26. Take Senge's Fieldbook to Meetings

The authors of Peter Senge's book, *The Fifth Discipline Fieldbook: Strategies and Tools for Building a Learning Organization* contribute 95 chapters, organized by the five disciplines of a learning organization and collected into 593 pages. Each chapter reveals useful tools or strategies that can be deployed to nurture learning organizations.

The authors titled it a fieldbook because they want readers to take it with them to business process team meetings. They want readers to use it in the field.

Let's turn to the English alphabet to conclude our discussion of learning tactics. The English alphabet consists of 26 little building blocks that can be combined and recombined to produce monumental results. Hopefully, the 26 learning tactics can be combined to nurture a learning organization, the kind needed for competitive advantage in the coming century.

REFERENCES

Mattison, R., and M. J. Sipolt. (1994). *The Object-Oriented Enterprise: Making Corporate Information Systems Work.* New York: McGraw-Hill.

Norman, D. A. (1993). *Things that Make us Smart.* Reading, MA: Addison-Wesley.

Oncken, W. (1954). *The Impact of Communications on Productivity.* The William Oncken Co.

Page-Jones, M. (1990, July/August). The seven stages of expertise in software engineering. *American Programmer,* p. 36–43.

Rummler, G., and A. Brache. (1990). *Improving Performance: How to Manage the White Space on the Organization Chart.* San Francisco: Jossey-Bass.

Senge, P. M. (1990). *The Fifth Discipline: The Art and Practice of the Learning Organization.* New York: Doubleday/Currency.

Spitzer, D. (1985, June). Misconceptions that produce bad training. *Training Magazine,* p. 104.

Tobin, Daniel R. (1993). *Re-educating the Corporation: Foundations for the Learning Organization,* p. 289. Oliver Wight Publications.

Video server big picture. (1994, October 31). *Information Week Magazine,* p. 63–72.

Yourdon, E., K. Whitehead, J. Thumann, P. Nevermann, and K. Oppel. (1995). *Mainstream Objects.* Englewood Cliffs, NJ: Prentice Hall.

PROFILES OF THE OBJECT TRAINING MASTERS

In this chapter we hear from the object training pioneers that have gained substantial experience in object-oriented education and training. These firms were selected to tell their stories and share the lessons they learned since first becoming involved in teaching and applying the technology.

Hewlett-Packard, IBM, ICONIX, Knowledge Systems Corporation, and Object International share their initial training experiences, mistakes, lessons learned, current training practice, and future directions. They tell us what they do and why they do it. These company profiles provide useful insights for corporations charting their paths up the object technology learning curve in business.

HEWLETT-PACKARD COMPANY

With Larry Marran, Joan Ochi, and Daniel Wu*

Abstract

If objects are such a good thing, how come everyone is having such a tough time learning about them?

In the following pages, we'll try to answer that question and give you some insight into Hewlett-Packard's approach to training and education. We'll describe the core issues surrounding the transition to object technology today, and share some stories from HP's own experience with objects within our company, as well as with some of the many customers who have relied on HP to educate them on object technology.

Technology transfer challenges: You can get there from here, but nothing is ever as easy as it looks—and some things are much harder than they look.

> *Object technology is the silver bullet that will solve the vital problems that we have in the software world today.*
>
> *All I need to do is to understand what an object is, and I will become an object developer.*
>
> *Since object languages include C++, Smalltalk, Simula, Ada, and others, all I have to do is to learn one of these languages and I must be qualified to be an object developer.*

All of these statements reflect common perceptions of object technology, and all of them underestimate what object technology is, what it means, and how it differs from traditional approaches to software development. Traditional methods are autocratic, typically following a linear thread of control. Object technology is based on the notion of distributed control—objects themselves are discrete units that cooperate in order to address complex problems. The challenge is making one's way from the traditional world to the new order dictated by object technology.

---

* In collaboration with Dave Deasy, Chris Dietrich, Patricia Gill, Lisa Guin, Brian McDowell, Linda Outlaw, and Morris Wallack

Object Technology Reflects the Real World

In the past, software development focused simply on the capabilities of the product. Today, functionality encompasses more than a product's ability to perform. Software must be user-friendly, contain graphical user interfaces, and integrate with other applications. To develop an entire software application, one needs to break the application down into many smaller ones, with each small part addressing at least one of a multitude of users' needs.

Different individuals may have different ways of dividing an application into pieces. This is no different from the way we comprehend our environment. People see and remember things, stories, and events in terms of symbols, which can be interpreted as "objects." Each person interacts with, and remembers, these objects in their own unique way.

Objects do not change often, but the interactions between them may change. Software development professionals can use object technology to address the challenge of creating a new application in the same way that all humans problem-solve and create in their everyday lives by changing the interactions between objects.

How a New Common Framework Can Help Speed Software Development

Without some common reference framework, however, it is unlikely that two different individuals will see the world as the same set of things, stories, and events. Something is needed to help different individuals look at the world in a similar way.

Biologists have developed a classification system to help organize the vast amount of information related to identifying, describing, and categorizing living organisms. Such a classification system seems quite natural, and is relatively easy to teach. Not only does it illuminate common facts (such as that both men and dogs have skeletons because they are both vertebrates), but it provides a common framework that is very helpful when analyzing a living organism. Many biologists also use this classification scheme to help focus their own skills and work.

Most software objects fall into a similar classification scheme (known as *inheritance hierarchy*), which provides similar benefits. Like biologists, programmers can use this inheritance mechanism to help provide focus or specifications to their own skills and work.

We have found that organizations that have applied object technology successfully have redefined the roles and responsibilities of their development and support staffs. Instead of having project managers, analysts, development programmers, and support programmers, they have object architects, class programmers, and application programmers.

With conventional technology and responsibilities, there is almost no reuse of code or design. It is not surprising that so many projects are slow or late—everyone is busy hurrying to reinvent the wheel. With object technology and a new division of responsibility, architects can specialize in developing and refining frameworks for classification and reuse as did the biologists who created and refined the biological classification scheme; class programmers can specialize in some domain as did the specialists who "know everything" about a small subset of the biological classification hierarchy; and application programmers, like the generalists who do most of the field research, can focus on reusing the work of others to rapidly solve practical problems.

Many real questions still come up:

- Is it possible to create a realistic schedule for software development?

- Can we leverage off what we have done in the past in terms of software development? Can we avoid starting everything from scratch?

- Are there many ways to do similar things?

With object technology, the answer to these questions can be yes. The challenge is to understand how to find the way to the answers.

The Hewlett-Packard Approach to Object Technology

Hewlett-Packard is a global provider of integrated object technology training, consulting, and mentoring services that range from single-point solutions to extensive, company-wide programs. HP's philosophy on object training has evolved over time and largely reflects our own experiences as an early user of object technology for internal software development.

Object technology has proven to be very effective in enabling HP to achieve the objectives we defined in our corporate wide software initiative. These objectives include the development of reusable code and a reduction in software maintenance costs. Over the past five years, hundreds of HP software professionals have been trained in object technology, including the HP Fusion object-oriented analysis and design methodology. As a result of our in-house efforts, we have learned a great deal about implementing object technology and training developers. Here are a few of the things we've learned:

- **Use real-life applications whenever possible.** Learning about objects is harder than it initially seems. Theoretical training often simplifies the problems and challenges to the point of trivializing them and is usually ineffective. One internal HP training organization will not even provide object training or consulting unless an actual project has been identified and requirements documents have been created.

- **Break it up.** Object technology takes time to learn: time for new concepts to soak in and time for individuals to realize what they don't yet understand. Each person seems to have many "ahas," and has them at different points in the learning process. Ideally, training consists of formal coursework interspersed with hands-on, real-life projects. This phased approach allows students to apply the skills they have learned. Often, students may not be sure of what they don't know until they've had a chance to get hands-on experience.

- **Use mentors.** Mentors with a broad range of object experience can help teams identify goals, assist students with object design and modification, and put all the pieces of an object puzzle together. The ongoing support of a mentor is key to generating multiple "ahas" throughout the learning process.

- **Encourage team training.** Object technology introduces concepts that are often at odds with the intuition that many students have developed over time. Students can learn a lot from each other. And commiserating can ease the burden of struggling to understand some new thing that seems so simple.

Team training is also good practice for real-life projects. Successful object technology projects require effective and constant communication within and among teams—objects cannot be created in a vacuum. Working as a group also encourages sharing of knowledge and best practices, and it allows team members to bring different perspectives to a problem. It is, however, important that a group of students have roughly the same level of knowledge when they begin training as a group.

- **Don't be discouraged by mistakes.** Creating a true object-oriented environment is a deceptively difficult process. Our experiences show that learning is an iterative process—failure often precedes true breakthroughs. Learning through trial and error often leads to greater success than getting it right the first time.

- **Allow time for reading and exploration.** Reuse requires search and study. In a traditional development environment, the majority of staff time is spent configuring new code. In an object world, reading, exploring, and experimentation is key. Often the solution for a question or problem may be found by researching class libraries and frameworks or other similar applications that use those classes and frameworks.

The Hewlett-Packard Integrated Methodology

Hewlett-Packard has adopted an integrated methodology in training our customers. A complete, coordinated program is essential to a smooth transition to object technology. This includes training, consulting, and mentoring, as well as ongoing evaluation to ensure the technology continues to support the organization's evolving business needs.

Hewlett-Packard's approach is to serve as an advisor throughout the stages of the customer's learning process. Many HP solutions begin at a high level, educating managers about object technology and helping them to evaluate the technology and the impact it can have on their business, and identify next steps. Because of the pervasive effect a transition to objects may have on a company's business, processes, and people, this frequently includes courses in change management along with object concepts and capabilities. Management must fully understand and support the organizational impact of object technology. Object training may also be one component of a larger technology initiative such as moving to a client/server environment.

A training needs analysis is another key element of HP's philosophy. In such an analysis, trained HP professionals assess an organization's existing skill set by conducting customized surveys and interviews with staff. This evaluation is then compared with the organization's desired outcome and a curriculum plan can be formulated based on this gap. This recommendation can take a variety of different forms, including standard classroom training, customized training at the customer's site, distance learning, self-paced training, mentored on-the-job training, and real-life, hands-on projects. HP's approach is summarized in Figure 4.1.

Start with the Basics

Deploying object technology without first building a base of conceptual knowledge is analogous to building a house without any underlying knowledge of home construction. Although it may seem obvious, we've seen it happen all too frequently. For example, eager to test the hot new technology that they've been reading about, companies send members of their development staffs to courses in C++ programming. But without the underlying "objects mindset," these companies are unlikely to achieve many of the benefits of object technology. In most cases, a solid foundation of courses in object concepts along with basic analysis and design techniques help ensure that students understand the big-picture implications of object technology.

Companies committed to a wide-scale implementation of object technology need to invest in programs such as HP's comprehensive jump-start program. For five or more weeks, students are immersed in a new technology such as objects or client/server. Courses, exercises, and projects are tailored to the customer's specific environment. After a thorough introduction to object concepts, individuals are given the opportunity to develop their skills through hands-on exercises such as designing and building an object-based application. Courses in object-oriented concepts and challenges, analysis and design methodologies, object programming languages, and product and tools training follow as needed. Whenever possible, case studies are employed to reinforce concepts. Ideally, "soak time," which allows students to absorb the information, is another important component of an object training solution. Self-paced training in a variety of media is another cost-effective way to allow students to reinforce their understanding on an ongoing basis.

Many organizations don't have the resources to adopt an extensive training program immediately. HP has partnered with organizations to create phased, integrated programs that allow individuals to develop their skills gradually and effectively. One major financial institution worked with HP and several other vendors to create a core curriculum for software developers who are new to the industry as well as those transitioning from a traditional mainframe environment. This curriculum included up-front training in information technology directions as well as

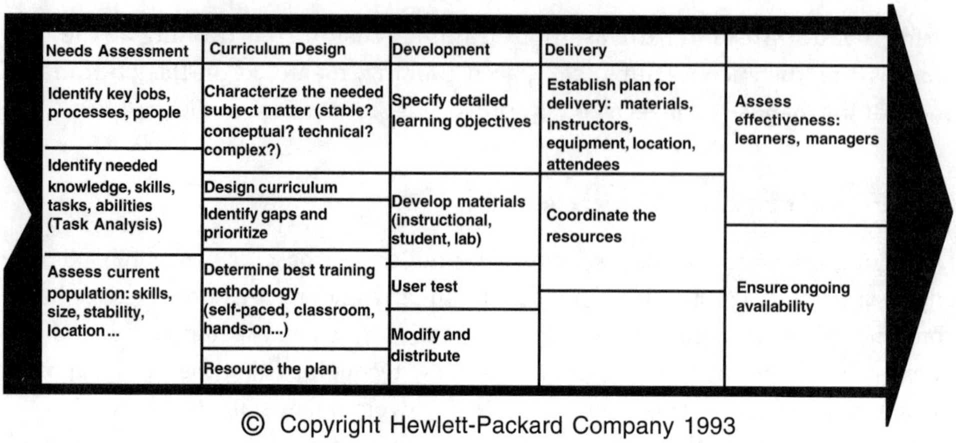

Needs Assessment	Curriculum Design	Development	Delivery	
Identify key jobs, processes, people	Characterize the needed subject matter (stable? conceptual? technical? complex?)	Specify detailed learning objectives	Establish plan for delivery: materials, instructors, equipment, location, attendees	Assess effectiveness: learners, managers
Identify needed knowledge, skills, tasks, abilities (Task Analysis)	Design curriculum Identify gaps and prioritize	Develop materials (instructional, student, lab)	Coordinate the resources	
Assess current population: skills, size, stability, location...	Determine best training methodology (self-paced, classroom, hands-on...) Resource the plan	User test Modify and distribute		Ensure ongoing availability

© Copyright Hewlett-Packard Company 1993

Figure 4.1 The Hewlett-Packard approach to tailored training and education—from needs assessment to effective knowledge transfer.

foundation courses in UNIX, C++, object concepts, and key products. Beyond this core training, project managers defined the skill sets their teams needed and recommended time frames for developing those skills. They then provided their employees with access to follow-on training.

Consulting and Mentoring Are Key to Effective Learning

More than almost any other technology, moving to objects requires reinforcing a new way of thinking. Ideally, HP's comprehensive consulting and mentoring services are integrated throughout the transition process. Our skilled instructors have provided consulting services integrated with training. In other cases, HP consultants work with HP instructors to ensure a well-integrated, effective learning and implementation processes. One successful HP engagement involved an HP consultant participating in the entire "classroom" portion of object analysis and design training. Upon completion of the course, analysts and designers went off to develop a real application with the consultant available to evaluate and review their work. Because the consultant had been present throughout the training, he knew exactly where the company was in terms of ability, design issues, and skill set. This

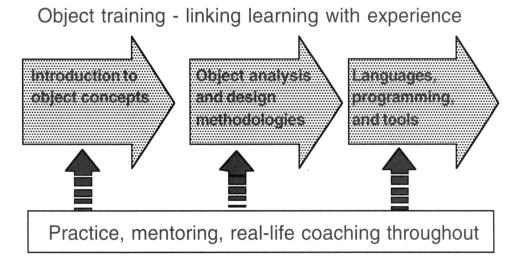

Figure 4.2 Hewlett-Packard's integrated approach and real-world experience.

ensured a smooth hand-off between instructor and consultant and consistency throughout the process.

Hewlett-Packard's strength stems from our ability to integrate object training into an overall open systems, client/server solution that includes evaluation, planning, and implementation services. Our long-standing, strong industry presence allows us to be a focal point and coordinator for our customers and to serve as an education consulting integrator (see Fig. 4.2). HP is a complete solutions provider and can deliver at both ends of the spectrum, from high-level consulting on an organization's IT strategy to hands-on implementation training. Our objective can be stated simply: to assist our customers in successfully implementing object technology within their organizations.

Conclusions

The future challenge in software development is getting managers responsible for deploying information technology to appreciate the power of object technology and its impact on their businesses. As demonstrated in this chapter, another significant challenge is in effectively retraining the legions of software developers who are currently "object-unaware." Although most good developers show a high capacity to learn new languages and approaches, understanding and mastering object technology often requires unlearning previous knowledge. This realization, combined with effective training, is essential to effectively using object technology in the working world.

IBM

With Chris Hotchkiss and Susan Von Bambus

Abstract

IBM consulted its own employees and customers worldwide to design the Object Technology University (OTU). For many years IBM has had object technology projects underway, and these provided valuable insight into what is and is not successful in making good "object thinkers." In the following pages IBM shares some of its experiences and some candid lessons learned during its initial object technology training efforts.

Introduction

IBM has long been a leader in the education and training business, dedicated to training its own employees and the employees of its customers. The company has offered programming and application development courses from a variety of perspectives to a diverse number of audiences. In 1994, 10,000 customers and IBMers worldwide attended IBM's object technology (OT) courses.

Object technology is a key technology focus area for IBM. Intent on becoming the preeminent supplier of object-oriented tools and services to its customers, IBM realizes the tremendous business advantages the move to object technology will provide. The promise of significantly faster time-to-market, rapid prototyping of business processes, higher-quality software, and the ability to adapt to changing business environments makes OT the business paradigm of the future.

IBM has considerable training experience and a firm corporate commitment to object technology. However, it will still be a significant challenge for IBM to fully integrate OT into all of its management, development, services, and marketing communities. It is a task IBM is compelled to perform because the ultimate rewards of object technology are clear. The investment in this transition will help IBM and its customers reengineer so that they can better address the pressures of today's highly dynamic business environment.

Although *object technology* has become a popular buzzword, the true implications of its adoption are not always obvious. The ramifications of making such a transformation are profound, and some of the most profound relate to the area of training. The availability of people skilled in object technology is perhaps the most significant challenge facing the industry today.

To address this challenge, IBM has committed to design innovative training programs that integrate residency (immersion) training, mentoring, just-in-time (JIT) classroom and self-study courses, advanced workshops, on-the-job "real world" experiences, case studies, and technology and industry updates. To assure a cohesive approach to this training worldwide and to create an environment where sharing of people, courseware, and training modules could happen, the Object Technology University (OTU) was created. The mission of the OTU is to provide IBM and its customers with segmented and targeted training programs that will make object technology a reality throughout the corporate enterprise.

Lessons Learned from Early OT Training Efforts

Lesson One: If software development is no longer to be business as usual, training can't be either.

It is the most natural thing in the world for human beings to gravitate to what they already know when they are trying to do something new. In deciding to make the move to object technology, a company has determined that it no longer wants to do business as usual. It is important to realize that the training required to facilitate and support the OT transformation cannot be business as usual either.

To achieve the reuse benefits of object technology, the process of software development must be different. The type of orientation or mindset change required to support an OT development environment cannot be achieved solely by providing product, language, and/or tool training in discreet, sporadic modules. There is certainly a place for such training, but by itself it cannot make the transformation to object thinking happen for software and application development professionals.

The training environment is critically important. Stringing together four or five object-related courses does not in any way accomplish the same result as an immersion training program that integrates and stages training in an environment where all activity is singularly focused on getting people to do good object thinking. Team interaction is of great importance as is the ongoing and immediate access to experienced OT masters.

Without this immersion training, what will be produced is people who write C++ procedural code and, surprisingly enough, procedural Smalltalk code. Failure to do the training right means that people will not change their procedural paradigms. They will not develop the skills needed to produce reusable artifacts that are essential for reaping the benefits of object technology.

Lesson Two: Implementation of object technology is not free, but is often misperceived as an undesirable expense rather than a worthwhile investment in the future.

Minimizing the investment in the development of skills is a temptation which businesses often cannot resist, but by succumbing, they run the risk of gaining in the short term at the expense of depleting their intellectual capacity in the long term. The ability to capitalize on reuse, for example, is developed as a result of integrated actions between training, development, and product delivery. Inadequate investment in this integrated approach will reduce the beneficial return of reuse.

Shortcuts aimed at minimizing the investment in time or money to accommodate work schedules or existing budgets will seriously jeopardize the implementation of object technology in an organization.

Lesson Three: OT training requires real-world application with mentoring to make it stick.

Making the time and dollar investments in the intensive immersion training for software developers is a great first step. However, the reality is that new trainees are easily frustrated in initial work encounters. This frustration causes them to revert back to what they already know and feel comfortable with.

Without an opportunity for immediate application of their new OT skills accompanied by expert mentoring, an unacceptable percentage of people will slide back into the procedural paradigm.

The need to infuse real-world experience with mentoring into the OT training led to the comprehensive training framework called the IBM Object Technology University Residency Program, where classroom, mentoring, and on-the-job experience are interwoven to increase the chances that the training will stick. Part of the entry qualification program for a prospective attendee of this program (described later) is that the person have a specific OT engagement or project assignment and mentor identified.

Within IBM this critical mentoring is provided for the IBM development community by an organization called the Object-Oriented Technology Center (OOTC). The OOTC has been supplying object expertise to IBM internal projects since 1992. "It is technology insertion," says Ken McCauley, manager of the OOTC. According to McCauley, "the OOTC is a technical support organization operating at a project level." The OOTC uses the existing OT knowledge and experience at the various IBM sites and, through mentoring, successfully completes projects and furthers the education of team members so that they, in turn, can become team leaders.

Lesson Four: Different levels of expertise in OT are required throughout a company or organization.

Training that meets individual or unique requirements is an important factor in establishing an effective delivery environment for object technology. Structuring individual training roadmaps according to level of skill at program entry, as well as to specific roles, is most effective. Obviously, the intensive immersion training discussed earlier is most appropriate and effective for application developers, but it is not necessary or even desirable for marketing specialists or executives. And what works for training marketing representatives will not achieve the right results with development managers.

For all audiences, however, from executives to coders, training is essential to provide the corporate environment where the transition to OT will be encouraged, supported, and rewarded. Not everyone needs to understand the underlying mechanisms of OT such as encapsulation, inheritance, and message passing, but everyone needs to know that object technology speeds development, improves quality, and provides applications that can adapt to changing business environments.

Furthermore, it is clear that grasping OT takes a lot longer than other technologies for all levels within an organization from corporate executives to the actual product and application developers.

These lessons, together with other pedagogical factors, resulted in the creation of the Object Technology University within IBM. The OTU focuses on all aspects of the transition to object technology and addresses the unique needs of multiple audiences from executives and managers to marketing and services specialists to system and application analysts, designers, and programmers.

The IBM Object Technology University

IBM's Object Technology University is composed of three major training programs, the Residency Program, the Continuing Education Program, and the Special Events

Program. Its mission is to develop and deliver leading-edge OT-related training for IBM employees and customers.

The OTU Residency Program

At the heart of the OTU is the Residency Program (see Fig. 4.3), IBM's "immersion in object thinking" program. It is a training framework or structure made up of two schools of thought, which are periods of knowledge and skills acquisition through dedicated formal training and several on-the-job training phases during which students actively engage in projects with mentors. This intensive educational program is specifically designed to create productive object technology project team members. As students increase their understanding and ability to apply object technology, they advance from the role of programmer to designer to team leader.

Not all students complete every level of the program. It is expected, for example, that the ratio of developers trained to team leaders will be about three to one. Not everyone will go on to be OT team leaders. Most importantly, however, all School One graduates continue through the mentoring phase to assure that they become productive, experienced object thinkers and programmers.

This unique program came about through the combined efforts of some of the most experienced educators and object experts within IBM. Dr. Robert Goldberg, the OTU program manager for IBM's development community has been one of the leading forces for technology transfer within IBM since the 1970s. Goldberg's chief concern in designing the IBM Development community program was how to manage technology transfer for such a large entity and how to optimize success? According to Goldberg, "First, we've got to educate the people who are going to be involved. We've got to deliver OT concepts through experience, with projects complex enough to be challenging. Training must built on real-world experience."

The need to infuse real-world experience into OT education led to the comprehensive curriculum that is the core of IBM's OTU Residency Program. Instead of relying on textbook learning to turn students into productive members of the OT community, the OTU will follow and guide its students for years.

To assure that students are well-prepared and to optimize their chance for success in the Residency Program, IBM has implemented for its own employees an entry qualification program. Prospective students must submit a readiness profile, take a prerequisite test, and have a committed OT project to which they will be assigned following graduation from School One. Students must be nominated by management and are accepted in the School One program based on the completeness and caliber of their entry qualification nomination package.

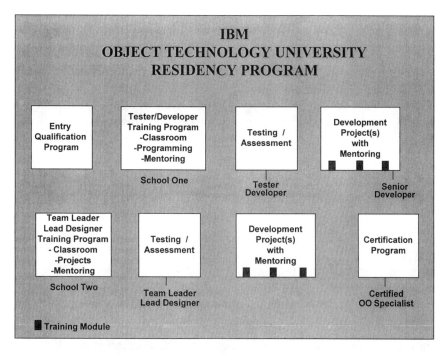

Figure 4.3 OTU entry qualification program.

OTU School One: Smalltalk (or C++) Developer/Tester Training

School One is a focused, intensive five-week on-campus program for application developers. Through an integrated set of lectures, mentoring, case studies, lab exercises, and discussions, students are prepared to contribute as developers on object technology projects. The School One environment accelerates the development of foundation skills in object technology and builds expertise in object programming.

Upon completion of School One, students are able to:

- Explain object-oriented concepts and terminology

- Describe the object-oriented application development life cycle

- Interpret design artifacts including object models, use cases, CRC cards, and object-interaction diagrams

- Recognize various notations used by major object-oriented methodologists

- Determine the quality and completeness of a given set of design artifacts as they relate to the usefulness as a blueprint for development

- Differentiate between interface objects and domain objects

- Build good domain and interface objects based on given design artifacts

- Write an application (in the language of study) and incrementally extend it

- Adhere to standard coding techniques

- Develop test methods to perform unit tests

- Participate in code reviews

- Create graphical user interface screens

- Function as a junior member of an object-oriented project team.

Jim Williams, one of the first non-IBM students to graduate from School One, is an object training specialist at a large insurance and financial services company that, he says, "is determined to pull off the object paradigm." They've decided to make the technology transfer to objects and have started early pilot projects, but the efforts are still isolated instances rather than company-wide initiatives. One of the first decisions they'll be making is about training.

Williams looked at the offerings of various OT training companies, but felt that most of them didn't go far enough. "You have to have pretty in-depth training even to be a beginner," he said. "We all view immersion training as the first step. It is the only way to get people across the initial bridge to object thinking."

Williams also sees the importance of mentoring and more advanced training as necessary to the larger training program. "We're looking for a polished curriculum and not a program where you have to deal with one short course at a time."

OTU Post–School One Testing and Assessment
Students who attend the School One program are tested for certain competencies at the end of their studies. Because School One focuses on developer skills, the testing procedures assess technical competencies such as ability to conceptualize object-

oriented designs and to write good object code. In addition, skills related to communicating work accomplished are assessed.

Development Projects with Mentoring

An important lesson was applied when IBM designed this portion of the Residency Program: the need for real-world application under the direction of an experienced mentor. During this phase of the Residency Program, students put into practice what they have learned in School One. Key lessons from the classroom are reinforced over many months of actual programming and design work.

"Mentoring is a well-designed, well-structured tracking event," says Timlynn Babitsky, a member of IBM's North America Object Technology Practice organization and the designer of the OTU's mentoring program. Babitsky, who is an experienced OT trainer and practitioner and one of the founding co-editors of *The International Object-Oriented Programming Directory,* points out that the existing skills and goals of each junior project team member or apprentice are different, and the mentoring program must reflect this. According to Babitsky, rather than play a passive role, mentors must help each apprentice design a custom program for developing skills in OT. "It is not simply ad hoc mentoring, sitting at the student's elbow; it is structured to their needs." Therefore, for students from the IBM Services and Consulting organizations, mentors are responsible for only two or three team members.

At the end of the mentoring program, apprentices have increased their confidence and proficiency in applying object technology to actual development projects.

An important part of the mentoring and project experience phase is to solicit feedback from mentors and apprentices on how well they are doing on the real-world projects and continually adjust the School One program based on this feedback.

OTU School Two: Team Leadership/Designer Training

School Two is an intensive and challenging five-week on-campus program for developing team leaders. Through mentored team sessions, individual research and design projects, student presentations and lectures, students build effective technical management, team leadership, and technical skills. School Two employs a mix of projects so that students begin to recognize patterns and opportunities for design re-use across different applications.

"School Two looks beyond the practical learning of School One to find leadership qualities," says Susan Lilly, an instructor in IBM's Education and Training organization, which is responsible for the OTU. According to Lilly, who is the lead designer of the School Two curriculum, "Creating top-notch OT team leaders and designers requires a lot of independent learning from the students that they must then turn around and teach to other students." In School Two, students are expected to bring their experience into the classroom and share it. The integration of on-the-job training experience and advanced OT topics is intended to produce object-savvy team leaders.

At the conclusion of OTU School Two, the student is able to demonstrate the following:

Technical skills:

- Create object-oriented analysis models from customer description of problem domain/requirements

- Create object-oriented design models

- Describe design issues of reuse and reuseability

- Describe design trade-offs of various object persistence strategies

- Write class specifications, including implementation guidance

- Develop testing and integration strategies and plans

Technical management skills:

- Work with a team to make a development plan that includes work products, assignments, milestones, dependencies

- Work with a team to make resource estimates for the work to be performed

- Determine, collect, and evaluate team measurements and metrics

- Coordinate and participate in reviews of analysis, design, and implementation work products

- Ensure adherence to team/project standards

- Manage and control changes

Team/leadership skills:

- Facilitate the effective work environment for the team

- Communicate plans and work product to team members, other teams, management and customer

- Find OT technical resources (e.g., published books, periodicals, electronic bulletin boards, subject matter experts).

Development Projects

Once again, students return to an object technology project as team leaders and lead designers. Following this phase of the program, students have the opportunity to become Certified Object Professionals.

The OTU Continuing Education Program

IBM realizes that not everyone requires an immersion in object technology. Managers, for example, need to understand the learning curves associated with adopting the object paradigm, know the reasons for not returning to earlier development techniques, and have the ability to compare and contrast OT methods. Executives, on the other hand, require an understanding of how OT can be successfully implemented to solve business problems. Programmers and developers need to stay abreast of technical breakthroughs following their initial immersion in OT. Because of these many different requirements, an important component of the OTU is the Continuing Education Program.

The Continuing Education Program is organized into sub-curriculum areas such as concepts, project management, executive and management topics, products and tools, programming languages, analysis and design, databases, and framework technology.

Through the use of common case studies threaded through the program, as well as a common methodology to teach analysis and design techniques and notations, the OTU Continuing Education Program presents an integrated and performance-based set of courses with a common "look, feel, and philosophy," but delivered in discreet modules.

From the learner's perspective, these integrated modules provide a sense of familiarity and continuity while allowing the students to learn in a JIT fashion. From a trainer's perspective, these similarly-developed offerings allow for easier reuse when building custom offerings.

Training in the Continuing Education Program is offered currently via public and private classes. Future plans include alternative delivery methods such as videos, self-study computer-based training, and multimedia.

The OTU Special Events Program

Realizing that object technology will continue to develop rapidly, IBM has designed the OTU Special Events Program to share the latest implementation and technical updates through timely special events such as conferences, symposia, seminars, and publications. These events will bring IBMers and customers together to discuss topics in object adoption and application and to engage in active dialogue on a spectrum of advanced topics and issues.

Special events, such as the conferences, will include presentations, hands-on workshops, product demonstrations, and panels aimed at a varying levels of attendee experience and interest. IBM will host several international conferences each year that will feature well-known industry and technology speakers.

Staffing the OTU

The OTU intends to maximize real-world experience for both students and instructors. IBM has many experienced OT instructors and mentors and some of these will become part of the OTU. Since a large percentage of OTU instruction depends on practical experience, IBM is supplementing the instructor ranks with specialists. These experts from IBM labs and the consulting and services organizations will serve as part-time instructors, guest lecturers, and mentors.

Just as the OTU curriculum must keep up with rapid developments in the OT world, so must its faculty. Real-world experiences are just as important for instructors as they are for students graduating from the Residency Program. Therefore, many instructors will return to the practice of object design and programming in actual OT projects and engagements. Others will take part as students in some of the more advanced courses at the OTU. The goal is to maintain a leading-edge knowledge of the subject coupled with a freshness in the approach to it. This freshness will be achieved by a lively rotation within the teaching faculty—teachers not only teaching but becoming students, project team members, mentors, and even researchers before coming back to teach some more; students becoming mentors and guest lecturers in OTU classes; consultants, practitioners, and developers becoming instructors in the OTU programs.

What Does the Future Hold?

For IBM, it is critical that the OTU maintain vitality so that it continues to provide help to clients who want to solve business problems through the use of object technology. As feedback from students and mentors is received, the OTU design and materials will be enhanced to assure that the program stays "real world" oriented and meets the needs of the OTU audiences. Once the initial cultural change has started throughout the enterprise, other issues and training will emerge from the experiences gained from implementing OT projects.

Over time, as the transition to objects becomes more pervasive throughout industry and academe, the job of the OTU will change. Upgraded skills among the general population will, for example, create higher expectations in terms of the prerequisite skills for the School One and the School Two programs and will cause these programs to tackle more complex subject matter.

Companies are beginning to realize the value of OT, and its adoption rate is accelerating. The challenge for IBM is to help clients capitalize on OT's higher returns. To do this, it must train its consulting and services organizations on how to use the technology to solve real customer problems and must provide training to customers so that they can successfully use the technology. It must also train its own staff of developers so that they can provide the preferred tools and enablers for development. IBM is confident that the OTU training model will be successful in transforming its own workforce as well as those of its customers worldwide.

ICONIX SOFTWARE ENGINEERING, INC.

With Doug Rosenberg

Abstract
Doug Rosenberg, president of ICONIX Software Engineering, tells how ICONIX became involved in the object-oriented arena and shares an early training experience that shaped ICONIX's approach to technology transfer and training.

Introduction
ICONIX, founded in 1984, had been selling object-oriented CASE tools for a few years, and it was becoming obvious that there was a real need for training in object-

oriented methods. In stark contrast to the old structured methods, where every-body knew what a dataflow diagram was, developers were very much still in the dark when it came to object-oriented methods and techniques.

According to Rosenberg, "We noticed that as people began moving to object-oriented development, they did not have a good grasp of the methods they were attempting to use. Because we wanted to be out in front of the CASE industry with our object-oriented tools, we had to get smart about object-oriented methods our-selves. It dawned on us that the knowledge we had amassed in object-oriented analysis and design tools was a marketable commodity in and of itself. Not only was this knowledge a marketable commodity, in most cases our customers required training in order to succeed with the object-oriented tools we were marketing."

This general lack of knowledge became clear during one early training experi-ence. Rosenberg had devised a pop quiz to give to one of his classes at a Fortune 500 company. He wanted to assess the level of knowledge of the people in the class, so he made up a quiz that had all of the four- and five-syllable object-oriented buzz-words on it: *encapsulation, polymorphism, inheritance,* and so on.

The quiz was tested with one of ICONIX's nontechnical employees, a college student who was designing some company brochures. She got 8 out of 10 right. She was a linguistics major and knew what polymorphism was. However, only 1 out of 12 students in the class for the Fortune 500 company did as well. Even a manager attend-ing the class did not do as well as the college student. This experience drove the point home about the widespread need for object-oriented training in the business world.

The company initially sold CASE tools for structured systems development. Over the next several years, ICONIX continued to develop its line of CASE tools, ICONIX PowerTools, to the 10 modules that it consists of today. In 1990, Mr. Rosenberg decided to move into object-oriented methods, setting "leadership in object-oriented methods" as a strategic direction for the company. Initially, PowerTools supported only Shlaer/Mellor-type object-oriented analysis methods using structured methodology tools such as entity-relationship diagrams, data-flow diagrams, and state diagrams in an object-oriented fashion. ICONIX then added support for Coad/Yourdon and Booch methods, and soon after added Rumbaugh OMT and Jacobson Objectory in response to market feedback.

Intent on maintaining its position in the growing object-oriented community, ICONIX became involved in object-oriented development in 1987. Since then, the company has developed over a quarter of a million lines of code built into the MacApp OO Applications Framework. Having overseen the development of the entire line of ICONIX PowerTools, Mr. Rosenberg was also responsible for expanding ICONIX's services into object-oriented training and consulting to meet the increasing demand for quality training.

From Training Services to Training Products

Since ICONIX had moved from a product-oriented background into training, Rosenberg felt that the next step in this progression was to develop their training services into training products. ICONIX produced a CD-ROM training course in object-oriented analysis and design methods: *An Object Methodology Overview.* The course is the first of its kind in the industry. The CD-ROM has served to position the company and Rosenberg recently announced plans to develop a whole family of CD-ROM training courses.

A Focus on Object-Oriented Methods

ICONIX provides a combination of methods and tools training in the early part of technology-transfer projects for its clients. Using a unique approach, called JumpStart Training, ICONIX consultants are able to spend less time on traditional teaching methods such as flip charts and lectures. Instead they can begin by applying theory in a lab situation involving the client's project. With the JumpStart program, students immediately begin to apply the theory learned in lecture to a real project assignment. Lab sessions involve real work as opposed to academic exercises.

The benefits of the JumpStart training are many: including employee downtime for training is less, students are more interested in the problem because it is relevant to their job, and students are rolling with methods and tools on real projects when the class is over. They have gained a jump start on a real project.

According to Rosenberg, using the client's project benefits both the trainer/consultant and the client. Real business projects are inherently more interesting for the trainer/consultant since the trainer is able to learn about new, unique applications each time she or he is called upon to teach.

ICONIX typically organizes its initial training day into a lecture in the morning and a lab in the afternoon to apply the newly learned methods and tools to the client's actual project. The second morning is devoted to more detail from the previous day's learning activities, the introduction of additional methods and techniques, and then another lab in the afternoon.

ICONIX does not espouse any single object-oriented method in its training. Instead, the company supports multiple methods. The trainer/consultant concentrates on teaching people how to integrate methods. According to Rosenberg, this lack of methods bias is essential to corporations as multiple methods are available that meet the needs of different business problem domains.

Technology Transfer Challenges

Rosenberg warns that there are certain traps to watch out for in object-oriented training. The object-oriented methods sometimes tend to take on certain "religious" aspects. There tend to be "high priests" who mix dogma with the actual substance of a method. Until the object-oriented approach becomes mainstream and is widely understood, such dogma is a real danger that businesses have to watch out for when selecting methods and training. Are participants getting solid methods guidance, or dogma? Rosenberg advises, "Beware the hype. Be skeptical of promises."

ICONIX makes a strong effort to stick to the most important aspects of each object-oriented development method. It is important to note that each embodies an incredible amount of detail. The bulk of a given method is actually fairly straightforward. The "90-10 rule" applies: If the 10% of the most complex, detailed portion of a method is deferred and the focus placed on the simpler 90%, understanding becomes much easier. Stated otherwise, 90% of the pay-off can be achieved with 10% of the effort, and learners have a much greater chance of initial success.

Strategies for Getting Started

ICONIX recommends one important strategy for businesses that are just getting started in object orientation. The recommendation is to hire a core team of experienced professionals. Rosenberg advises, "Do not try to institutionalize a cookbook approach to selecting training and tool providers and expect it to all somehow magically work. Hire experienced, competent people, professionals who have heard all the hype before and are capable of separating hype from substance."

Future Directions

One of the problems that arises when making the transition from a traditional mainframe to an object-oriented, client/server environment is the tremendous volume of information that needs to be absorbed. According to Rosenberg there usually comes a point where sitting down and reading all of the needed books takes longer than the lifespan of the project.

One of the promising developments for the future, which ICONIX is just beginning to tap, is information delivery with multimedia, CD-ROM-based training. Rosenberg believes strongly in the potential for CD-ROM training to tackle the problem of absorbing the large amount of information.

ICONIX plans to expand its line of CD-ROM training courses. The current CD-ROM training course in object-oriented methods provides training that is informative and convenient, and prepares learners before formal training actually begins. Rosenberg explains, "One example is a class of 10 people which I recently taught. Prior to my teaching the class, everyone took the CD-ROM course. When the scheduled class began, participants had already gotten the basics from the CD-ROM, we were able to proceed directly to more advanced material and the client's actual project."

KNOWLEDGE SYSTEMS CORPORATION

With John Cribbs and Ron Schultz

Abstract
Knowledge Systems Corporation (KSC) is one of the object-oriented industry's oldest and largest consulting and training organizations. KSC's services span the spectrum of activities required by today's software engineering efforts. KSC assists and facilitates organizations and development projects that have chosen object orientation as their software development approach with Smalltalk as their primary implementation language. The following section

1. Introduces why KSC entered the object-oriented technology (OOT) training market

2. Presents KSC's unique (and, at the time it was first offered, revolutionary) multistep approach to OOT training

3. Discusses how the KSC approach to OOT training has evolved as the market has matured

4. Characterizes KSC's training offerings based on the business requirements of client organizations

5. Predicts some of the significant directions that OOT training will take in the near future

Introduction

KSC was founded in 1985 to pursue the then-hot technology of the time, artificial intelligence (AI). Financing for the company came from maxing out credit cards and proceeds from the sale of the founder's home. Initially these sacrifices bore fruit. KSC won a number of consulting jobs involving expert-system evaluation and development, including several with Digital Equipment Corporation. Unfortunately, these early successes were short-lived.

Less than two years after the company's founding, KSC hit the wall. There were many reasons for this, but the primary ones were that the successes enjoyed by AI in the research community were not being repeated in the commercial sector and KSC lacked the business focus that might have allowed it to compete successfully in the reality of this new and smaller-than-projected market.

Months of soul searching ensued while the company struggled to find a new direction. Most of the staff deserted the company and by January of 1988 only two employees remained. As fate would have it, the answer to the company's salvation and its path to the future were literally "at its fingertips."

KSC won a contract to develop a business process modeling system for Hewlett-Packard. The implementation language used for the contract was ParcPlace Systems' Smalltalk-80; the same object-oriented language that had been instrumental in many of the company's AI development efforts. Smalltalk allowed KSC to compress the projected development schedule for HP's system from three to five person-years down to a single person-year. The successful use of Smalltalk on this and subsequent projects enabled the KSCers to turn their business around. In so doing, they compiled an impressive list of Fortune 1000 company success stories.

As KSC's consulting business grew and the Smalltalk market evolved, the organization made two critical observations. First, the types of systems that clients were asking for were moving toward mission-critical business applications and away from the early model of advanced technology or proof-of-concept projects. And second, this market move toward mainstream MIS was attracting more significant competitors than KSC had been accustomed to (i.e., the "tier 1" consulting companies).

To distinguish its services from its competition KSC adopted a business strategy of enabling client OOT self-sufficiency. KSC developed a technology transfer program that provided both theory and project-focused training, supplemented by consulting services to meet the demanding deadlines typical of this class of projects. Thus KSC expanded its business focus and became a technology transfer agent.

What follows are:

1. A short description of the key factors KSC believes are critical for successful technology transfer

2. An overview of KSC's approach to successful technology transfer

3. A brief listing of likely directions that technology transfer will take in the near future.

Technology Transfer Road Map

Challenges are encountered any time a company significantly modifies its core business practices. Chaos can result if the impact of these changes on the organization is not properly anticipated. OOT introduction is no exception. The factors described here form a short list of items that should be considered when forming a technology transfer or introduction plan.

Like any new technology, object orientation has, and is going through, what we refer to at KSC as the "show-me" states. These states consist of clients asking:

1. **Show Me the Language/Tools.** Newcomers to object technology are often enamored with the tools and technology available. While this initial exuberance is what initially motivates organizations to even consider a new technology, this line of questioning is quickly replaced by "show me delivery."

2. **Show Me Delivery.** At this stage, organizations are attempting to validate the hype associated with objects. Real examples and case histories are reviewed and considered. If the technology passes this phase of review, the next state entered is "show me how I can deliver."

3. **Show Me How I Can Deliver.** In this state the organization is actively trailing the technology (e.g., a pilot project is started) and seeking assistance in education, training, and mentoring, to demonstrate internal delivery based on the technology. Many organizations have today passed this phase and are dealing with "show me how to manage delivery."

4. **Show Me How to Manage Delivery.** At this point, clients are past proving the technology to themselves and are now willing to deal with institutionalizing the technology. Issues such as project management, reuse, software quality assurance, and configuration management move to the forefront. Training the trainer programs become important as the organization fully embraces self-sufficiency and establishes its own object-oriented training and mentoring capabilities or partners strategically with an OOT training institution to provide such services.

5. **Show Me How I Can Optimize My Delivery.** Organizations in this state are providing complete suites of tools, training, technology, and reuse libraries to support object technology. Detailed understanding and training and automation of object-oriented processes is provided as is technology training.

KSC has dealt with clients in the first four states, and is currently driving itself into level five (an issue dealt with later in this section). The following addresses what an organization must go through to start this path.

Understand Your Organization

First and foremost, articulate the business case for the changes you are proposing. What business problem(s) are you attempting to solve? Technology for technology's sake (even if it is OOT) has been found to be a poor reason for potentially disrupting the development activities of an entire organization. And it is probably not an argument that any responsible manager will support. For example, say your company is falling behind the competition because your software development life cycle is too long. Your solution is to model key components of your business as objects and then implement them as reusable components that can be used across multiple projects. This saves time during both development and maintenance. The rationale supporting OOT deployment can be used as the starting point for building a solid OOT business case.

A word of warning: Be careful not to throw technology at what is basically a process problem. For example, let us go back to the problem of the development life cycle being too long. What if after analyzing the problem we find that the development team is spending too much time implementing software that does not address the needs of the user community because no formal requirements statement exists? Or say that significant time is being wasted fixing bugs after the system has been put into production because insufficient testing was done prior to product release. Problems such as these would better be addressed by improving the requirements gathering process or the testing process rather than throwing an object-oriented programming language into the mix.

A final word on understanding your organization. When building a business case don't forget to give some thought to the political environment (Block, 1983). What people or groups will support your proposal? What groups will oppose you and why? We're not advocating that people become political animals, just politically aware. Usually it's not too difficult to make relatively minor modifications to a proposal so that potential opponents become allies. Look for win-win situations wherever possible.

Understand the Target Technology

To the best of your abilities, make sure that there's a good fit between the business problem you're trying to solve and the technology you're proposing as a solution. Or put another way, just because you have a hammer in your toolbox doesn't mean every problem is a nail. This issue frequently occurs with technologies that are supposedly hot, as object orientation is today. Technology-enamored individuals will try to force fit a solution so they have an opportunity to use the technology. Sometimes they are successful, sometimes not. Either way, the project-associated risk is significantly increased.

Also, do not underestimate the complexity of introducing a new technology into an organization. A significant paradigm shift is required of individuals and groups moving from a traditional to an OOT-centric environment. Choose your initial OOT projects wisely. Recent history is littered with the failed wreckage of high-visibility, tight-deadline, mission-critical development efforts in which OOT was positioned as the "silver bullet" that would save the project. Unfortunately, a theme common to many of these projects has been to blame OOT instead of the foolhardy souls who underestimated the challenge at hand.

Understand the Impact on Your Development Process

An organization's development process can be divided into macro- and micro-process models which are used primarily to support the project management function. The macro-process, or life cycle, model is a coarse-grained partitioning of the primary tasks necessary for system development. Valid inter-task transition paths are also part of the model. A macro-process model associated with traditional development efforts is the sequential waterfall model (Berard, 1993). Note that some variations of this model allow for corrections to prior activities, that is, to "go up" the waterfall (see Figure 4.4).

A macro-process model more commonly associated with OOT development projects is the spiral model (Figure 4.5). A significant difference from the sequential waterfall model is the spiral's support for iteration (i.e., feedback) between development tasks. The spiral model was originally proposed as a risk mitigation strategy, but it has also proved effective in managing the iteration inherent in object-oriented development efforts. The original Boehm model has been further adapted for OOT by leaders in the object community such as Rebecca Wirfs-Brock.

OOT life cycle models typically rely on iteration as an integral model component. If the model used by your organization does not support fine-grained iteration between tasks, OOT adoption may require significant modifications to your group's approach to project management.

Significant changes will also be required at the micro-process level. Micro-processes refer to the component tasks that, when taken together in the appropriate sequence and combination, form the macro or life-cycle process. Figure 4.6 shows a simplified task list of one iteration in an object-oriented development effort. Iterations are usually tied to a specific object or collection of objects. Thus a single project may exhibit tens or even hundreds of simultaneous iterations as the objects comprising the system are developed. If the micro-process tasks in Figure 4.6 look familiar, they should. OOT is not magic, nor does its adoption require us to forget everything that we've ever known about software engineering, but it does require that its adopters reevaluate their approaches to analysis, design, project manage-

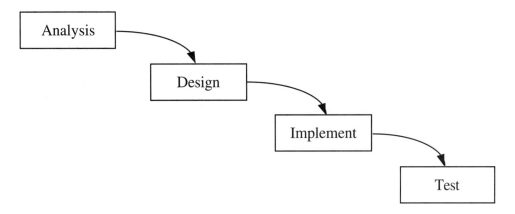

Figure 4.4 The sequential waterfall model.

ment, testing, etc. to ensure an optimal process fit with the different development focus required by this paradigm.

Set Expectations Appropriately

A major task for anyone introducing OOT into an organization is to appropriately set the expectations of all impacted groups. For instance, the first object-oriented effort may take as long, if not longer, than developing the project using conventional means. Object-oriented training, familiarization, and infrastructure changes all require effort and time. Setting expectations includes not only the developers but management and the user community as well. If management, users, or others within your organization have unreasonable expectations regarding the new technology and what it can deliver your efforts on the development side may be for naught when you fail to fulfill their pipe dreams.

Provide a Total Organization Training Plan

All object industry experts agree on the need to provide OOT training to all individuals in an organization that will be involved in the development activity (Cohen et al., 1994; DeNatale et al., 1990; Korson et al., 1991). Role-specific training is required for all team members. For example, users may require only a short introductory course on object-oriented concepts. Developers probably require object-

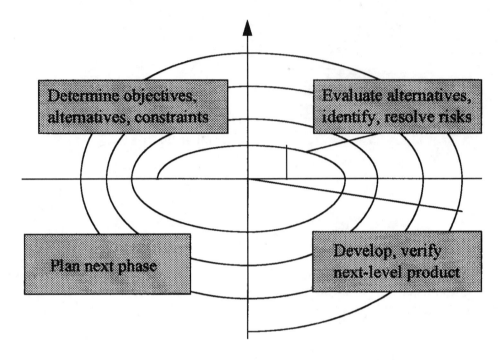

Figure 4.5 The spiral model (Boehm, 1988).

oriented analysis and design courses as well as programming language, tools, and testing courses. Managers typically require education in object-oriented concepts and project management. More detailed education recommendations will be discussed in the next section.

KSC's Solutions

Figure 4.7 depicts KSC's process for transitioning organizations and individuals from traditional development environments to OOT-based projects. This is referred to as KSC's multistep training program. The program begins with theory-focused training and hands-on exercises presented in a traditional classroom environment. Development team members are then given an opportunity to apply the theory that they've been taught to a project of their choosing. This project-focused training is centered around KSC's Smalltalk Apprentice Program (STAP). Following the STAP are a series of mentoring activities where the development team receives custom, individualized mentoring as necessary to supplement the more formal training activities.

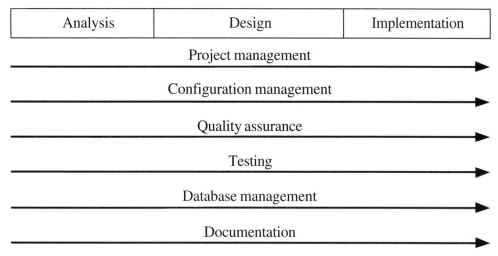

Analysis	Design	Implementation

Project management

Configuration management

Quality assurance

Testing

Database management

Documentation

Figure 4.6 Parallel threads in iteration "N".

Theory-Focused Training

KSC offers a wide variety of courses geared to meet the needs of software engineers and managers involved in Smalltalk-specific implementation efforts. A subset of the available courses and their recommended order of attendance for different project roles is shown in Table 4.1.

KSC courseware shares a common educational philosophy of learning by doing. In keeping with this approach, hands-on exercises comprise between 50–60% of class time. In classes where computers are necessary, students have their own machines to maximize the opportunity to explore topics independently. KSC

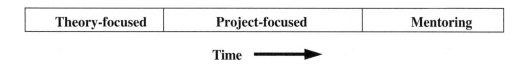

Theory-focused	Project-focused	Mentoring

Time ➡️

Figure 4.7 The KSC Multi-Step Process. KSC's approach starts with transferring knowledge about object-oriented fundamentals and then transitions to the application of the fundamentals on a client project. Mentoring activities complement the overall strategy.

Table 4.1 Recommended Object-Oriented Training Curriculum

Course	Manager [a]	Project Lead [a]	System Architect [a]	Developer [a]	Senior Developer [a]
Introduction to Objects for Managers	1				
Introduction to Objects for Developers		1	1	1	1
Object-Oriented Software Engineering	2	2	2	2	2
Object-Oriented Project Management	3	3			
Object-Oriented Analysis and Design	Optional	4	3	3	3
Introductory Smalltalk Programming		Optional	4	4	4
Advanced Smalltalk Programming			5	Optional	5
Supplemental Tools Training		Optional	Optional	Optional	Optional

[a] The numbers indicate the sequence of courses for each development role.

instructors encourage student discovery by giving hints instead of direct answers to questions, thereby furthering the learning by doing approach. Pragmatic problem solving is encouraged by the requirement that all KSC instructors have real-world experience in the subject matter they are certified to teach.

Project-Focused Training

KSC's project-focused training takes over where the classroom education ends. Project-focused training goals are to help client developers apply the theory learned in the classroom to a project they've been tasked to deliver by their management. These activities help students internalize the previously presented lessons while facilitating significant progress on the organization's development tasks. The core activity in KSC's project-focused model is its Smalltalk Apprentice Program (STAP).

The ideal student-teacher ratio for an apprentice program is 3:1 (although under special circumstances KSC will support 2:1 and 4:1 models). The instructor for a STAP is referred to as the STAP Master. The STAP Master acts both as an instructor and also project leader for the term of the STAP. The STAP model is shown in Figure 4.8. The STAP is ten weeks in length with half of that time spent onsite at KSC and the other half working at the client's home office on the project.

The rationale for the time spent at KSC is two-fold. First, it is virtually impossible for any one individual to possess all the technology expertise required by today's typical application development project. The time at KSC allows the STAP Master to draw on additional KSC staff that have the expertise required to ensure the success of the STAP students. Second, apprentice programs are designed to be intense, high-productivity learning events. Removing the students from their offices and any associated distractions (e.g., meetings, phone calls, faxes, etc.) allows them to concentrate on the task at hand, that is, OOT technology transfer and the application of OOT to their project.

The initial activity in the STAP is the finding domain objects (FDO) workshop. The objective of the FDO is to produce an initial domain model for subsequent use in an apprentice program. The resulting model includes domain object definitions, class definitions, class relationships, responsibilities and contracts. The FDO is typically given at the client's site where one KSC design "master" facilitates the activities of six or more client developers and users.

The FDO is immediately followed by a week of independent development and exploration (IDE). IDEs are interspersed throughout the apprentice program. They serve as unsupervised times where client developers work independently of their KSC mentors to extend the results of the supervised sessions (e.g., models, software, etc.). This time helps the students gain confidence in their abilities to use the OOT techniques and technologies on an independent basis.

Project-focused

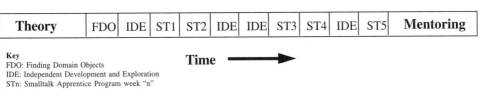

Figure 4.8 Smalltalk Apprentice Program (STAP) provides an intense, project-focused education event to make real the object-oriented training received.

Following the IDE week is the STAP itself. The STAP is divided into three segments each of which is separated by IDE weeks. The initial two-week segment is spent extending and implementing the domain model that was a by-product of the FDO. After having two weeks to work independently, the students return to begin work on their application models. This development phase will include implementation of the GUI interfaces and any interfaces to external databases. There is an additional IDE week followed by the final week of the STAP. This last week is typically spent on performance tuning, system packaging, and planning for the next iteration in the development life cycle.

A variation on the STAP that is useful with larger development teams is the Parallel STAP shown in Figure 4.9. In this model, all members of the development team participate in the same FDO. One additional deliverable from the FDO is a partitioning of the domain model between the project sub-teams that will be working in parallel apprentice programs. STAPs then progress in parallel. Periodically as the STAPs move forward the teams are brought back together to share the work that they've done independently. This ensures that at the end of the STAP the individual application components can be smoothly integrated to form the basis of a working system.

Parallel STAP activities can also be supplemented with additional contract development resources if the development schedules are aggressive to the point that the students would be unlikely to make their deadlines on their own.

Figure 4.10 shows the STAP just-in-time model. This model is most useful when the client's application is reasonably complex and will use sophisticated tech-

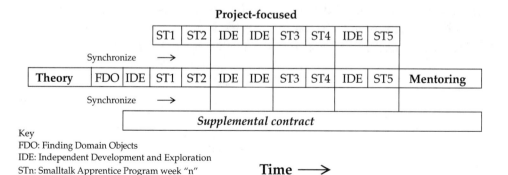

Figure 4.9 Parallel Smalltalk Apprentice Programs are useful in large integration efforts, or when many developers must be prepared for an effort rapidly.

Project-focused

| Theory | FDO | IDE | ST1 | ST2 | AST | IDE | ST3 | ST4 | ODB | IDE | ST5 | ST6 | Mentoring |

Key
AST: Advanced Smalltalk Training
FDO: Finding Domain Objects
IDE: Independent Development and Exploration
ODB: ODBMS Training
STn: Smalltalk Apprentice Program week "n"

Time →

Figure 4.10 Smalltalk Apprentice Program just in time.

nologies beyond what are normally available in an off-the-shelf Smalltalk development environment. The basic idea is to defer the classroom education events until the point in the STAP when they are to be used. Then replace the appropriate IDE weeks with the desired classroom training activities.

In Figure 4.10, it was determined that the target application will need to use some of the techniques taught in an advanced Smalltalk course. Also, the application will be using an object-oriented database management system (ODBMS) and training will be required in this technology prior to its use. Instead of front-loading all the classroom education events, they are interspersed throughout the STAP at times closest to their project introduction.

A final apprentice program-like activity is the practicum (Figure 4.11). Practicums are for organizations that require an intense, project-focused learning experience but do not have an internal project to drive the experience. Under these circumstances, KSC has developed a number of case studies specific to targeted horizontal and vertical application domains. The client organization simply chooses an application domain that is relevant to its business domain. This application then becomes the target application for the education experience.

Project-focused

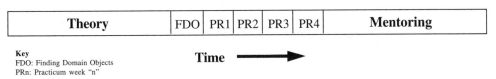

| Theory | FDO | PR1 | PR2 | PR3 | PR4 | Mentoring |

Key
FDO: Finding Domain Objects
PRn: Practicum week "n"

Time →

Figure 4.11 Practicum.

Mentoring

KSC assigns two definitions to the word *mentoring*. As a verb, *mentoring* is the process by which an experienced OOT technician provides periodic, on-site guidance to an object-oriented development team on matters spanning the entire software engineering spectrum. The goal of these activities is to further the teams' successful use of OOT. Typical mentoring activities include

- Software engineering process critiques

- Project planning seminars

- Team capability assessments

- Project progress reviews

- Design and code reviews

- Performance and tuning workshops

- Configuration management process optimization

- Custom training on project relevant advanced technology topics (e.g., memory management optimization, design patterns recognition, and real-time event processing)

As a noun, *mentoring* is the final event in KSC's multistep approach to technology transfer (as shown in Figures 4.7–4.11). Its goal is to deliver mentoring (the verb) services in a manner such that the clients' development teams attain OOT self-sufficiency. Typical mentoring begins four to six weeks after the end of an apprentice program. During this period, the team has continued work on their project. The team's former apprentice master then schedules a series of three-to-five day visits that span a six-month period. The visits provide an opportunity for sanity checks on the group's progress during their weeks of independent development.

Future Directions

It's been said that the only sure things in life are death and taxes. For at least the decade of the nineties this list should be amended to include "intense competitive pressures in most business activities." As the economies of the world become more and more intertwined and deregulatory pressures sweep the globe, business will continue its unending search for competitive advantage. A focal point for many companies will be better use of data processing systems.

Many of the promised benefits of object-oriented technologies will directly benefit companies in their quests to become more competitive. Higher productivity, lower maintenance costs, increased reuse and more flexible software architectures (to name a few) can all significantly impact companies' competitive positions. But these benefits will not be realized if organizations do not effectively equip their staffs so they can best leverage the technology.

The challenge for OOT technology transfer companies is to maintain and improve the quality of education services while meeting the urgent needs of a rapidly expanding market. One option is to better leverage computer-based training (CBT) technology. KSC plans to extend its training sequence as shown in Figure 4.12. Note the addition of computer-based training as a means of dealing with course prerequisites and introductory materials into the sequence.

CBT can best be used to cost-effectively reach large audiences on introductory topics. For example, courses such as KSC's introduction to objects for developers are ideal candidates for migration to a CBT format. CBT enables large numbers of programmers to master such material at a time and place most convenient for their individual work schedules. There's no technical reason that introductory material on more specific OOT topics (languages, databases, development tools, etc.) could not be disseminated in a similar manner.

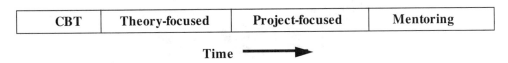

Figure 4.12 Extended training sequence.

Conclusions

By all accounts the ground swell of support for OOT continues unabated through-out the industry. In part, this popularity can be traced back to the elegance and conceptual simplicity of the concepts that serve as the technology's foundation: objects, abstraction, encapsulation, inheritance. Now that objects have been "mainstreamed," our set of base concepts is expanding to deal with the complexities of real-world computing. We now need to know about and understand distributed objects, object request brokers, language independent object models, object-oriented databases and design patterns; to name a few.

If the OOT industry is to continue its recent growth, new approaches must be discovered to facilitate the introduction of newcomers to this increasingly complex world. Earlier in this article the states of object-oriented adoption were considered. The fifth state, that of optimizing the delivery of object orientation, is the current target of KSC's internal efforts. KSC is embarking on an effort to merge software engineering disciplines and goals with Smalltalk culture and technology to create what we refer to as Smalltalk Engineering (Figure 4.13). This effort is bearing fruit in refining current training materials, adopting new practices regarding software reuse, project management, quality assurance, and testing, as well as positioning KSC to advance the state of the art in object-oriented technology adoption and use.

Current KSC activities are directed at developing and deploying business practices that will merge the best of Smalltalk development, object-oriented technology, and software engineering. Many challenges and much work lie ahead.

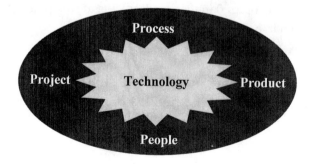

Figure 4.13 Smalltalk Engineering addresses all the aspects of object-oriented software engineering.

References

Berard, E. V. (1993). *Essays on Object-Oriented Software Engineering,* Vol. I. Englewood Cliffs, NJ: Prentice-Hall.

Block, R. (1983). *The Politics of Projects.* Englewood Cliffs, NJ: Prentice-Hall.

Boehm, B. W. (1988). A spiral model of software development and enhancement. *Computer* 21(5):61–72.

Cohen, J., et al. (1994). Training professionals in object technology, *OOPSLA '94, ACM SIGPLAN Notices* 29(10):46–50.

DeNatale, R., et al. (1990). OOP in the real world. *OOPSLA/ECOOP '90, ACM SIGPLAN Notices,* 25(10):299–302.

Korson, T., et al. (1991). Managing the transition to object-oriented technology. *OOPSLA '91, ACM SIGPLAN Notices,* 26(11):355–358.

OBJECT INTERNATIONAL

With Peter Coad and Mark Mayfield

Abstract
Object technology presents a tremendous learning challenge. Those who have studied transitions to the technology cite education as the major obstacle.

What if we had a power approach to learning and applying the technology? What if we deployed accelerated methods of learning? Pursuit of these kinds of questions led to the founding of Object International and drives the company today and in the future.

Object International was established as companies were beginning to embrace object technology to solve new and complex business problems. The following pages tell the story of Object International to provide insight into the successful strategies for adopting object technology in business. The accelerating technology has required accelerated learning to keep up.

A Little History

The history of Object International reflects the birth and evolution of the commercial adoption and use of object technology. Much has happened since the company was founded 1986. Much more lies ahead.

Business interest in object-oriented technology became a ground-swell in the late 1980s. Caught up in the force, Peter Coad founded Object International to contribute to the development of the ideas, teach the emerging object disciplines, and eventually put the ideas into print.

Coad recounts the systems analysis project in 1987 that turned his thinking to objects. While suffering through the modeling tools and approaches of the project team, the usual disagreements over entity relationship diagrams and data flow diagrams ensued. To stop the arguing and overcome the conceptual problems of either business modeling tool, Coad proposed that the team work with one model. The combined model charted things in the problem domain under study (e.g., as vehicle, owner, title, and registration) and then layers were added to this single model to identify data (e.g., owner, name, and address) and to name services (e.g., add, calculate, and renew). When one of the domain experts, a business expert, was asked what this one model would mean to her, she said, "Well, then I'd understand what you people talk about all day long." This response sharpened Object International's focus on its mission of developing the object-oriented ideas into business practice. The overriding goal was and is to help software developers do a better job in thinking about architecting, effectively working on the conceptual side of building software systems.

During the first years at Object International, the materials were taught in the standard lecture format that people expected, and the teaching methods included the usual flip charts and small case-study exercises. It was all very nice and neat, until 1991. A Christmas retreat to the family cabin would change Object International's approach to teaching and learning. Coad's dad is a teacher and during the retreat he revealed that he had recently challenged everything he had done over his long teaching career. In applying a new approach to teaching a logic class, he formed small teams among his students, taught them just enough to get started, and made them responsible for their own learning. Although comfortable with the platform teaching he had done for years, Coad's dad reported that lessons were better learned and better retained. The platform is no longer a fixture in Coad's classes.

This revelation put Object International on a search for more powerful ways and means to teach object thinking, more engaging ways of teaching and learning with small, empowered teams maximizing actual learning. The *example* teaches, and Edgar Guest once pondered if anything else ever does:

> *I'd rather see a sermon than hear one any day;*
> *I'd rather one should walk with me than merely tell the way.*
> Sermons We See, *by Edgar A. Guest (1934)*

The search for power learning lead to Mrs. Dale Carmichael, a teacher at Hill Elementary School and innovator in integrated learning systems for reading, writing, and spelling. The system she uses, called Spalding, is used in elementary schools with stellar results. Two of Mrs. Carmichael's guiding principles had a major impact on the training approaches developed and used by Object International. First, the learning situation must engage the learner. Learners should be made to see it, hear it, touch it, taste it, and smell it. Such multisensory engagement demands full attention and amplifies the information being brought to the brain from multiple sources. With all senses active at once, the material is quickly burned in. Second, teaching something can occur only at the moment that it can be applied with success. This means that pages of books and hours of lecturing about object-oriented theory and philosophy, the typical approaches to learning the subject, are not the least bit effective for accelerated learning. Accelerated object learning is doing, doing objects, with just enough teaching to get on with the doing.

Today, Object International's books and workshops are centered on multisensory engagement and teaching by example. The book *Object-Oriented Programming* is written entirely by example (Coad and Nicola, 1993). The new book, *Object Models*, teaches the reader object modeling entirely by examples, spelling out the strategies and patterns along the way (Coad et al., 1995). The materials in these books were developed in workshops that are entirely example-based, hence perspectives of the books. In both the books and the workshops, lessons are taught just at the moment that the learner can apply them with success.

Continuing the search for the power learning methods needed for transitioning to object think, another surprise happened along the way. In 1992, some Object International staffers enrolled in an accounting course provided by the Professional Training Group. The course title, "The Accounting Game," is eye-catching. The course has been taught for about ten years, and it is truly unique. What is amazing about The Accounting Game is that it teaches a 48-hour college-level accounting class in just 8 hours! And it's fun!

It was immediately obvious that this power learning method had direct application to learning object thinking and problem solving. No more flip charts. No more lectures. They are insufficient to meet the overwhelming educational challenge. Through collaboration and study of the methods used in The Accounting Game, Object International developed The Object Game and added it to the growing accelerated methods used in their workshops. Many of the disciplines that have been incorporated in the design of The Object Game are based on Howard Gardner's work, *Frames of Mind* (Gardner, 1985). The concepts have been explained and further expanded in many practical ways by Thomas Armstrong, especially in his work, *Seven Kinds of Smart* (Armstrong, 1993).

Gardner describes seven intelligences, where intelligence is the ability to produce something of value within a certain cultural context. Of the seven intelligences, linguistic and mathematical/logical are the two most commonly promoted and revered in Western society, and so much so in the field of information systems that these two intelligences may be considered as the foundation. From this perspective, the other five are amplifiers. Thus, in a learning situation, we begin with mathematical/logical and linguistic, and add in spatial, musical, bodily kinesthetic, intrapersonal, and interpersonal intelligences. The idea is to get multiple intelligences engaged at the same time. Since the foundation intelligences are already engaged, one of more of the other intelligences is used to amplify the learning experience.

This history of Object International may be surprising. Some may have thought that the history of such a company would have been a story of astonishing technical developments and amazing technology widgets. Instead, this history tells the true story of the challenges that must be faced by businesses wanting to transition to object-oriented technology. It's a formidable learning challenge that requires an overwhelming response, not corporate training as usual.

Like Object International, other companies that are succeeding with object technology have committed to continuous learning, and they deploy power learning methods that are up to the task. When it comes to learning object thinking and acquiring object-oriented technology skills, successful companies have recognized the need for accelerated learning. First, they have come to grips with the scope and depth of the learning challenge. Second, they can easily calculate the incredibly high cost of traditional training using traditional learning methods. The bottom line is that accelerated learning is probably the only practical and affordable way to learn to develop and deploy object-oriented information systems.

Accelerated learning is a cornerstone strategy for transitioning to objects. Recognition of the need for accelerated learning has been demonstrated by the invited lectures series of tutorials that Peter Coad has delivered at OOPSLA (Coad, 1994), ACM's annual conference on Object-Oriented Programming Systems and Languages. For three years running, conference attendees are eager to listen, observe, and apply practical, accelerated learning of techniques to object technology and expand their knowledge of strategies they can apply in their organizations to encourage people by making education engaging, more effective, and fun. Fun is very definitely a key part of accelerated learning, and accelerated learning is a key part of adopting object technology.

Tools to Support Hands-On Learning

Object International develops tools to support the learning process. They even offer a tool that is free for classroom and personal study (a small shareware fee applies when the software is used for other purposes). It's called Playground, an object model "whiteboard" for domain experts and object modelers. Object International also offers Together/C++, a commercial development tool for continuously up-to-date object modeling and C++ programming.

The Technology Transfer Challenges

The learning challenge posed by object technology is so great that nothing less than power learning methods and techniques are required. Object International and its clients are united in the common belief that hands-on, engaging learning approaches are essential to accelerated object learning. Furthermore, the hands-on learning situations must be based in real projects in the problem domain of the participants. If "toy" case studies are the basis of study, learners face the classic questions, "What do I do to apply object technology in my business area when I go back to work next Monday morning? How do I build an object model in my domain?" Answering such fundamental questions is essential.

The focus of training, of learning, must be on producing frequent, tangible, working results within the learning experience itself. These results must be actual project results, results that are for real and that matter. Achieving such learning outcomes requires accelerated learning methods. What's at stake is making technology transfer happen.

Another challenge in succeeding at technology transfer is the need to accomplish team learning. Object-oriented information systems development is a team endeavor. New information systems are being developed by multidisciplinary teams. It is very helpful to have work teams learn the technology together, as a team. Direct relevance of the problem domain is assured, and the team that learns together works well together to produce outstanding results together. We are challenged to train competent work teams, not just individuals. Underestimating the scope of the learning effort can be a major pitfall.

One of the most difficult ways to get new ideas into an organization is to send an employee to a public seminar, and expect them to come back to the workplace and impart the knowledge. It is unrealistic to think that one person could spark and tend the fires needed to insert new technology. And, it is important to have the multiple perspectives of a team so that the application knowledge is well balanced.

Another challenge to adopting object technology has been the thinking, "if we just buy the right tools, everything will be okay." This thinking is not uncommon, especially in the United States business community. But, what good is a tool without the knowledge or skill to use it? A fool with a tool, is still a fool. If limited resources force that a choice be made, pay for education, get hand-on training, get the job done, then, get the tools if you can.

Object International's staff have seen people hurt themselves by not investing in education first. While neglecting the learning, they purchased sophisticated tools that got them into trouble faster. Still others have gained initial object knowledge and training, and decide their training is over. They feel that they can simply apply what they have just learned and build applications. They show little interest in continuing their education. Yet, the willingness to continue learning and growing is essential to mastery of the object-oriented methods and techniques. The challenge to the business who wants to deploy the technology is a challenge to apply accelerated learning methods, and sustain learning over time.

Strategies That Work

Having investigated the evolution of object technology in business and the challenges of technology transfer, this discussion can be advanced by considering some of the education and training approaches that show promise for power learning.

For accelerated technology transfer to occur, training and mentoring must be combined into the same activity. As shown in Figure 4.14, this fusion involves

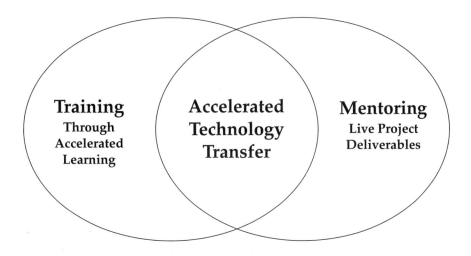

Figure 4.14 Accelerated technology transfer.

1. The use of accelerated learning methods to achieve mastery of the object disciplines in limited time

2. Mentoring projects and hands-on workshops—not classes—that are directly tied to project results.

With these two conditions for learning in place, small corporate work teams learn rapidly by working on real problems, with real deadlines, and a real need to know how to get the job done. Object International and other successful businesses have learned that consulting and training are one and the same activity.

Object International conducts workshops using the technology transfer approach discussed above. Tools such as Together/C++ and Playground are used throughout the results-based workshops. Although current object modeling workshops run from 5 to 10 days, clients are requesting longer time frames, say 2 to 4 weeks of extended training and consulting all the way through. In keeping with the results orientation of the workshops, language-specific training is taught in terms of style of thinking as well as the subsets of the language or tool that is effective to use. For example, subsets matching the requirements of the problem domain are taught. By introducing a subset of C++, the learner can stay out of trouble within this rich and diverse language, and subsets of Smalltalk can allow the team to focus on getting the job done while suppressing some of the language features that are not needed to build effective information systems in the given problem domain.

New users of object technology are wise to insist on some basics when evaluating sources of training. They will be well served if they insist on hands-on training wrapped around their needs and training that is complete only when real project results are delivered. Anything less will not bring about the desired results.

Object technology is a paradigm shift, not in just the world of technology, but throughout the world of business. Both business and technology leaders need a working knowledge of the technology and its business implications. Object International provides mentoring to business executives through its one-day workshop, The Executive Decision to Adopt Object Technology. Successful transitions to object technology as a business tool requires that management maintain a working knowledge of object-oriented business reengineering and technology.

Successful transitions require education and training from top to bottom. And since the technology and its business uses continue to rapidly evolve, executive briefings are needed to keep management abreast of the latest developments. Management must stay beyond the hype of new technology and new management theories. They must have sufficient understanding of the technology to know that it can be used to reduce risk in a chaotic business world. The impact of object-oriented approaches to business engineering will be grasped by the successful companies, and the technology will be deployed to harness the potential.

Keeping abreast of emerging technologies and business practices is essential as the pace of change shows no sign of slowing. Learning must continue over time. Object International stays in touch with clients and uses e-mail and the World Wide Web as means of continuing the dialogue. Successfully making the initial transition to object technology is the beginning, not the end, of a long, challenging, and rewarding journey.

Future Directions

From the experiences of and observations made by Object International to date, some needs and trends are coming into focus. In the future, domain experts, business users of the technology, must be more directly involved in building object models, maybe even going so far as to assume ownership of business modeling. The business, technical, and other models should be views of one and the same model. If it is one model, it is easy to argue that ownership of the modeling process rests with the business user, not the technologist.

Object methods, techniques, and tools continue to evolve very rapidly. The object modeling workshops in coming years will evolve accordingly. Tools such as Borland's Delphi95 will give us drag-and-drop ways to build a human interface and domain objects, develop database hooks, and press a button to see something that works. Such tools create confidence that people feel when they build an object model that ends up as working software. As more and more advanced tools become available, the distance between the model and the software becomes shorter and shorter.

Multimedia provides new opportunities for applying accelerated learning techniques. Multimedia programs may provide powerful support to hands-on workshops and facilitate annual skill updates.

Conclusion

Accelerated learning has become the secret weapon of companies that make successful transitions to object-oriented technology. Many advances have already been made, and power learning methods are now available. Just as companies have used accelerated learning for objects to gain a competitive advantage, they must continue with power learning to sustain that advantage over time.

References

Armstrong, T. (1993). *Seven Kinds of Smart.* New York: Plume Books.

Coad, P. (1993). *The Object Game.* Austin, TX: Object International, Inc.

Coad, P. (1994, October). *Amplified Learning: Using Multi-Intelligence Engagement.* OOPSLA Tutorial.

Coad, P., and J. Nicola. (1993). *Object-Oriented Programming.* Englewood Cliffs, NJ: Prentice Hall.

Coad, P., D. North, and M. Mayfield. (1995). *Object Models: Strategies, Patterns, and Applications.* Englewood Cliffs, NJ: Prentice Hall.

Gardner, H. (1985). *Frames of Mind: The Theory of Multiple Intelligences.* New York: Basic Books.

Guest, E. A. (1934). Sermons see. *Collected Verse of Edgar A. Guest.* New York: Contemporary Books.

Object International, Inc. (1994). The executive decision to adopt object technology. Austin, TX: Object International, Inc. 1994. [A special report with the same title is included as an appendix in Coad (1994).]

Professional Training Group. (1992). *The Accounting Game.*

THE ESSENTIAL OBJECT-ORIENTED LIBRARY FOR BUSINESS AND OTHER LEARNING RESOURCES

This appendix presents a shortlist of effective learning resources. Books have been screened for readability and their applicability to business. The chapter also includes a directory of publishers and consultants mentioned in the book.

THE ESSENTIAL OBJECT-ORIENTED LIBRARY

New books in the fields of object-oriented technology, business reengineering, and human-computer interaction are appearing with great frequency. Some publishers have specialized in these topics. SIGS Books specializes in object-oriented technology books, Oliver Wight specializes in business reengineering, ASQC Quality Press in total quality, and Future Strategies, Inc. in workflow technologies.

Meanwhile, some long-established publishing houses, including Addison-Wesley, John Wiley, McGraw-Hill, and Prentice Hall, to name a few, have focused in these areas. Getting on the mailing lists for announcements from these companies is one way to keep up with the new titles. Addresses are provided later in this appendix.

The flood of new books creates a problem for businesses trying to keep up. Many titles, especially those in the field of object-oriented technology are written for science and engineering audiences, not business. Some very interesting and eye-catching titles turn out to be extremely technical discussions of arcane subjects. The number of computer science titles on object-oriented technology alone represents a bewildering choice, and most such books are far too complex or obscure to be of use in business information systems development.

This appendix was developed to chart a business path through the literature. In the pages that follow I've complied an annotated list of books that is representative of the works of leading thinkers and developers of these fields of study.

The list is not intended to include all books in print, and some excellent new books may have been overlooked. The list does provide many of the titles that should be in corporate libraries and on the desktops of information systems developers.

Many of the titles included here are rated as "required reading" or "required reference" and are marked (R). This rating means that it is difficult to conceive of an object-oriented information systems developer that is not at least familiar with the work.

Some books are first reads, and they are marked accordingly. These titles will be especially useful for readers that are just getting started in a subject such as C++ programming. Complete bibliographic references appear in Appendix C, "Classified Bibliography: An Extended Object-Oriented Library for Business."

To provide easy reference, The Essential Object-Oriented Library for Business is categorized as follows:

- New world order of business

- Introduction to object technology and business reengineering

- Learning to object think and program

- Business process reengineering

- Human cognition and work

- Object-oriented systems development

- Object-oriented programming

- The learning organization

New World Order of Business

Barker, Joel Arthur. (R) *Future Edge: Discovering the New Paradigms of Success*. W. Morrow. 240 pp. 1992. Since the pace of change shows no sign of slowing, successful businesses will learn to stay alert to and systematically study paradigm shifts. Barker instructs the business to watch for the surprises, not extrapolate the past.

Bradley, Stephen P., Jerry A. Hausman, and Richard L. Nolan. *Globalization, Technology, and Competition: The Fusion of Computers and Telecommunications in the 1990s*. Harvard Business School Press. 400 pp. 1993. The authors explore the dramatic influences of globalization and technological innovation on the structure of industries, the strategies of firms, and their organizational forms.

Champy, James. *Reengineering Management: The Mandate for New Leadership*. HarperBusiness. 212 pp. 1995. In a follow-up to the publication of *Reengineering the Corporation*, Champy asserts that a familiar pattern has emerged in the application of reengineering: too often reeengineering stops in its tracks at the executive suite. He provides the guidelines needed by managers to lead, measure, and reward the new work created by reengineering.

Davidow, William H., and Michael S. Malone. (R) *The Virtual Corporation: Structuring and Revitalizing the Corporation for the 21st Century.* Harper Collins. 294 pp. 1992. The authors provide an integrated picture of the customer-driven company of the future. The book is at the cutting edge and describes the future global marketplace that depends on corporations producing virtual products high in added value and available to customers instantly. Compaq Computer thought highly enough of this book to give copies to present and prospective customers.

Gelernter, David. *Mirror Worlds or: The Day Software Puts the Universe in a Shoebox . . . How it Will Happen and What it Will Mean.* Oxford University Press. 237 pp. 1991. In what could easily be mistaken as a piece of science fiction, the chairman of the computer science department at Yale University takes the reader on a prose ride into the future, to the day software puts the universe in a shoe box. Gelernter takes the reader on a tour of the information world being constructed with advanced networked information technology. The reader will not learn object technology but will learn what is ultimately being built with the technology.

Goldman, S. L., R. N. Nagel, and K. Preiss. *Agile Competitors and Virtual Organizations: Strategies for Enriching the Customer.* Van Nostrand Reinhold. 400 pp. 1994. The publisher of this book practices what the book preaches by offering corporate customers with customized editions to meet their specific needs. This book explains the business impact of mass customization and what it does to the legacy of mass production where one size fits all.

Hamel, Gary, and C. K. Prahalad. *Competing for the Future: Breakthrough Strategies for Seizing Control of Your Industry and Creating the Markets of Tomorrow.* Harvard Business School Press. 336 pp. 1994. The authors challenge executives to stop the unrewarding process of dead-end downsizing and enter the realm of dynamic business transformation. The book reframes what it means to be strategic.

Kelly, Kevin. *Out of Control: The Rise of Neo-biological Civilization.* Addison-Wesley. 521 pp. 1994. Reengineered processes lead to redesigned organizations. This work makes a significant contribution to organizational design as it applies to the business enterprise of the coming century.

Keyes, Jessica. *Infotrends: The Competitive Use of Information.* McGraw-Hill. 221 pp. 1993. This book points executives toward the aggressive use of information for competitive advantage. Nine key trends in information technology are discussed. They include downsizing, alliances, competitive intelligence, turning data into knowledge, and surrounding the business core with technology.

Martin, James. *The Great Transition: Using the Seven Disciplines of Enterprise Engineering to Align People, Technology, and Strategy.* AMACOM. 503 pp. 1995. Martin synthesizes the best of the next-generation management technologies into a meaningful framework for success.

McKenney, James L. *Waves of Change: Business Evaluation Through Information Technology.* Harvard Business School Press. 240 pp. 1995. McKenney, a Harvard professor, builds and applies a framework for an information technology based business strategy. Using cases from two corporations to build the framework, he applies the model to three additional companies, revealing the entire spectrum of issues involved in the deployment of information technology.

Peters, Tom. *Liberation Management: Necessary Disorganization for the Nanosecond Nineties.* Macmillan. 1992.

Pinchot, Gifford and Elizabeth Pinchot. *The End of Bureaucracy and the Rise of the Intelligent Organization.* Berrett-Koehler Publishers. 399 pp. 1994. Although many management books strive to make "bureaucracy" work better, these authors show how to replace it with various principles for organizing and coordinating work.

Sakaiya, Taichi. *The Knowledge-Value Revolution, or A History of the Future.* Kodabsha International. 379 pp. 1991.

Senge, Peter M. *The Fifth Discipline: The Art and Practice of the Learning Organization.* Doubleday/Currency. 424 pp. 1990. Senge's focus on "systems thinking" represents a discipline central to reengineering business processes. This seminal work has had a major impact on business reengineering.

Strassmann, Paul A. *Information Payoff: The Transformation of Work in the Electronic Age.* Collier Macmillan. 298 pp. 1985.

Strassmann, Paul A. *The Business Value of Computers.* Information Economics Press. 522 pp. 1990.

Tappscott, Don, and Art Caston. (R) *Paradigm Shift: The New Promise of Information Technology.* McGraw-Hill. 337 pp. 1993. Tappscott and Caston provide an in-depth explanation of how a new era of information technology is enabling corporate rebirth. The book covers the impact of work-group computing, enterprise computing, interenterprise computing, open systems, network-based systems, and the shift from software craft to software manufacturing.

Wang, Charles B. (R) *Techno Vision: The Executive's Survival Guide to Understanding and Managing Information Technology.* McGraw-Hill. 198 pp. 1994. Wang, founder of the $2 billion company, Computer Associates, asserts that there is a fundamental "disconnect" between corporate management and technology executives that sets the stage for serious, even catastrophic errors. He attempts to close the gap and help realign business and technology. The introduction is written by Peter Drucker, and the book is a must reading for CEOs and CIOs.

Introduction to Object Technology and Business Reengineering

Hammer, Michael, and J. Champy. (R) *Reengineering the Corporation: A Manifesto for Business Revolution.* Harper Business. 1993, 1994 updated paperback edition. Hammer is a founder of the reengineering movement, and this is the opening volley of the reengineering attack. The central thesis of the book is that American corporations must undertake nothing less that a radical reinvention of how they do their work. Whether one agrees with the radical approach or not, this work is widely known and referenced in business discussions.

Love, Tom. (R) *Object Lessons: Lessons Learned in Object-Oriented Development Projects.* SIGS Books. 256 pp. 1993. Love's highly readable book focuses on building large-scale commercial software projects using objects. The book provides clear insight into the issues and trends as opposed to specific products and services. Love brings over a decade of experience to this work. The book examines the many questions that technical leaders and managers face as they transition to object technology.

Mattison, Rob, and Michael J. Sipolt. (R) *The Object-Oriented Enterprise: Making Corporate Information Systems Work.* McGraw-Hill. 400 pp. 1994. This book is aimed directly at corporate information systems. Its in-depth coverage of large-scale business information systems makes the book indispensable for business and technology professionals. The book considers immediate and tactical applications of object technology and the use of design methods and CASE tools. Over two and a half years of research went into this book. The results are presented in a thorough discussion of the topic of objectification, the process of migrating to object-oriented corporate information systems. The book covers logical and physical architectures and the development of an object-oriented infrastructure.

Sims, Oliver. *Business Objects: Delivering Cooperative Objects for Client/Server.* McGraw-Hill. 348 pp. 1994. Sims' approach is the application of business-sized objects to the user interface, where cooperative business objects correspond to an on-screen object needed by the user. The book also explains the need for middleware between applications and the operating system.

Taylor, David. *Object-Oriented Technology: A Manager's Guide.* Addison-Wesley. 146 pp. 1991. This brief and lucid primer is ideal for the busy manager. It explains the concepts, the business impact, and the advantages and disadvantages of object-oriented technology.

Learning to Object Think and Program

Ambler, Scott. (R) *Objects Primer: The Application Developer's Guide to Object-Orientation.* SIGS Books. Forthcoming title. Ambler's primer is directed to mainframe programmers and developers working on their first object-oriented projects. The book is to the point and time saving while covering a complete development life cycle instead of just object-oriented programming. The book will be followed by two additional volumes: *Advanced OO Design, Construction, and Testing,* and *Management Issues for OO Development.*

Coad, Peter. *The Object Game.* Object International. 1993. This is a board game that teaches "object think." Object International adopted the theories and methods of The Accounting Game to the world of objects.

Coad, Peter, and J. Nicola. *Object-Oriented Programming*. Prentice Hall. 260 pp. 1993. Book and disk. This book represents a breakthrough in learning to "object think" and program. Coad and Nicola used accelerated learning methods to craft this book into a very effective learning resource. It provides an object-oriented programming primer, a graduated series of four examples, language summaries for both Smalltalk and C++, source code for the examples, and patterns of program design.

Coad, Peter, David North, and M. Mayfield. (R) *Object Models: Strategies, Patterns, & Applications*. Prentice Hall. 450 pp. 1995. This book teaches totally by example and uses accelerated learning methods to amplify learning. The book makes a significant contribution to the world of business computing by providing familiar business application examples, and strategies and patterns that make it easy to extend the practitioner's current knowledge. The application examples include point-of-sale, warehousing, order-processing, and data acquisition. The disk features an on-line version of the strategies and patterns in the form of a Windows help file.

Cogswell, Jeffery M. *Simple C++: Learn C++ While You Build the Incredible Robodog*. The Waite Group. 252 pp. 1994. The title says it all. An entertaining first introduction from the company that publishes some very serious object-oriented programming books. Have fun.

Hamilton, Margaret. *Object Thinking: Development Before the Fact*. McGraw-Hill. 320 pp. 1994. This book/CD-ROM combination explores the "development before the fact paradigm" and features tools to put the paradigm to immediate use.

Khoshafian, Setrag. *Object Orientation: Concepts, Languages, Databases, and User Interfaces*. Wiley. 434 pp. 1990. This book is a solid introduction to the main concepts of object-oriented systems suitable for a technical audience of software developers.

Korienek, Gene, and Tom Wrench. *A Quick Trip to ObjectLand: Object Oriented Programming with Smalltalk/V*. (R) Prentice Hall. 192 pp. 1993. This book uses an actual dialogue between two characters to help the reader solve problems in the object-oriented paradigm and implement solutions using Smalltalk/V. This unique book is a must-read for those who want to learn Smalltalk.

Mattison, Rob, and Michael J. Sipolt. *The Object-Oriented Enterprise: Making Corporate Information Systems Work.* McGraw-Hill. 400 pp. 1994. This book is aimed directly at corporate information systems. Its in-depth coverage of large-scale business information systems makes the book indispensable for business and technology professionals. The book considers immediate and tactical applications of object technology and the use of design methods and CASE tools. Over two and a half years of research went into this book. The results are presented in a thorough discussion of the topic of objectification, the process of migrating to object-oriented corporate information systems. The book covers logical and physical architectures and the development of an object-oriented infrastructure.

Orfali, Robert, Dan Harkey, and Jeri Edwards. *Essential Client/Server Survival Guide.* Wiley. 527 pp. 1994. This book is witty, approachable, and comprehensive, covering everything from operating systems and communications to application architectures that incorporate database, transaction processing, groupware, and distributed objects. While rich in content, it is also fun to read and contains almost 200 illustrations. Over 100 pages of the book are devoted to distributed object computing, the next generation of client/server.

Orfali, Robert, Dan Harkey, and Jeri Edwards. (R) *The Essential Distributed Objects Survival Guide.* Wiley. 1995. The authors help the Martian, Zog, on an intergalactic tour of client/server and object orientation including CORBA, Business Objects, OpenDoc, OLE, ODBMS and Component suites. Don't let the friendly and fun nature of the book fool you. It contains serious information and in-depth coverage of the next generation: distributed object computing.

Taylor, David. *Object-Oriented Information Systems: Planning and Implementation.* Wiley. 384 pp. 1992. Taylor's books have been well received and widely read. This overview of object-oriented information systems is aimed at MIS managers and delivers a good introduction and decision-making framework.

Business Process Reengineering

Andrews, Dorine C., and Susan K. Stalick. *Business Reengineering: The Survival Guide.* Yourdin Press. 302 pp. 1994. This is a step-by-step, how-to book. It covers when to reengineer, the basic principles, obstacles and problems, and making the transition to continuous improvement. The authors make a plea for executives to read their book, since leadership from the top is the single most important success factor.

Baba, Marietta, D. Falkenberg, and D. Hill. "The Cultural Dimensions of Technology-Enabled Corporate Transformations," research paper, March 28, 1994. In *Technological Innovations and Cultural Processes: New Theoretical Perspectives.* Edited by Santos, M. Josefa and R. Diaz Cruz. National University of Mexico.

Boar, Bernard H. *Practical Steps for Aligning Information Technology with Business Strategies: How to Achieve a Competitive Advantage.* Wiley. 353 pp. 1994. This book provides an in-depth discussion of aligning information technology with business and the strategic planning techniques for achieving that goal. The book includes charts and templates for immediate use, and guidelines on how to design an internal information technology economy.

Bounds, Greg, et al. *Beyond Total Quality Management: Toward the Emerging Paradigm.* McGraw-Hill. 817 pp. 1994.

Braithwaite, Timothy. *Information Service Excellence Through TQM: Building Partnerships for Business Process Reengineering and Continuous Improvement.* ASQC Quality Press. 145 pp. 1994. This to-the-point primer describes how TQM thinking can be applied to the information systems setting.

Champy, James. *Reengineering Management: The Mandate for New Leadership.* HarperBusiness. 212 pp. 1995.

Ciborra, Claudio. *Teams, Markets and Systems—Business Innovation and Information Technology.* Cambridge University Press. 250 pp. 1993.

Clemmer, Jim, Barry Sheehy, and Achieve International/Zengler Miller Associates. *Firing on All Cylinders: The Service/Quality System for High-Powered Corporate Performance.* Business One Irwin. 392 pp. 1992. This book was recommended by practitioners on the business process reengineering discussion group on the Internet (BPR-L@duticai.twi.tudelft.nl).

Davenport, Thomas. *Process Innovation: Reengineering Work Through Information Technology.* Harvard Business School Press. 337 pp. 1993. Ernst & Young. Davenport shows how to implement the reengineering process by fusing information technology with new ways of managing people. He provides an in-depth study of the strategic and operational dimensions, and the book is one of the first to provide a step-by-step guide to reengineering.

Deming, W. Edwards. *Out of the Crisis.* Cambridge University Press. 507 pp. 1982.

Dimancescu, Dan. *The Seamless Enterprise: Making Cross Functional Management Work.* HarperBusiness. 249 pp. 1992.

Donovan, John J. *Business Reengineering with Information Technology.* Prentice Hall. 224 pp. 1994. Donovan includes objects as one of the weapons of the future for business reengineering. The book provides information technology strategies, a method for reengineering business processes, and the impact of client/server architectures.

Dunn, Robert H., and Richard S. Ullman. *TQM for Computer Software.* 2nd Ed. McGraw-Hill. 364 pp. 1994. The second edition of this widely read book includes quality implications of object-oriented programming as well as solutions for the entire development life cycle. It emphasizes the roles of technology, people, and management in creating customer satisfaction and controlling software projects.

Fallon, Howard. *How to Implement Information Systems and Live to Tell About It.* Wiley. 291 pp. 1995. Fallon's techniques are aimed at today's cross-functional, multi-platform environments. His Joint Implementation Process is a group planning technique that helps keep implementation on track.

Fisher, Kimball, and the Belgrad-Fisher-Rayner Team. *Tips for Teams: A Ready Reference for Solving Team Problems.* McGraw-Hill. 250 pp. 1995. This book about teams was written by a team. It is a problem-solving guide for teams and offers 416 tips.

Fried, Louis. *Managing Information Technology in Turbulent Times.* Wiley. 339 pp.

1995. This book is based on the best practices of chief information officers from more than a thousand corporations. It deals with the changing role of the CIO, business process redesign, the impact of object technology on software management, outsourcing, protecting information assets, and keeping users satisfied.

Gunn, Thomas G. *In the Age of the Real-Time Enterprise: Managing for Sustained Performance with Enterprise Logistics Planning.* Oliver Wight Publications. 166 pp. 1994. This well-written management primer's enterprise resource planning method is especially relevant to manufacturing organizations.

Hamel, Gary, and C. K. Prahalad. *Competing for the Future: Breakthrough Strategies for Seizing Control of Your Industry and Creating the Markets of Tomorrow.* Harvard Business School Press. 336 pp. 1994. The authors challenge executives to stop the unrewarding process of dead-end downsizing and enter the realm of dynamic business transformation. The book reframes what it means to be strategic.

Handy, Charles B. *The Age of Paradox.* Harvard Business School Press. 303 pp. 1994.

Handy, Charles B. *The Age of Unreason.* Harvard Business School Press. 278 pp. 1989.

Hastings, Colin. *The New Organization: Growing the Cultural of Organizational Networking.* McGraw-Hill. 178 pp. 1993. Motivated by Peter Drucker's classic Harvard Business Review article, "The Coming of the New Organization," Dr. Hastings wrote this book to sketch a picture of what the large business organization will look like 20 years from now. He provides five core capabilities that must be developed in the organization of tomorrow: collective individualism, soft networking, project working, sharing know-how, and hard networks through communications technology.

Hofstede, Greet. *Cultures and Organizations: Software of the Mind.* McGraw-Hill. 1991.

Hunt, V. Daniel. *The Survival Factor: An Action Guide to Improving Your Business Today.* Oliver Wight Publications. 300 pp. 1994. This book delivers ten survival factors that can be implemented by leaders, managers, and teams.

Hunt, V. Daniel. *Reengineering: Leveraging the Power of Integrated Product Development.* Oliver Wight Publications. 300 pp. 1993. This practical guide to reengineering includes advice and guidelines from such leading companies as Hewlett-Packard, AT&T, Saturn, and McDonnell Douglas.

Institute of Industrial Engineers. *Beyond the Basics of Reengineering: Survival Tactics for the 90's.* Institute of Industrial Engineers. 250 pp. 1994. In addition to the essentials, this book includes more than ten real-life stories that detail the pitfalls and critical success factors involved in reengineering implementations.

Jacobson, Ivar, Maria Ericson, and Agneta Jacobson. (R) *The Object Advantage: Business Process Engineering with Object Technology.* Addison-Wesley. 1994. This landmark work provides one method to integrate the work of reengineering a business, its processes, and the underlying information systems. Going beyond the theory, the authors provide actual deliverables and a formal object-orient method.

Jayachandra, Y. *Reengineering the Networked Enterprise.* McGraw-Hill. 290 pp. 1994. This book brings reengineering and enterprise networking topics under one cover and combines technology with business process automation and work-flow. Technical treatments of object-oriented methods, client/server, EDI, E-mail, and distributed computing are included.

Johansson, H. J., et al. *Business Process Reengineering: BreakPoint Strategies for Market Dominance.* John Wiley. 1993.

Katzenbach, Jon R., and Douglas K. Smith. *The Wisdom of Teams: Creating the High-Performance Organization.* Harvard Business School Press. 291 pp. 1993. This book examines numerous teams to determine what works, and then provides a detailed plan for building and managing successful teams.

Kelly, Kevin. *Out of Control: The Rise of Neo-Biological Civilization.* Addison-Wesley. 521 pp. 1994. Reengineered processes lead to redesigned organization. This work makes a significant contribution to organizational design as it applies to the business enterprise of the coming century.

Keyes, Jessica. *Solving the Productivity Paradox: TQM for Computer Professionals.* McGraw-Hill. 300 pp. 1994. The theme of this book is how to make computer investments pay off by using TQM strategies. Each chapter includes a parable based on interviews with Fortune 100 firms.

Khoshafian, Setrag, B. Baker, R. Abnous, and K. Sheperd. *Intelligent Offices: Object-Oriented, Multi-Media Information Management in Client/Server Architectures.* 424 pp. Wiley. 1992. Neither science fiction nor hype, this book with a long title provides an excellent description of the state-of-the-possible with information technology.

Lipnack, Jessica, and Jeffrey Stamps. *The Age of the Network: Organizing Principles for the 21st Century.* Oliver Wight Publications. 256 pp. 1994. This work provides a practical view of how to think about business reinvention without losing the value and knowledge that is embedded in the current organization. Principles of effective teams is one key focus of the book.

Lowenthal, Jeffrey N. *Reengineering the Organization: A Step-by-Step Approach to Corporate Revitalization.* ASCQ Quality Press. 185 pp. 1994. This work provides a four-phase, 13-step approach to streamlining, customer focus, and evaluation of improvements. Offers a simple explanation of change theory.

Martin, James. *Enterprise Engineering—The Key to Corporate Survival Vol. I-IV.* Savant Institute. 1994. Martin clearly explains the do-or-die fundamentals of business reengineering and offers a comprehensive set of techniques to implement change.

Nolan, Richard L., and David C. Croson. *Creative Destruction: A Six-Stage Process for Transforming the Organization.* Harvard Business School Press. 272 pp. March 1995. According to Nolan and Croson, the next generation of corporate organization is the information technology enabled network. They propose a six-stage process to achieve stability in the turbulent business environment.

Raymond, Larry. *Reinventing Communication: Visual Language for Planning, Problem Solving and Reengineering.* ASQC Quality Press. 167 pp. 1994. Raymond introduces a concept called *visual language* that uses visual images for extending communication and analysis capabilities. The approach strives to take reengineering out of the realm of technology and management methods and make it accessible to project teams.

Roberts, Lon. *Process Reengineering: The Key to Achieving Breakthrough Success.* ASQC Quality Press. 195 pp. 1994. This book surveys the many issues and facets of process reengineering, and defines the scope, meaning, and philosophy of reengineering.

Rummler, Geary, and Alan Brache. *Improving Performance: How to Manage the White Space on the Organization Chart.* Jossey-Bass. 227 pp. 1990. The authors explore three avenues to deal with performance issues that affect the interactions between departments and function, the "white space" on traditional organization charts. This white space is approached from the perspective of the organization, processes, and individual jobs.

Senge, Peter M. (R) *The Fifth Discipline: The Art and Practice of the Learning Organization.* Doubleday/Currency. 424 pp. 1990. Senge's focus on "systems thinking" represents a discipline that is central to reengineering business processes. This seminal work has had a major impact on business reengineering. This work has been so influential that an Internet discussion group has been established to carry on the discussion. It is a lively discussion and happens at learn-org@world.std.com.

Shekerjian, Denise. *Uncommon Genius—How Great Ideas Are Born.* Penguin Books. 244 pp. 1990. Guy Kawasaki of Apple Computer has this to say about this work: "Most books about creativity are cuties with exercises, brainteasers, and cartoons. They are supposed to tickle you into creativity. Then there's Shekerjian's book. It is a complete, radical, and welcome departure from any book I've ever read about creativity." This is a serious business book about the real dimensions of creativity, including years of dedicated work and enduring years of uncertainty and frustration.

Simon, Alan R. *The Computer Professional's Survival Guide.* McGraw-Hill. 176 pp. 1992.

Simon, Alan R. *Workgroup Computing: Workflow, Groupware, and Messaging.* McGraw-Hill. 350 pp. 1994. Simon provides step-by-step discussions of workflow, workgroup, and combined paradigms, applications development, and a survey of available groupware products and services.

Spurr, Kathy, P. Layzell, L. Jennison, and N. Richards, Eds. *Software Assistance for Business Reengineering.* Wiley. 1994. This book was derived from the work of the British Computer Society CASE Group. It answers fundamental questions about business reengineering and provides discussions of methods and tools. Part four is a sampling of automated tools available.

Strassmann, Paul A. *The Politics of Information Management.* Information Economics Press. 523 pp. 1994.

Taylor, David A. (R) *Business Engineering with Object Technology.* Wiley. 188 pp. 1995. Many powerful concepts are presented in these few, lucid pages. Taylor's "convergent engineering" presents a framework for integrating business and software engineering. The essence is expressing business concepts directly in executable software objects.

Tomasko, Robert M. *Rethinking the Corporation: The Architecture of Change.* AMA-COM. 213 pp. 1993.

Weinberg, Gerald M. *An Introduction to General Systems Thinking.* Wiley. 279 pp. 1988. A readable and insightful book.

Wheatley, Margaret. *Leadership and the New Science: Learning About Organization from an Orderly Universe.* Berrett-Koehler Publishers. 164 pp. 1992.

White, Thomas E., and Layna Fischer, Eds. *New Tools for New Times: The Workflow Paradigm. The Impact of Information Technology on Business Process Reengineering.* Future Strategies Inc. 1994. This anthology with twenty-one contributors arose from a quest for more meaningful information about workflow technology and business process reengineering. In addition to answering some very fundamental questions, the book provides case studies, a vendor directory, and a "who's who" of industry enablers.

Zuboff, Shoshanah. *In the Age of the Smart Machine: The Future of Work and Power.* Basic Books. 468 pp. 1988.

Zuboff, Shoshanah. *Psychological and Organizational Implications of Computer-Mediated Work.* Center for Information Systems Research, Alfred P. Sloan School of Management, MIT. 26 pp. 1981.

Human Cognition and Work

Bass, Len, and Prasun Dewan, Eds. *User Interface Software.* Wiley. 201 pp. 1993. This collection of papers provides an authoritative overview of new technologies and what they mean for the developer. Coverage includes techniques for multimedia, multiuser, animation-based, and direct-manipulation user interfaces.

Ehn, Pelle. *Work-Oriented Design of Computer Artifacts.* 2nd Ed. Arbetslivscebtrum. 1989.

Hix, D., and R. Hartson. *Developing User Interfaces: Ensuring Usability Through Product & Process.* Wiley. 416 pp. 1993. This book is based on a course that has been widely taught by the authors. It discusses representation techniques and a variety of object-oriented tools.

Lakoff, George. *Women, Fire, and Dangerous Things: What Categories Reveal About the Mind.* The University of Chicago Press. 614 pp. 1987. Since classification is a foundation of object-oriented problem-solving, Lakoff is a must-read for object-oriented developers.

Lakoff, George, and M. Johnson. *Metaphors We Live By.* The University of Chicago Press. 614 pp. 1987.

Laurel, Brenda. *Computers as Theatre.* Addison-Wesley. 1993. This book presents a dramatic theory of human-computer activity. Laurel compliments the notion of direct manipulation with direct engagement as a means to fuse the design of applications and human interfaces as a single integrated process.

Laurel, Brenda. *The Art of Human-Computer Interface Design.* Addison-Wesley. 523 pp. 1990. This book includes works from more than fifty of the major thinkers and explorers in the field. The first section offers insights into the general issues, and is followed by "sermons" from those who have deeply influenced the field of human-computer interaction: Donald Norman, Nicholas Negroponte, Ted Nelson, Alan Kay, Jean-Louis Gassee, Timothy Leary, and Ben Schneiderman.

Minsky, Marvin. (R) *The Society of Mind.* Simon & Schuster. 339 pp. 1986. To Minsky, founder of MIT's Artificial Intelligence Lab, the mind is a "society" that arises out of ever-smaller agents that are themselves mindless. This classic work is made up of one-page sections, that together arise to offer a revolutionary explanation of how the mind works.

Nielsen, Jakob, and Robert L. Mack, Eds. *Usability Inspection Methods.* Wiley. 413 pp. 1993. Nielsen coined the term "usability inspection," and this book provides comprehensive treatment of strategies, tools, and techniques. Methods include heuristic evaluation, pluralistic walkthroughs, and cognitive walkthroughs.

Norman, Donald A. (R) *Design of Everyday Things.* Doubleday. 257 pp. 1990.

Norman, Donald A. (R) *Things That Make Us Smart.* Addison-Wesley. 1993.

Norman, Donald A. *Turn Signals are the Facial Expressions of Automobiles.* Addison-Wesley. 205 pp. 1992.

Norman, Donald A. *User-Centered Systems Design.* Lawrence Erlbaum Assoc. 1986. Norman has contributed so much to cognitive science and human-centered design that it is difficult to write large enough words about his work. Developers of computer systems are well advised to read as much of Norman's work as they can get their hands on.

Preece, Jenny, et al. (R) *Human-Computer Interaction.* Addison-Wesley. 640 pp. 1994. This textbook (instructor's guide also available) was created from course materials developed by a UK Open University team chaired by Preece. The book offers a comprehensive account of the multidisciplinary field of human-computer interaction. It balances technical and cognitive issues particularly in emerging fields like multimedia, virtual environments, and computer mediated cooperative work.

Rubin, Jeffrey. *Handbook of Usability Testing: How to Plan, Design, and Conduct*

Effective Tests. Wiley. 416 pp. 1993. Rubin provides the basics and assumes no prior engineering or human factors training. Step-by-step design are included as well as proven testing tools and techniques.

Shneiderman, Ben. *Designing the User Interface: Strategies for Effective Human-Computer Interaction.* 2nd Ed. Addison-Wesley. 573 pp. 1992. This book is a complete and current introduction to human interface design. Coverage includes the human factors of interactive software, interaction styles, design considerations, and methods to develop and test the user interface.

Shneiderman, Ben. *Sparks of Innovation in Human-Computer Interaction.* Addison-Wesley. 387 pp. 1993.

Suchman, Lucy. *Plans and Situated Actions: The Problem of Human-Machine Communications.* Cambridge University Press. 203 pp. 1987.

Tognazini, Bruce. *Tog on Interface.* Addison-Wesley. 331 pp. 1992. While focusing on the Macintosh, the book captures the underlying principles of graphical user interfaces. The work uses ideas from diverse sources including information theory, Carl Jung, and even professional beekeeping to provide a framework for achieving a deep understanding of user-interface design. Tog's gives insight into the central issues of human-computer interaction including the challenges of multimedia, agents, virtual reality, and future technologies.

Wiener, Norbert. *The Human Use of Human Beings: Cybernetics and Society.* Da Capo Press. 1954. Avon Books. 1979. This book is a classic and is a must read for anyone developing information systems for humans.

Winograd, T., and C. F. Flores. (R) *Understanding Computers and Cognition—A New Foundation for Design.* Addison-Wesley. 207 pp. 1987. This deeply thought-out work is concerned with the design of computer-based systems to facilitate human work and interaction. It definitely contributes to the ongoing discussion about what it means to be a machine and what it means to be human.

Winograd., Terry A., and Paul S. Adler, Eds. *Usability: Turning Technologies Into Tools.* Oxford University Press. 208 pp. 1992.

Object-Oriented Systems Development

Andleigh, Prabhatk, and Nichael R. Gretzinger. *Distributed Object-Oriented Analysis.* Prentice Hall. 260 pp. 1992.

Andriole, Stephen J. *Getting it Right: Information Systems Design Principles for the 90s.* AFCEA Int. Press. 117 pp. 1990. Although not a book about object-oriented technology, Andriole provides a realistic framework that describes the interdisciplinary expertise required to build the robust information systems of the future.

Berard, Edward. *A Project Management Handbook for Object-Oriented Software Development.* Prentice Hall. 600 pp. 1994. Berard's handbook discusses the project management issues associated with object-oriented development, provides the guidelines and tools, and identifies common project management problems.

Berard, Edward. *Essays on Object-Oriented Software Engineering.* Prentice Hall. 544 pp. 1993. Berard explores object-oriented software engineering methods, documentation, and testing strategies based on experience gained from engineering large projects. Topics include testing, domain analysis, requirements analysis and specification, and object coupling and cohesion.

Booch, Grady. *Object Solutions: A Source Book for Developers.* 2nd Ed. Addison-Wesley. 589 pp. 1994. The first four chapters of this book describes the process of object-oriented development in terms of inputs, outputs, products, activities, and milestones. The remaining chapters provide advice on key issues including management, planning, reuse, and quality assurance.

Booch, Grady. (R) *Object-Oriented Analysis and Design With Applications.* 2nd Ed. Addison-Wesley. 589 pp. 1994. The first edition of this book in 1991 had a major impact on the adoption of object-oriented technology. The first 160 or so pages provide gentle, yet comprehensive concepts and notions. Later he develops his method and notation and concludes with a number of case studies based in specific object programming languages. This work has been incorporated into other methods, reflecting the contributions Booch has made.

Burleson, Donald. *Practical Applications of Object-Oriented Techniques to Relational*

Databases. Wiley. 1994. Burleson writes a practical, how to do it guide to applying object-oriented techniques to relational database systems. He shows how legacy databases can function within the scope of an object-oriented application.

Cardenas, Alfonso F., and Dennis McLeod. *Research Foundations in Semantic and Object-Oriented Databases.* Prentice Hall. 432 pp. 1990. Advanced research.

Carmichael, Andy, Ed. *Object Development Methods.* SIGS Books. 347 pp. 1994. Carmichael introduces different methods to uncover the commonalty of the models produced and the changes introduced by object-orientation. Methods are compared and contrasted using a framework of three dimensions: behavioral or dynamic; static or structural; and architectural. Six methods are compared: Booch, Coad/Yourdin/Nicola, Martin/Odell, Rumbaugh, Shlaer/Mellor, and Wirfs-Brock.

Catell, R. G. G. *Object Data Management: Object-Oriented and Extended Relational Database Systems.* Addison-Wesley. 389 pp. 1994.

Chorafas, Dimitris N. *Intelligent Multimedia Databases.* Prentice Hall. 350 pp. 1994. Covers physical and logical multimedia database solutions, object-oriented databases, and the contributions of fuzzy logic to them. This advanced book includes the innovation in database operations through knowledge artifacts.

Chorafas, Dimitris N., and Heinrich Steinmann. *Object-Oriented Databases: An Introduction.* Prentice Hall. 375 pp. 1993. A technical introduction to object-oriented databases.

Coad, Peter, and Edward Yourdin. *Object-Oriented Analysis.* 2nd Ed. Prentice Hall. 255 pp. 1991.

Coad, Peter, and Edward Yourdin. *Object-Oriented Design.* Prentice Hall. 244 pp. 1991.

Coleman, Derek, P. Arnold, S. Bodoff, C. Dollin, H. Gilcrist, F. Hayes, and P. Jeremaes. *Object-Oriented Development: The FUSION Method.* Prentice Hall. 400

pp. 1994. Lines formed at the 1993 OOPSLA conference to buy this book. It heralded a second generation of object-oriented development methods, fusing the best features other methods into an industrial-strength, full life cycle process. The authors also compare some of the most widely used analysis and design methods, and provides focus on reuse and management goals. Several object-oriented CASE tools support the method, and the authors list sources of training and support.

Connell, John L., and Linda Shafer. *Object-Oriented Rapid Prototyping.* Prentice Hall. 250 pp. 1994. This book outlines an approach to applying rapid prototyping concepts to object-oriented development.

Davis, Alan M. *Software Requirements: Objects, Functions, States, Revision.* Prentice Hall. 448 pp. 1993. This book compares and contrasts problem analysis techniques, notation, and requirements specification techniques. especially suited for requirements analysts and requirements specification writers.

DeBoever, Larry R. *Enabling Technologies for Client/Server: Implementation of Adaptive Systems.* McGraw-Hill. 400 pp. 1994. Drawing from his consulting work with Fortune 1000 companies, DeBoever provides a road map for using client/server computing and reengineering methods in integrated ways. He shows how to apply sixteen principles of implementation and maintenance of information systems.

deChampeaux, D., D. Lea, and P. Faure. *Object-Oriented Systems Development.* Addison-Wesley. 532 pp. 1993. The authors go beyond particular methods and focus on a mature process to put key object-oriented concepts to work in software construction. The book is geared to software professionals and offers a detailed technical perspective on the object-oriented software development process.

Embley, David W., Barry D. Kurtz, and Scott N. Woodfield. *Object-Oriented Systems Analysis: A Model-Driven Approach.* Prentice Hall. 256 pp. 1992. This book provides how-to instructions to create and maintain analysis models and object-oriented system specifications. It covers capturing objects and their relationships, modeling behavior of individual objects, and organizing large system models.

Firesmith, Donald G. *Object-Oriented Requirements Analysis and Logical Design.* Wiley. 574 pp. 1993.

Firesmith, Donald G. *Object-Oriented Methods, Standards, and Procedures.* Prentice Hall. 1994.

Firesmith, Donald G. *Testing Object-Oriented Software.* SIGS Books. Forthcoming. Firesmith writes a column in SIGS Publication's *Report On Analysis and Design (ROAD)* and is maintainer of the ASTS Development Method (ADM).

Gamma, E., R. Helm, R. Johnson, and J. Vlissides. (R) *Design Patterns: Elements of Reusable Object-Oriented Software.* Addison-Wesley. 416 pp. 1995. Lines formed at the 1994 OOPSLA conference to buy this book. The authors show how object-oriented systems exhibit recurring patterns and structures that let developers reuse successful designs and architectures without having to rediscover solutions.

Graham, Ian. *Object-Oriented Methods.* 2nd Ed. Addison-Wesley. 473 pp. 1994.

Gray, Peter, K. G. Krishnarao, and N. W. Patton, Eds. *Object-Oriented Databases: A Semantic Data Model Approach.* Prentice Hall. 300 pp. 1992. An advanced book on database design, this book will be useful in the design of large, complex, multi-media, and object-oriented databases.

Halliday, Steve, and Mike Wiebel. *Object-Oriented Software Engineering.* Prentice Hall. 320 pp. 1993. Going beyond C++ programming, this book shows readers how to engineer software products using object-oriented principles.

Henderson-Sellers, B. *A Book of Object-Oriented Knowledge: Object-Oriented Analysis, Design, and Implementation: A New Approach to Software Engineering.* Prentice Hall. 240 pp. 1991. This introduction focuses on the basic concepts underlying the object-oriented paradigm, while emphasizing analysis and design, rather than programming. It includes a running example of a bank account to illustrate the concepts and notions.

Henderson-Sellers, B., and J. M. Edwards. (R) *Book Two of Object-Oriented Knowledge:*

The Working Object (MOSES Method). Prentice Hall. 540 pp. 1994. This book describes the second-generation object development method MOSES, which encompasses business planning and delivery stages as well as the more technical components of systems development. Moreover, the method includes critical aspects of development: maintenance and object-oriented metrics. The method is designed to evolve and adapt to specific application domains and new ideas from the object community.

Hutt, Andrew T. F., Ed. *Object Analysis and Design: Description of Methods.* Wiley. 216 pp. 1994. This book presents the results of a survey conducted by the Object Management Group. It describes twenty-one different object analysis and design methods, from "B to Z" (Booch to Z++).

Hutt, Andrew T. F., Ed. *Object Analysis and Design: Comparisons of Methods.* Wiley. 224 pp. 1994. This OMG survey shows how sixteen different object-oriented analysis and design methods are used and with what results. It segments analysis and design into a number of areas that can be studied separately.

Jacobson, Ivar, Maria Ericson, and Agneta Jacobson. (R) *The Object Advantage: Business Process Engineering with Object Technology.* Addison-Wesley. 347 pp. 1994. This landmark work provides one method to integrate the work of reengineering a business, its processes, and the underlying information systems. Going beyond the theory, the authors provide actual deliverables and a formal object-orient method. The method describes all the details about a business and its processes by viewing customers as users and business processes as cases.

Jacobson, Ivar, P. Jonsson, and G. Overguard. (R) *Object-Oriented Software Engineering: A Use Case Driven Approach.* Addison-Wesley. 524 pp. 1992. Jacobson has been working with objects for over 20 years. Today, just about every object developer uses Jacobson's breakthrough *use case* driven approach. Analysis and design models are organized around users interactions and actual usage scenarios. Jacobson's method is Objectory (a contraction of *object factory*). The value of the use case approach is demonstrated by it being incorporated into many other formal methods.

Khoshafian, Setrag. *Object-Oriented Databases.* Wiley. 1993. This book is a comprehensive overview of next-generation database management systems. Contents include modeling and designing for object-oriented databases, persistence, concurrency, recovery, and versioning.

Khoshafian, Setrag, B. Baker, R. Abnous, and K. Sheperd. (R) *Intelligent Offices: Object-Oriented, Multi-Media Information Management in Client/Server Architectures.* Wiley. 424 pp. 1992. This work describes in detail the computing components needed to construct the next generation of "intelligent offices." Shows how the object-oriented model helps users organize their information flow while offering multimedia solutions to future office needs.

Kilov, Haim, and J. Ross. *Information Modeling: An Object-Oriented Approach.* Prentice Hall. 320 pp. 1994. By using an object-oriented approach, Kilov seeks to make systems analysis as disciplined as programming. They show how the systems analyst can use concepts programmer use such as abstraction, precise understanding of behavior, and reuse. The concepts are applicable to many methods.

Loomis, Mary E. S. *Object Databases: The Essentials.* Addison-Wesley. 256 pp. 1995. This book is relevant to both technical and management audiences. Not only does it provide the technology information it also discusses competitive impact of information.

Lorenze, Mark, and Jeff Kidd. *Object-Oriented Software Metrics.* Prentice Hall. 200 pp. 1994. The authors derived metrics that apply to object-oriented software projects from experience gained from actual projects. The book covers completion metrics and design metrics for Smalltalk, C++, and those common to both.

Martin & Co. *White Paper: Extending Information Engineering With Rules and Objects.* James Martin & Co. 30 pp. 1993.

Martin, James, and James Odell. (R) *Object-Oriented Analysis and Design.* Prentice Hall. 400 pp. 1992.

Martin, James, and James Odell. (R) *Object-Oriented Methods: A Foundation.* Prentice Hall. 513 pp. 1995.

Martin, James, and James Odell. *Object-Oriented Methods: The Pragmatics.* Prentice Hall. Forthcoming.

Martin, James. (R) *Principles of Object-Oriented Analysis and Design.* Prentice Hall. 448 pp. 1993.

Martin, James. (R) *The Great Transition: Using the Seven Disciplines of Enterprise Engineering to Align People, Technology, and Strategy,* AMACOM. 503 pp. 1995. The challenge of business reengineering and object-oriented technology has given rise to a keen new interest in the disciplines of information engineering. Martin and Odell have objectified information engineering and their Object-Oriented Information Engineering Method (OOIE) is being adopted by corporations making enterprise transitions. Using the vocabulary of the Object Management Group, the collection of works speaks to the business layman, the business modeler, object architects, and object developers. The method is backed by Intellicorp's Object Management Workbench and PTech's process-centered CASE tools. Business process models execute in the early analysis stages and throughout the iterative development process.

Meyer, Bertrand. *An Object-Oriented Environment: Principles and Applications.* Prentice Hall. 231 pp. 1994.

Meyer, Bertrand. *Object-Oriented Software Construction.* Prentice Hall. 534 pp. 1988. This book is one of the first descriptions of object-oriented ideas. The book uses Eiffel as a program design language. Meyer is one of the developers of Eiffel.

Montgomery, Stephen L. *Object-Oriented Information Engineering: Analysis, Design, and Implementation.* Academic Press. 324 pp. 1994. Montgomery discusses reengineering techniques and practices as well as programming, database management, client/server and cooperative computing.

Mowbray, Thomas J., and Ron Zahavi. (R) *The Essential CORBA: System Integration Using Distributed Objects.* John Wiley & Sons. 316 pp. 1995. The book deals directly with the application of CORBA specifications to distributed object systems development. Systems architecture is stress throughout.

Orfali, Robert, Dan Harkey, and Jeri Edwards. (R) *The Essential Distributed Objects Survival Guide*. John Wiley & Sons. 604 pp. 1995. Just buy it.

Rao, Bindu Rama. *Object-Oriented Databases: Technology, Applications, and Products*. McGraw-Hill. 253 pp. 1994. Rao provides an in-depth look at contemporary object-oriented databases and presents examples of three commercial object-oriented data base management systems.

Rumbaugh, James, M. Blaha, W. Premerlani, F. Eddy, and W. Lorensen. (R) *Object-Oriented Modelling and Design*. Prentice Hall. 528 pp. 1991. The object modeling techniques established by this work are widely used. The method is based on modeling objects from the real world and then using the model to build a language independent design. Thus it focuses on the high-level front end conceptual process of analysis and design to provide a practical rather than theoretical perspective. Case studies, examples, and exercises are provided.

Selic, Bran, G. Gullekson, and P. Ward. *Real-Time Object-Oriented Modeling*. Wiley. 525 pp. 1994. This book is an essential text for real-time systems developers. Dr. Ward is the co-developer of the Ward-Mellor approach to the development of real-time systems.

Schur, Stephen. *The Database Factory: Active Database for Enterprise Computing*. Wiley. 320 pp. 1994. This book is a comprehensive guide to the tools and their uses in active client/server databases.

Shlaer, S., and S. Mellor. (R) *Object Lifecycles: Modeling the World in States*. Prentice Hall. 200 pp. 1992.

Shlaer, S., and S. Mellor. (R) *Object-Oriented Systems Analysis: Modeling the World in Data*. Prentice Hall. 192 pp. 1988. These classic works are very widely used when the problem domain is that of real-time systems. The first book describes the first in a three-step process. The second book describes subsequent steps.

Starr, Leon. *Practical Guide of Shlaer/Mellor OOA*. Prentice Hall. 300 pp. 1994. This book was written for readers who have been introduced to Shlaer/Mellor and are now in the process of applying it. This problem-solving guide covers organizational and political obstacles as well as technical barriers.

Sullo, Gary C. *Object Engineering: Designing Large-Scale Object-Oriented Systems.* Wiley. 325 pp. 1994. Sullo believes that the object-oriented design is an evolutionary, not revolutionary process. He develops a method that builds out of conventional design approaches. Cross-references are made to other object-oriented notations and techniques.

Sully, Philip. *Modelling the World With Objects.* Prentice Hall. 200 pp. 1993. This book introduces the concept of objects for the systems analyst/designer. It introduces object-oriented notation to help express a perception of the real world.

Tkach, Daniel, and Richard Puttick. *Object Technology in Applications Development.* Benjamin/Cummings. 225 pp. 1994. Both authors are with IBM's International Support Center and focus on technology transfer. Their book provides a high-level road map of object-oriented application development, describes the role of CASE tools, uses frameworks for reuse, and describes how legacy code can be reused in object-oriented environments.

Wilkie, George. *Object-Oriented Software Engineering: The Professional Developer's Guide.* Institute of Software Engineering: Addison-Wesley. 399 pp. 1993.

Wirfs-Brock, Rebecca, B. Wilkerson, and Lauren Wiener. (R) *Designing Object-Oriented Software.* Prentice Hall. 368 pp. 1990. This landmark work established the widely used responsibility-driven design process, which can be applied to any software effort, even those not using object-oriented languages. Topics include objects and other basics, classes, responsibilities, collaborations, hierarchies, subsystems, protocols, and implementing the design. This is an excellent book from which to learn the fundamentals of object-oriented technology.

Object-Oriented Programming

Anderson, Arthur E., Jr., and William J. Heinze. *C++ Programming and Fundamental Concepts.* Prentice Hall. 480 pp. 1992.

Anderson, Arthur E., Jr., and William J. Heinze. *Object-Oriented Programming and Design Using C++*. Prentice Hall. 500 pp. 1993. This book shows how to incorporate object-oriented features of C++, including inheritance and dynamic binding, into complete C++ applications. It provides learn-by-doing examples, and can serve as a reference.

Bar-David, Tsvi. *Object-Oriented Design for C++*. Prentice Hall. 350 pp. 1993. This guide concentrates on design and implementation. It introduces design from both a language independent and C++ perspective.

Cargill, Tom. *C++ Programming Style*. Addison-Wesley. 233 pp. 1992. Using the same style as Kernighan and Plauger's classic *The Elements of Programming Style*, Cargill discusses programming style problems and, through example, offers better expressions in C++.

Coad, Peter, and Jill Nicola. *Object-Oriented Programming*. Prentice Hall. 260 pp. 1993. This book represents a breakthrough in learning to "object think" and program. Coad and Nicola used accelerated learning methods to craft this book into a very effective learning resource. It provides an object-oriented programming primer, a graduated series of four examples, language summaries for both Smalltalk and C++, source code for the examples, and patterns of program design.

Cogswell, Jeffery M. *Simple C++: Learn C++ While You Build the Incredible Robodog*. The Waite Group. 252 pp. 1994. This is a good first book. It is fun and lighthearted while establishing fundamentals of object-oriented programming and C++.

Connell, John L., and Linda Shafer. *Object-Oriented Rapid Prototyping*. Prentice Hall. 250 pp. 1994. Even when object-oriented techniques are used, requirements cannot be complete until an example of the proposed application (a prototype) is available for experimentation. This book outlines an approach to applying rapid prototyping concepts to object-oriented software development.

Coplien, James. (R) *Advanced C++ Programming Styles and Idioms*. Addison-Wesley. 520 pp. 1992. Readers will experience the works of the C++ masters if they can get through this book. A required reference for advanced C++ program developers.

Cox, Brad, and A. J. Novobilski. *Object-Oriented Programming: An Evolutionary Approach.* 2nd Ed. Addison-Wesley. 270 pp. 1991. The first edition of this book was published in 1986, and introduced object-oriented technologies to a broad audience. It shows how software can be assembled from standard, interchangeable, reusable components.

Dewhurst, Stephen C., and Kathy Stark. *Programming in C++.* 2nd Ed. Prentice Hall. 320 pp. 1995. These developers of an AT&T C++ compiler cover data abstraction, programming paradigms, class inheritance, memory management, and the use of collections of reusable software components.

Eckel, Bruce. *Thinking C++.* Prentice Hall. 500 pp. 1995.

Ellis, Margaret, and Bjarne Stroustrup. (R) *The Annotated C++ Reference Manual.* Addison-Wesley. 447 pp. 1990. This is the ultimate language reference book for C++. It is not for beginners, but it belongs on the desk of every professional C++ programmer.

Goldberg, Adele, and D. Robson. *Smalltalk-80: The Language and Its Implementation.* Addison-Wesley. 715 pp. 1983.

Goldberg, Adele. *Smalltalk-80: The Interactive Programming Environment.* Addison-Wesley. 516 pp. 1984. Some of the classic works on Smalltalk.

Gorlen, K. E., Sm M. Orlow, and P. S. Plexico. *Data Abstraction and Object-Oriented Programming in C++.* Wiley. 403 pp. 1990. This advanced book focuses on the National Institutes of Health Class Library in examples. It is not a beginner's book.

Korienek, Gene, and Tom Wrench. *A Quick Trip to ObjectLand: Object Oriented Programming with Smalltalk/V.* (R) Prentice Hall. 192 pp. 1993. This book uses an actual dialogue between two characters to help the reader solve problems in the object-oriented paradigm and implement solutions using Smalltalk/V. This unique book is a must-read for those who want to learn Smalltalk.

Korienek, Gene. *An Excursion to ObjectLand.* ObjectLand, Inc. Forthcoming.

Lafore, Robert. *Object-Oriented Programming With Turbo C++.* The Waite Group. 741 pp. 1991. The Waite Group offers a full line of object-oriented and C++ texts. Lafore's work is one of the most popular.

Lalonde, Wilf, and John Pugh. *Smalltalk in Action.* Prentice Hall. 1994.

Lalonde, Wilf, and John Pugh. *Smalltalk V: Practice and Experience.* Prentice Hall. 185 pp. 1993.

Lalonde, Wilf, and John Pugh. *Inside Smalltalk, Vol. 1,* 507 pp., and *Vol. 2,* 553 pp. Prentice Hall. 1990, 1991.

Lalonde, Wilf. *Discovering Smalltalk.* Addison-Wesley. 549 pp. 1994. Lalonde and Pugh have written some of the classics in Smalltalk books. Both are professors of computer science at Carelton University and columnists for the *Journal of Object-Oriented Programming.* Their works are widely known and used.

Lippman, Stanley B. *C++ Primer.* (R) Addison-Wesley. 614 pp. 1992. Although the examples and content keep this book from being a primer for commercial information systems professionals, it belongs in the library of the C++ programmer. Lippman is editor of the *C++ Report* and a leading authority on the language.

Lorenz, Mark. *Rapid Software Development with Smalltalk.* SIGS Books. 210 pp. 1995. Object-oriented analysis, design and implementation techniques with Smalltalk. Emphasizes Responsibility-Driven Design methods, software architecture, project design patterns and metrics. Discusses case tools, levels of reuse and gives development tips. Familiarity with Smalltalk and object-oriented programming assumed.

Marchesi, M. *Object-Oriented Programming in Smalltalk/V.* Prentice Hall. 400 pp. 1992. This book assumes that the reader is already familiar with a conventional programming language, but not necessarily object-oriented programming.

Mark, Dave. *Learn C++ on the PC. With Semantec ThinC++.* Addison-Wesley. 425 pp. 1994. A first book.

Mark, Dave. *Learn C++ on the Macintosh. With Semantec ThinC++.* Addison-Wesley.

425 pp. 1994. Mark's previous books have been widely used due to their clear presentation and hands-on approach. He continues his tradition of highly readable, highly effective work in these two new books. Software and code are included. Required reading (and doing) for newcomers that want an easy to follow, but comprehensive introduction to object-oriented programming in C++.

Meyers, Scott. *Effective C++: 50 Specific Ways to Improve Your Programs and Designs.* Addison-Wesley. 206 pp. 1992. This book is designed for the C++ programmer that wants to master the more complex interactions between the features of the language.

Microsoft. *Microsoft C++ Tutorial.* 1992. Widely recognized first book on C++.

Mitchell, Ed. *Object-Oriented Programming from Square One.* Que. 654 pp. 1993. This is a first book.

Mullin, M. *Object-Oriented Program Design with Examples in C++.* Addison-Wesley. 303 pp. 1989. This book provides useful insights and reflects some Smalltalk influence. It is not for beginners.

Mullin, M. *Rapid Prototyping for Object-Oriented Systems.* This book provides a high-level walk-through of the generation of a prototype system.

Murray, Robert. *C++ Strategies and Tactics.* Addison-Wesley. 282 pp. 1993. Murray, a researcher at AT&T Bell Labs and founding editor of the *C++ Report,* compares the novice C++ programmer to the chess player who knows only how the pieces move. Unless you know the successful strategies traps lie ahead.

Pappas, Chris H., and William H. Murray. *The Visual C++ Handbook.* McGraw-Hill. 982 pp. 1994.

Pohl, Ira. *Object-Oriented Programming Using C++.* Benjamin/Cummings. 496 pp. 1993. Pohl focuses on abstract data types (ADTs) and polymorphism as keys to understanding the object-oriented programming paradigm. Topics include parameterized types, exception handling, templates, and iterator abstraction.

Rao, Bindu Rama. *C++ and the OOP Paradigm.* McGraw-Hill. 188 pp. 1993. This book provides an in-depth treatment of object-oriented programming concepts and C++ implementations. Separate chapters cover the basic concepts that constitute object-oriented programming: classes, inheritance, polymorphism, and multiple inheritance.

Rudd, Anthony. *C++ Complete: A Reference and Tutorial to the Proposed C++ Standard.* Wiley. 486 pp. 1994. As the title indicates, this is a combined tutorial and reference. Its broad coverage includes templates, exception handling and the C++ library. Each topic is explained in both theoretical terms and with practical illustrations.

Saks, Dan. *C++ In Detail.* Prentice Hall/R&D Publications. 300 pp. 1994. This book draws together techniques from major computing journals. It provides practical tools and shows how to avoid the traps of complex object-oriented programming.

Saviac, Duesko. *Object Oriented Programming with Smalltalk/V.* Ellis Horwood. 340 pp. 1990. Experienced programmers and systems developers will find this book to an in-depth introduction.

Schildt, Herbert. *Mastering C++ and Instructor's Manual.* Glencoe/Macmillan/ McGraw-Hill. 316 pp. 1994.

Schildt, Herbert. *C++: The Complete Reference.* Glencoe/Macmillan/McGraw-Hill. 784 pp. 1994.

Schildt, Herbert. *C++ From the Ground Up.* Glencoe/Macmillan/McGraw-Hill. 512 pp. 1994. These books are designed for the college classroom market.

Shammas, Namir Clement. *Secrets of the Visual C++ Masters.* SAMS Publishing. 824 pp. 1993.

Shapiro, Jonathan. *A C++ Toolkit.* Prentice Hall. 231 pp. 1991. Shapiro's book focuses on C++ as a problem-solving tool, and explores the language's abilities to construct reusable software tools. Coverage includes storage management and reference-counted garbage collection.

Skublics, Suzanne, E. Klimas, D. Thomas, and A. Bradley. *Smalltalk With Style.* Prentice Hall. 160 pp. 1996.

Smith, David N. *Concepts of Object-Oriented Programming: With Examples in SmallTalk.* 2nd Ed. McGraw-Hill. 187 pp. 1991. 320 pp. 1994. Smith is a senior programmer and researcher at IBM's Thomas J. Watson Research Center, and has been involved with object-oriented programming since 1983. This book is designed so that it does not overwhelm the reader with detail or try to teach programming. Instead it uses Smalltalk examples to show what the object approach means and how to take advantage of the object programming paradigm.

Smith, David N. *IBM Smalltalk: The Language.* Benjamin/Cummings, Addison-Wesley. 577 pp. 1995.

Stevens, Al. *C++ Database Development.* MIS Press. 1992.

Stroustrup, B. (R) *The C++ Programming Language.* 2nd Ed. Addison-Wesley. 669 pp. 1991. This is the definitive book on the C++ language by its developer. The book is definitely not for beginners.

Watson, Mark. *C++ Power Paradigm.* McGraw-Hill. 218 pp. 1995. Book and disk. This book provides reusable classes for nontrivial object-oriented programs. It is meant to be explored. Each of the four sections may be read independently of the others. Applications include constraint programming, genetic algorithms, and neural networks for making buy/no buy decisions for home consumer goods.

Weinberg, Gerald M. *Quality Software Management: Three Volumes: Vol. 1,* 318 pp. *Systems Thinking—Vol. 2,* 345 pp. *First-Order Measurement—Vol. 3,* 315 pp. *Congruent Action.* Dorset House. 1991. Weinberg has and continues to make significant contributions to general systems thinking and software development. He has the unique ability to find the patterns that underlie recurring problems and solutions. Tough issues are covered: management, corporate culture, error detection and fault attribution, hierarchical power, customer demands, what and how to measure in project management including human factors.

Welstead, Stephen T. *Neural Network and Fuzzy Logic Applications in C/C++*. Wiley. 493 pp. 1994. Book and disk. This book is aimed at having its reader actually design and implement neural and fuzzy programs. Applications include financial forecasting and interest rate modeling.

Winder, R. *Developing C++ Software*. Wiley. 400 pp. 1991. An introductory work.

Woollard, Rex, Robert Lafore, and Harry Henderson. *Master C++: Let the PC Teach You Object-Oriented Programming*. The Waite Group. 391 pp. 1992. An introduction with the computer serving as the turor.

The Learning Organization

Bouldin, Barbara M. *Agents of Change: Managing the Introduction of Automated Tools*. Yourdon Press. 198 pp. 1989. Bouldin's work deals with the resistance of users to new technologies, describes the many forms of resistance, and offers practical advice on overcoming resistance.

Capper, P. *Organizational Learning: A Review of Current Theory and Practice in the USA*. Christchurch, NZISRD. 1994.

Davis, Stanley M., and Jim Botkin. (R) *The Monster Under the Bed: How Business is Mastering the Opportunity of Knowledge for Profit*. Simon & Schuster. 1994.

Davis, Stanley M., and Bill Davidson. *20/20 Vision*. Simon & Schuster. 223 pp. 1991.

Masie, Elliott. *The Computer Training Handbook*. 2nd Ed. Lakewood Publications. 276 pp. 1994.

Pedler, Mike, John Burgoyne, and Tom Boydell. *The Learning Company: A Strategy for Sustainable Development*. McGraw-Hill. 213 pp. 1991. The authors provide 101 glimpses of the learning company, including case studies, activities, ideas, and a company diagnostic. The book is written with a down-to-earth style and includes a diagnostic framework that can be used to determine if a company is a learning company.

Quinn, James B. *Intelligent Enterprises*. Free Press. 472 pp. 1992.

Rose, Colin. *Accelerated Learning*. Dell Publishing Company. 246 pp. 1987.

Senge, Peter M. (R) *The Fifth Discipline: The Art and Practice of the Learning Organization*. Doubleday/Currency. 424 pp. 1990. Senge's focus on "systems thinking" represents a discipline that is central to reengineering business processes. This seminal work has had a major impact on business reengineering. This work has been so influential that an Internet discussion group has been established to carry on the discussion. It's a lively discussion and happens at learn-org@world.std.com.

Senge, Peter M., et al. *The Fifth Discipline Fieldbook: Strategies and Tools for Building a Learning Organization*. Doubleday/Currency. 593 pp. 1994. This book is a collection of tools, techniques, and methods categorized into the five disciplines of a learning organization.

Shekerjian, Denise. *Uncommon Genius—How Great Ideas Are Born*. Penguin Books. 244 pp. 1990. Guy Kawasaki of Apple Computer has this to say about this work: "Most books about creativity are cuties with exercises, brainteasers, and cartoons. They are supposed to tickle you into creativity. Then there's Shekerjian's book. It is a complete, radical, and welcome departure from any book I've ever read about creativity." This is a serious business book about the real dimensions of creativity, including the need for years of dedicated work and enduring years of uncertainty and frustration.

Tobin, Daniel R. *Re-educating the Corporation: Foundations for the Learning Organization*. Oliver Wight Publications. 289 pp. 1993. Former education manager at Digital, Dan Tobin brings more than twenty years of training and development experience to the pages of this widely read book. The book provides a complete blueprint and practical tools to create virtual training opportunities and to build a dynamic learning organization.

Van Oeech, Roger. *A Kick in the Seat of the Pants: Using Your Explorer, Artist, Judge, and Warrior to Be More Creative*. Perennial Library. 153 pp. 1986.

Van Oeech, Roger. *A Whack on the Side of the Head: How You Can Be More Creative.* Warner Books. 196 pp. 1990.

Van Oeech, Roger. *Creative Whack Pack: A Pack of Cards Which is a Creative Thinking Workshop in a Box.* Available from Resources for Organizations, Inc. The titles of these books and materials speak for themselves. Releasing individual and team creativity is a key challenge of business reengineering efforts. Van Oeech can help.

Wick, Calhoun W., and Lu Stanton Leon. *The Learning Edge: How Smart Managers and Smart Companies Stay Ahead.* McGraw-Hill. 232 pp. 1993. Based on the authors' rigorous 12-year study of how managers actually learn, this book provides a blueprint for intentional learning in the workplace. It takes an in-depth look at learning strategies used by five major corporations.

BOOK PUBLISHERS, PERIODICALS, AND CONSULTANTS

The compilation that follows contains the names and contact information for companies mentioned in this book. A complete directory of object-oriented resource providers is contained in *The Object Buyer's Guide* published by SIGS Publications (see below).

Book Publishers

Academic Press
525 B Street
Suite 1900
San Diego, CA 92101-4495
Tel. (617) 669-6390
Tel. (800) 321-5068
Fax. (800) 336-7377
Catalog includes a major section on computer science.

Addison-Wesley
One Jacob Way
Reading, MA 01867
Tel. (617) 944-3700
Fax. (617) 944-7273
Email. info@aw.com
Addison-Wesley produces a specialty catalog, *Professional Computing Series*, as well as larger computing catalogs.

ASQC Quality Press
Customer Service Department
P. O. Box 3066
Milwaukee, WI 53201-3066
Tel. (800) 248-1946
Fax. (414) 272-1734
The publishing arm of the non-profit American Society of Quality Control (ASQC).

The Benjamin/Cummings Publishing Company, Inc.
390 Bridge Parkway
Redwood City, CA 94065
Tel. (800) 322-1377
Email. bookinfo@bc.aw.com

Borland International
1800 Green Hills Road
Scotts Valley, CA 95067-0001
Tel. (408) 438-8400
Borland produces a number of videos on object-oriented topics.

Future Strategies, Inc.
3640 N. Federal Highway
Lighthouse Point, FL 33064
Tel. (305) 782-3376
Future Strategies specializes in workflow technology and business process reengineering publications.

McGraw-Hill, Inc.
Professional Book Group
Order Service Dept. S-1
Princeton Road
Hightstown, NJ 08520-1450
Tel. (800) 722-4726
Fax. (609) 426-5924
Email. info@mcgraw-hill.com
McGraw-Hill publishes a catalog of professional, technical, and reference books and another catalog of computer books. These catalogs are updated twice a year.

Microsoft Press
One Microsoft Way
Redmond, WA 98052-3895
Tel. (206) 936-3895

Oliver Wight Publications
85 Allen Martin Drive
Essex Junction, VT 05452
Tel. (800) 343-0625
Fax. (802) 878-3384
Oliver Wight specializes in business reengineering and total quality publications.

Prentice Hall
Professional Reference Division
Box 11073
Des Moines, IA 50381-1073
Tel. (201) 592-2498
Fax. (201) 592-2249
Email. orders@prenhall.com
Prentice Hall produces a catalog, *Object-Oriented Resources for Professionals.*

SIGS Publications and Books
71 West 23rd Street
New York, NY 10010
Tel. (212) 242-SIGS (7447)
Fax. (212) 242-7574
SIGS is devoted exclusively to object-oriented and client/server publications (see Periodicals below).

Springer-Verlag
175 Fifth Avenue
New York, NY 10010
Tel. (212) 460-1500
Tel. (800) springe
Fax. (201) 348-4505
The *Springer Newsletter of Computer Science* is produced annually.

The Waite Group
200 Tamal Plaza
Corte Madera, CA 94925
Tel. (415) 924-2575

John Wiley & Sons
Dept. 5-6099
P. O. Box 6793
Somerset, NJ 08875
Tel. (800) 225-5945
Tel. (Canada) (800) 263-1599

Periodicals

interactions Magazine
The Association of Computing Machinery (ACM)
P. O. Box 12114
Church Street Station
New York, NY 10257
Tel. (800) 342-6626
Tel. (212) 626-0500

Fax. (212) 944-1318

Internet. ACMHELP@ACM.org

This magazine was created in 1993 in response to the growing interest and rapid advancements in the field of human-computer interaction.

Object Magazine

SIGS Publications

71 West 23rd Street

New York, NY 10010

The people who are shaping the future of object-oriented technology regularly contribute to this popular magazine. With a managerial outlook, it looks at the implications of using object technology in the workplace.

Journal of Object-Oriented Programming (JOOP)

SIGS Publications

71 West 23rd Street

New York, NY 10010

JOOP is written by and for programmers and developers using object technology. International in scope, editorial features are code-intensive, technical, and hands-on. The editors and contributing writers are the most advanced and best-known names in object technology.

C++ Report

SIGS Publications

71 West 23rd Street

New York, NY 10010

As a code-intensive publication, this magazine is packed with new ideas and developments, tips, tricks, and usable advice provided by the leading authorities on C++: Stroustrup, Lippman, Booch, Dewhurst, Cargill, Meyers, and Koenig. It is designed for C++ program developers at all levels.

Report of Object Analysis and Design (ROAD)

SIGS Publications

71 West 23rd Street

New York, NY 10010

ROAD presents a language-independent exploration of object-oriented analysis, design, and modeling. It is aimed at practicing professionals and educators.

The Smalltalk Report
SIGS Publications
71 West 23rd Street
New York, NY 10010
This code-intensive magazine reports on applications and developments as well as analysis and design issues. Articles address teaching and implementing Smalltalk, designing and managing class libraries, metrics, effective use of tools, and language issues.

OBJEKTspktrum
SIGS Publications
71 West 23rd Street
New York, NY 10010
OBJEKTspktrum is the only German-language magazine devoted to object technology. It is written for software managers and programmers/developers.

TOOLS Conference Proceedings
(Technology of Object-Oriented Languages and Systems)
Prentice Hall
Professional Reference Division
Box 11073
Des Moines, IA 50381-1073
Tel. (201) 592-2498
Fax. (201) 592-2249
Email. orders@prenhall.com

Business Change and Reengineering: The Journal of Corporate Transformation
Quarterly. Established in 1993 by John Wiley Publishers.
P.O. Box 6793
Somerset, NJ 08875
Tel. (800) 225-5945
Tel. (Canada) (800) 263-1599

Object-Oriented Consultants

Carm Group, Inc.
7200 Wisconsin Avenue
Suite 410
Bethesda, MD 20814-4809
Tel. (301) 961-7273
Email. carm@acm.org
The Carm Group specializes in human-computer interaction and interface design.
See profile in Appendix B.

CBT Systems Ltd.
400 Oyster Point Blvd.
Suite 401
South San Francisco, CA 94080
Tel. (415) 737-9050
Tel. (800) 929-9050
Fax. (415) 737-0377
CBT offers a complete line of information technology training that can be delivered
over client's networks. CBT's catalog includes curriculum planners for major sub-
ject areas.

Digitalk, Inc.
5 Hutton Centre Drive
Santa Ana, CA 92707
Tel. (714) 513-3000
Fax. (714) 513-3100
Email. info@digitalk.com

Enix Limited
3 The Green
Richmond
Surrey TW9 1PL UK
Tel. (44-181) 332-0210
Fax. (44-181) 940-7424
Email. miers@enix.co.uk

Enix road tests business process reengineering tools and reports its findings in its quarterly *Process Product Watch*.

Hewlett-Packard Company
Professional Services Division
100 Mayfield Avenue
Mountain View, CA 94043
Tel. (415) 691-5828
Fax. (415) 691-5484
See profile in Chapter 4.

IBM
Object Technology University
19th Floor Dept 1CA
1 IBM Plaza
Chicago, IL 60611
Tel. (708) 876-9150
Fax. (312) 245-2477
Email. susanvb@vnet.ibm.com
See profile in Chapter 4.

ICON Computing, Inc.
12343 Hymeadow Drive
Suite 3c
Austin, TX 78750
Tel. (512) 258-8437
Fax. (512) 258-0086
Email. info@iconcomp.com

ICONIX Software Engineering, Inc.
2800 Twenty-Eighth Street
Suite 320
Santa Monica, CA 90405
Tel. (310) 458-0092
Fax. (310) 396-3454
See profile in Chapter 4.

James Martin & Company
2100 Reston Parkway
Suite 300
Reston, VA 22091
Tel. (703) 620-9504
Fax. (703) 476-1335
James Martin & Company offers a comprehensive business reengineering program, is a leader in information engineering, and provides training and consulting in object-oriented information engineering methods. Tools include the IE-Expert® and Intellicorp's Object Management Workbench.

Knowledge Systems Corporation
4001 Weston Parkway
Cary, NC 27513
Tel. (919) 481-4000
Email. salesinfo@ksccary.com
See profile in Chapter 4.

National Education Training Group (NETG)
1751 West Diehl Road
Naperville, IL 60563-9099
Tel. (708) 369-3000
Tel. (800) 457-6993
Fax. (708) 983-4518
NETG offers media-based training on a variety of technology and management subjects including object-oriented development, client/server computing, and business process reengineering.

Object International, Inc.
8140 N. MoPac 4-200
Austin, TX 78759
Tel. (512) 795-0202
Fax. (512) 795-0332
Email. info@oi.com
WWW Home Page. http://www.oi.com/oi_home.html
See profile in Chapter 4.

Object Management Group, Inc.
Framingham Corporate Center
492 Old Connecticut Path
Framingham, MA 01701
Tel. (508) 820-4300
Fax. (508) 820-4303
Email. info@omg.com
The Object Management Group is a nonprofit international organization dedicated to establishing industry guidelines and standards for object technology.

ParcPlace Systems, Inc.
999 East Arques Avenue
Sunnyvale, CA 94086-4593
Tel. (800) 759-7272
Tel. (408) 481-9090
Fax. (408) 481-9095
Email. info@parcplace.com

QUOIN, Inc.
124 Mt. Auburn Street
Suite 200 North
Cambridge, MA 02138
Tel. (617) 576-5885
Fax. (617) 576-5876
Email. jbkain@quoininc.com

Semaphore
800 Turnpike Street
North Andover, MA 01845
Tel. (508) 794-3366
Tel. (800) 937-8080
Fax. (508) 794-3427

SIGS Conferences
71 West 23rd Street
New York, NY 10010
Tel. (212) 242-7515
Fax. (212) 242-7578
Email. sigsconf@ix.netcom.com
SIGS Conferences sponsors and presents *Object Expo, XWorld, C++ World, Object Expo Europe, OOP/C++ (Germany), Smalltalk Solutions,* and the *Client/Server Applications Tour.*

Technology Exchange Company
One Jacob Way
Reading, MA 01867
Tel. (617) 944-3700
Tel. (800) 662-4282
Email. joannes@aw.com
The Technology Exchange Company is an Addison-Wesley company. Many of the instructors are authors of the books on which the courses are based.

The Technical Resource Connection
12320 Racetrack Road
Tampa, FL 33626
Tel. (813) 891-6084
Tel. (800) TRC-2992
Fax. (813) 891-6138
Email. info@trcinc.com
Web. http://www.trcinc.com/
The Technical Resource Connection focuses on technical implementation of distributed object computing. Work centers on object architectural assessments and implementing mission critical, distributed object projects for Fortune 500 companies. The firm is well known for its white-paper series, *Next Generation Computing*™.

A GUIDE TO USABLE INTERFACE DESIGN FOR OBJECT-ORIENTED SYSTEMS

With Richard Chimera, The Carm Group

The art and science of designing useable user interfaces is essential to developers of successful object-oriented information systems. User interfaces to traditional commercial information systems were generally simple menus served up by the system to guide the user to a data-entry or report screen. Essentially the user interface was a static view of the information system. Object-oriented information systems emphasize dynamic interaction of the user and the system where the user starts with a goal and, based on a conceptual model of the problem domain, formulates strategies to reach the goal.

Such dynamic human interfaces require multidisciplinary knowledge if they are to be designed successfully. These disciplines include human-factors engineering, cognitive science, human-computer interaction, graphics and media design, and object-oriented software engineering. Developers new to the world of object technology are usually new to these disciplines as well. Further, some of these disciplines have not yet adopted object-oriented notions, and thus the literature is sparse. (David Collins' book, *Designing Object-Oriented User Interfaces* is one of the first in this growing field. See Appendix A.) This practical guide has been included to highlight the importance of dynamic user interfaces in the design of successful object-oriented systems and to provide a useful development process.

ABSTRACT

Interfaces that people can use effectively and confidently are the keys to market share for any software product whether it is for sale or is an internal productivity tool. Force-feeding idiosyncratic, proprietary systems to customers is a strategy that cannot survive in today's more competitive, open-systems marketplace.

What features make interfaces more usable? What steps are necessary for creating more usable interfaces? Is ensuring usability cost-effective? What roles can object technology play?

The following pages step through the interface development process used by Carm Group consultants. Relevant interface design and usability issues and approaches, and pivotal human-computer interaction principles are described. Throughout the description of the process, information resources are provided. These references can be used as a road map for further study of the field of human-computer interaction.

INTRODUCTION

Computer users often cite examples of interfaces that are difficult to use, frustrating, inconsistent, surprising, or illogical. A favorite anecdote, and this is not being made up, is the user who is trying to get past the initial startup screen message. When asked why he was frantically searching the keyboard and could not move on, the hapless user responded, "The program says to hit any key to continue, but I cannot find a key with the label *any*." While this is an extreme example, it points out key issues that designers and developers must overcome to create usable and used interfaces.

Users simply want to complete their tasks without the interface getting in the way. Developers' more sophisticated knowledge of computers and the interface they have programmed for months can produce "developer blindness" to interface problems—or more positively stated, alternate perspectives—users may have. The alternatives often pertain to getting started, interaction paradigms, information views, and layout of objects and their associated actions. These many perspectives can inhibit developers' ability to remember that many users

- are not computer savvy,

- do not possess a mental model of the interface (and if they do, it is probably not the same model the developer has in mind),

- do not have an intrinsic desire nor the time to explore the program (even though exploration is a good strategy for users to understand an interface better).

Successful developers overcome the blindness and provide users with interfaces they understand and can use. Well-designed interfaces fade from users' conscious attention.

Interface usability can be measured by the amount of training users require, the speed with which users can perform tasks, the rate at which users make errors, the ability of users to retain their knowledge over time, and users' subjective satisfaction with the interface (Kreitzberg, 1994). Interface usability will become more important as the Information Age blooms. *Ubiquitous computing* is the latest term for the trend of more workers encountering computers on the critical path of completing their tasks (Weiser, 1991). Providing usable interfaces alone is not enough. Computer literacy, appropriate partitioning of tasks between humans and computers, plus investment in superior quality information technology are needed. Object technology is leading the way toward next-generation software systems and applies directly to designing and implementing usable interfaces (McDaniel et al., 1994).

Designers and developers could always use more time and bigger budgets, but they also need a better understanding of how important usable interfaces are plus the information resources to learn and apply the principles to their work. Formed in 1993, the Carm Group is a human-computer interaction and information technology consulting company that sees what happens in the trenches out in the real world, and it is not a rosy picture.

Principal consultant for the Carm Group, Richard Chimera recently created graphical user interface (GUI) guidelines and standards for a major financial firm on Wall Street. Chimera worked for five years at the Human-Computer Interaction Laboratory, which is headed by Dr. Ben Shneiderman. Here he learned much of what is shared in these pages—from Ben, from staff and graduate students, from European and Japanese visiting researchers, and from electronic communications with colleagues on the Net. In addition to his scholarly activities at the University of Maryland and Carnegie Mellon University, Chimera organized panel discussions and authored papers for major international computer conferences, including Computer-Human Interaction (CHI), User Interface Software and Technology, the International Conference on Software Engineering, and the Hawaii International Conference on System Sciences.

Chimera's recommended strategy for learning about usability issues and human-computer interaction is to stay abreast of research in scholarly journals, major conferences, and books. Trade magazines still do not focus much on usability and often do a poor job when they do. An excerpted list of human-computer interaction information resources originally compiled by Dr. Ben Shneiderman is available from the author or from http://www.cs.umd.edu:80/projects/hcil/.

Recognized thinkers and writers include Fred Brooks (software systems), Aaron Marcus (traditional and GUI graphic design; color), Don Norman (cognitive psychology), Bruce Tognazzini (HCI), Edward Tufte (visual design), and Terry Winograd (HCI).

Consultants and research organizations can bring their expertise to bear on specific issues and goals not only to improve an interface product, but to improve the development process and educate team members in a most efficient manner. Interface usability comes in degrees. While it is true that one only gets out what one puts in, providing more usable interfaces can be done cost effectively and with modest effort.

A Practitioner's Guide to Designing Usable Interfaces

The first of the four parts following describes the product life cycle and the broader context into which the interface must fit. By seeing a more global view of a software product and its interface, priorities can be set better and a wholeness can be ascribed to the undertaking. The second part discusses interface design approaches that are the foundations for creating more usable interfaces. The third part covers development and implementation strategies that promote efficient production of usable interfaces. The fourth part presents usability testing procedures that can dramatically improve interfaces with relatively modest effort and cost.

Product Life Cycle

Before knowing how to design usable interfaces, the systems developer must understand where software and its interface fit into the big picture of company productivity. An interface can be a weak link, but it can never be the entire chain. Everything the customer encounters should be usable, from product installation, documentation, and use to technical support. And developers must commit unconditionally to usability throughout the entire product life cycle.

This means that usability cannot be "sprinkled on" as a product nears completion. As Charlie Kreitzberg explains, "These managers believe that if the product can be dressed up with some nice colors and decorated with a few graphics, users will love the result. This idea strikes me as roughly equivalent to used car dealers who spiff up a clunker with polish and dazzle the prospective buyer by displaying it under a string of colored floodlights. With both software and cars this technique can make the sale but leave the user angry and frustrated in the end. . . . Like automobiles, toasters, and pipe wrenches, [interfaces] are tools. Tools must be usable to be useful. And because software is structurally complex, usability engineering must be an integral part of the software architecture. It is not a refinement to be added at the end but must be a requirement embraced from the beginning" (Kreitzberg, 1994).

Even though the following aspects of development are discussed separately, each affects the others and no phase is considered finished until the whole project is complete. This methodology uses a *spiral* model of development as introduced in 1988 by CASE expert Barry Boehm (Boehm, 1988). The traditional waterfall model, as specified by MIL-STD-2167A and required by federal government defense system contractors, is out. In fact, DOD-STD-2167A has been replaced by MIL-STD-498, which will be replaced, some time in the future by IEEE-1498. This model had each phase completely separate from the others with little communication and no iteration. The spiral model was not embraced immediately, for it involves significant changes and was not supported at first by computer tools. This will change with time.

Two critical aspects in the initial phase of a project are to identify the target user population and to determine the business tasks the interface is to address. Other practical issues include setting constraints on hardware, time, training, and budget. Only after this initial analysis can the project can enter the design, implementation, and testing phases. Object technology can play a significant role in reducing complexity and speeding completion of design and implementation. Both training procedures and documentation (on-line and printed versions) should be created concurrently with product design, implementation, and testing.

Before initial product delivery is made, complete and attractive product packaging, a simple installation guide, and a quick-start guide must also be designed and tested. It is a good idea to embark on a beta delivery to friendly customers. This is a trial run with actual users who discover sometimes unforeseeable problems. Of course, within minutes of receiving a product, some customers will call technical support. An 800 number, electronic communication, and problem-tracking system should all be in place. If a product is a new version of an existing product, surely existing data can be imported and some help is offered for learning the new system based on the old system. A good treatment of updating legacy systems is found in Telles (1990).

Design

Designing the User Interface: Strategies for Effective Human-Computer Interaction is one of the best books on interface design (Shneiderman, 1992). The very readable book contains excellent topic coverage. It describes the three-pillars approach to interface development. The approach starts with two foundations, theories and models of human-computer interaction and controlled experimental research. This foundation tells what is usable and what is not. The three pillars on top of the foundation are guidelines documents (both internal and external), user interface management systems, and usability labs and iterative testing.

The process of interface design is being increasingly focused in a task-oriented manner. Not too long ago a user-centered design was considered ideal. In many situations a user-centered perspective has migrated to a micro-level, while a task-centered perspective is almost always at a macro-level. Peter Drucker advocates task-focused business teams that are formed as needed to solve problems (Drucker, 1988). The highest priority goal is that the task must be solved efficiently, and the interface must be created to gain task-efficiency.

Keeping abreast of the rapidly advancing field of human-computer interaction requires significant reading and participation in major conferences. Information in this field expanded manyfold during the early 1990s. ACM's journal *interactions* provides insight and valuable information geared for practitioners rather than researchers.

Perhaps more digestible than scholarly journals are guidelines documents. They have distilled the wisdom of international researchers as well as outlined their own territory and direction for interfaces. Guidelines documents can help dramatically in creating interfaces that are consistent within themselves and with each other, two more key components of usable interfaces (Chimera, 1993b).

Three commercial organizations have produced excellent guidelines: *Apple Human Interface Guidelines; IBM System Application Architecture: Common User Access, Advanced Interface Design Guide* (and other IBM SAA CUA documents); and the less-rich *OSF/Motif Style Guide*. A more platform-free, although older, guidelines document is Smith and Mosier's highly acclaimed *Guidelines for Designing User Interface Software*, a public work commissioned by the MITRE Corporation. This guidelines document, as well as a comprehensive human-computer interaction bibliography can be found via anonymous ftp at the site ftp.cis.ohio-state.edu in the directory pub/hci. Smith and Mosier can be found in the subdirectory Guidelines.

Iteration of design, implementation, and testing is a powerful methodology for ensuring better usability. This process goes hand in hand with rapid prototyping approaches. Typically it starts with interface mock-ups of the key screens, which can be on paper or created on the computer with drawing programs or user-interface management systems (UIMS) (discussed later). While the interface may be minimally interactive, there is usually little application-specific functionality at this stage. The idea is to determine through user testing how users comprehend and react to screen designs and interaction paradigms. Successive iterations of refinements plus additional application-specific functionality are again user tested, incrementally bringing the program closer to completion.

The Elements of Friendly Software Design is another highly readable book on usable interfaces. It borrows from other disciplines (as the usable interface design discipline should do) such as filmmaking and literature. The book is written by Paul Heckel (1991), the originator of the card-and-stack metaphor popularized by Apple's HyperCard system. Heckel's main points are that interface design is most purely an exercise in communication and that the process necessarily involves much revision.

Visual Basic for the PC Windows platform and HyperCard for the Macintosh are two popular tools in use today for prototyping. These tools provide a palette of objects with which to create interfaces and a simple, interpreted language to execute "scripts" (one hesitates to call them "programs") at runtime. The advantage in using such tools is that prototypes of standard interfaces can be created easily by nonprogrammers in a matter of days. Flaws can be discovered early in the product life cycle and corrected. Perhaps an idea can be communicated as a prototype instead of words.

A major disadvantage of this class of prototyping tools is that they are not suitable for developing the final product (although some may disagree). They are tools for prototyping only and interfaces created with them do not evolve from prototype to final product. UIMS, on the other hand, usually have the power and flexibility to evolve a prototype to a final product.

The process and the environment used to develop usable interfaces does not guarantee success. Neither would a tome on Michaelangelo's process and style guarantee that one could paint a masterpiece. While usable interface design is still more an art than a science, adherence to the basic design principles should allow the developer to avoid the more obvious pitfalls and traps.

One reason usable interfaces are difficult to produce is that today's programming languages and environments are themselves not designed for the task of creating usable interfaces. This point is part of a lucid article describing why interfaces are difficult to design and implement (Myers, 1994). Further, the fact that an interface is delivered in a GUI environment does not make it usable. Just as many (perhaps even more) subtly bad or horrendous design decisions can be made in a direct manipulation GUI environment as in a command language text-oriented display.

Design Principles

Interface design principles are covered in-depth in the works that have been referenced. A high-level discussion is useful here to provide a framework for further study.

1. Strive to be externally consistent with metaphors and social/cultural norms. Work more diligently to be internally consistent within the interface itself (Chimera, 1993b):

   - Like objects should look and behave alike.

   - The same words should be used in equivalent situations.

   - Equivalent objects should be placed in similar locations on different screens.

   - Colors are used consistently and with restraint. Color for the sake of flash is a sure loser.

2. The design should be harmonious with the organization's culture and attitudes plus the physical environment.

3. One must seek actual target users' input, to observe them in real-life situations, and to understand their perspective and then to know which users' issues not to accommodate.

4. A direct manipulation interaction paradigm is natural to use and easy for both designer and user to extend to many types of applications. Direct manipulation interfaces are characterized by

   - Continuous representation of the objects and actions of interest

   - Physical actions instead of complicated syntax

   - Rapid incremental reversible operations whose effect on the object of interest is immediately visible.

5. Provide interaction feedback. Always

   - Use the busy/working cursor for every action.

- Consider a status/message line at the bottom of the screen.

6. Promote the concept that interfaces are predictable tools, which users are able to master and control to perform tasks. Interfaces are not magical. People accomplish tasks, computers and interfaces do not.

7. For large data spaces use the principle of progressive disclosure. Provide an overview of all data to see the whole picture, allow the user to zoom and to filter the data while supporting exploration, and bring up data details on user demand.

8. Avoid letting implementation difficulties affect the interface design, which should remain pure.

9. Make simple activities simple, and make popular functionality obvious.

10. Lay out objects on an invisible grid to reduce distraction.

11. Provide redundant ways to navigate and to perform actions.

12. Error messages should be as specific as possible but terse. Explain the problem and, more importantly, provide solution steps.

13. Provide a help system that is at least screen specific and hopefully object specific.

Ideally an interface would recede out of a user's conscious attention to allow for concentration on the task at hand. The ironic anthem designers should strive to hear from their users is, "Of course it is designed that way, how else would it be done?"

Implementation Strategies

Newer implementation models and technologies allow usable interfaces to be created more efficiently and achieve higher levels of robustness. A major advance in this regard is the technology of user-interface management systems (UIMS), which are programming environments that are specialized for creating interfaces. They typically provide a set of primitive GUI building blocks, or widgets, plus additional infrastructure (above that of normal programming) for specifying widget behaviors. The latter typically takes the form of automatic resizing behavior, and establishing conditions to enable and disable objects.

UIMS take away much of the burden from interface developers at the lower level of primitive objects and allows more time and effort to be placed at the higher-level design and interactions. Object technology plays a major role in partitioning interface development into higher and lower levels so that focus and concentration are more easily applied to simpler issues. Most UIMS use object technology both internally and in the object hierarchy available for developers' use. Some UIMS support subclassing of objects as primary functionality.

The Carm Group was commissioned by NASA Goddard Space Flight Center in 1993-1994 to review leading commercial and academic tools for building interfaces (with the particular perspective of how they visualize widget behaviors and relationships). Several high-quality commercial and academic UIMS were identified as part of this project. The commercial tools tend to concentrate in the CASE area (computer-aided software/systems engineering) while the academic tools tend to be UIMS that focus on a subset of UIMS issues.

Three highly acclaimed academic systems that are free for the ftp'ing (in no particular order) are SUIT (Simple User Interface Toolkit) by Randy Pausch at the University of Virginia (Pausch, 1991), Garnet by Brad Myers at Carnegie Mellon University (Myers, 1990), and UIDE by James Foley at Georgia Tech (Foley, 1993). A leading commercial system is James Rumbaugh's OMTool, which relies heavily on object technology. It has now been combined with Software through Pictures, developed by Tony Wasserman and based on his Rapid/USE research systems at Interactive Development Environments (IDE).

One new branch of commercial GUI builders (typically less functional than UIMS) deals specifically with creating interfaces that run on multiple window systems using the exact same source code (which raises them to be more functional than UIMS). These systems are invaluable to those who know they will deliver an interface on multiple platforms. Three exemplary systems (ranked by this author through an extensive study) include Galaxy by Visix Software, Open Interface by Neuron Data, and XVT by XVT Software. The last two are covered by Chimera (1993a) and information about the first system can be obtained directly from the author.

UIMS and GUI builders also separate interface code from application code. This can bring large efficiencies when changes are made. Often changes are made only to the interface or mostly in the application. When those two conceptual code modules are already separated, modifications are made quicker and more reliably. In the case of platform-independent development environments, further separation is made between interface code and particular window systems. This allows interfaces to be ported across window systems in a matter of hours or days rather than months.

Other advantages besides speed of porting are

- increased reliability as there is only one set of interface source code,

- reduced team size as typically only one expert per window system is needed (sometimes none),

- guaranteed conformance to and consistency with window system look and feel issues, which allow users to apply their existing knowledge of particular window system interaction.

One obvious though infrequently used strategy for creating usable interfaces is to reuse what has been proved usable in the past. This can apply to whole-application metaphors and interaction paradigms all the way down to libraries of individual widgets. The bonuses of software reuse include

- time savings from not having to reimplement widgets,

- high-quality software that has been tested extensively in real-use situations,

- improvements made to library widgets propagate to many applications at once.

Reuse has not been widely achieved since modifying traditional library objects for reuse in a new interface may not be trivial. Object technology can make such modifications easier by isolating changes to particular objects, possibly in either their data or methods only. Another factor contributing to low reuse is that sometimes better generalizations must be made to a library object to allow certain specializations to be made for a new interface. Reuse through object technology can yield a big advantage.

USABILITY TESTING

While designing for usability is difficult to codify, testing for usability has become more of a science. Even the terminology points this out: usability engineering and usability defects. The late 1980s saw a surge of usability review and testing methods introduced. Jakob Nielsen, a leading authority in the field of usability engineering formerly at Bellcore and now at Sun Microsystems, wrote an excellent book on the subject with a focus on achieving results with minimal cost (Nielsen, 1993). He lays out his empirical methods for straightforward application by practitioners well. Clayton Lewis at the University of Colorado offers a more theoretical approach called *cognitive walk-throughs* (Lewis, 1990). Deborah Hix and Rex Hartson at Virginia Tech wrote an excellent book full of prescriptive information on building usable interfaces and evaluating them (Hix and Hartson, 1993). To quiet the usability review nay-sayers, Chris Marshall et al. at Hewlett-Packard share their experience of a real product just before rollout (Marshall et al., 1990). Various usability reviewers using various methods all correctly predicted common major usability defects.

The usability experts agree on the following:

- There is no substitute for running tests with *real* users. While twenty real users would usually be statistically sufficient, use fewer if that is all that can be tested.

- Although no single usability method is best, most current methods will find a large subset of the more severe usability defects.

- The earlier that usability testing is performed, the more cost effective making changes will be.

- Task-oriented interfaces developed by interdisciplinary teams have a better chance of success.

When performing usability tests, capturing usability testing data is important. At a minimum, user events (mouse and keyboard input) and user reactions should both be time stamped and recorded. The "think aloud" protocol, whereby users vocalize everything they are thinking in real time (sometimes the users need to be reminded to do this), can be quite helpful for understanding users' mindsets and goals. Analyzing and replaying event sequences can be enlightening for all involved in development. Events can be captured automatically by the computer. Audiotapes and videotapes capture user activities during usability testing very well. Test administrators must not help users in any way during usability tests because it would defeat the whole purpose of discovering how users deal with the interface on their own.

Developers and managers alike must see real users struggling with an interface before they truly understand the pervasiveness and effects of usability problems. This cannot be understated. Ideally they should watch users during actual usability testing, though videotape is adequate.

From square one, many users do not know what to do, where to look, how to proceed. Users also do not care *why*. They should not be forced to figure out the interface. They simply want to complete their tasks using an interface (apparently) streamlined for them for their purposes. Once designers and managers see users in action, they understand for the first time the difference between their view of the interface and that of their users. Then bridges can begin to be built by endeavoring to create usable interfaces.

A more thorough approach to usability testing is to build one's own usability lab or rent such a facility. A usability lab typically consists of a control room with monitoring, recording, and editing equipment plus a testing room that mimics the environment in which a typical user would be: the computer, the application being tested, hard copy documentation, and for the zealous test administrators, fake colleagues chattering, simulated background phone calls and so on. A one-way mirror usually separates the two rooms. Three camera angles should be simultaneously recorded, a view of the screen, a view of the keyboard, and a view of the user's face to catch the contorted and bewildered expressions.

The cost to build and staff a high-quality usability lab in 1994 was around $300,000 (Kumar, 1994). This cost is approximately equally split between equipment and infrastructure and staff. This is not as large of an investment as it may seem for the payoff it could provide. The savings in technical support effort and software patches and updates for just one product could amount to a larger sum of money. The value of not acquiring a bad reputation from the customers' viewpoint must also be considered in the investment analysis.

FUTURE DIRECTIONS

Using order-of-magnitude estimates, we are in the fourth generation of computers. The fifth and sixth generations will not have reliable speech recognition, artificial intelligence, malleable agents, and gophers, nor will there be virtual reality interfaces that are useful for getting work done. What will happen is ubiquitous computing (Weiser, 1991). Computers will be as prevalent as pieces of paper and pencils are today. Software tools and widgets that can be fitted together like pipe segments from different plumbing supply stores will rule the interface landscape. Object technology, in the hands of intelligent interface designers and developers, will be the enabler in the (r)evolution leading up to and shaping that landscape.

Information will dominate. The need for instant information retrieval will lead to even more information overload for the increasing hordes of knowledge workers. Information visualization and filtering with comprehensible, usable, and malleable interfaces will be the key to success.

For the foreseeable future, hardware advances and greater access to online information will continue to outpace advances in software. Commercial off-the-shelf (COTS) software will provide an even smaller percentage of the applications necessary to gain competitive advantage in business.

Businesses must have vision and commitment to chart their own course into innovative interfaces and empower knowledge workers with more resources than they need. Rapid advances in interface software will continue. UIMS functionality will grow and we will see a resurgence in interpreted development and runtime environments with hundreds of compatible building blocks.

CONCLUSIONS

Users are never wrong. They do what they do without being judged. On the other side of the coin, designers are wrong if they do not take into account users' tasks, training, mindset, motivation, and mental and physical capabilities. Then, through their own intelligence, information gathering, interdisciplinary outreach, and due diligence they can strive to create a truly usable interface. This is how it should be.

Myopic designers will be out of a job. Managers who do not strive for usable interfaces will be placed elsewhere. Organizations that do not provide managers with the mandate and appropriate resources to develop usable interfaces will not prosper.

The *any* key example presented earlier was more humorous than practical. In recent years, the VCR provides an everyday example of interface design that has failed. As comedians remind us, many people are not able to set the clock on their VCRs. Some electric companies are now sending time information through electric wires to homes so that VCRs can set the time themselves!

In addition to the difficulty of setting the time, people cannot program VCRs properly to record television shows. Some high-tech entrepreneurs built a solution by assigning a numerical code with a television show's listing and providing a device that accepts that code and programs the VCR automatically. The thought that interfaces are made this way to provide future business opportunities is of grave concern.

If businesses are to gain competitive advantage, high-quality interfaces to information systems are essential. Successful developers must continually strive to provide usable interfaces. Simply stated, usable interfaces empower people and business organizations.

REFERENCES

Boehm, B. (1988). A spiral model of software development and enhancement. *IEEE Computer, 21*, 5, 61–72.

Chimera, R. (1993). Evaluatión of platform independent user interface builders. Working report at Human-Computer Interaction Laboratory at the University of Maryland, 1993 (also available from the author).

Chimera, R. (1993) User interface consistency: An evaluation of original and revised interfaces for a videodisk library. In Ben Shneiderman (Ed)., *Sparks of Innovation*. Norwood, NJ: Ablex Publishing.

Drucker, P. (1988). The coming of the new organization. *Harvard Business Review, 66,* 1, 45–53.

Foley, J., P. Sukaviriya, and T. Griffith. (1993). A second-generation user interface design environment: The model and the runtime architecture. *Proceedings of the Conference on Human Factors in Computing Systems INTERCHI '93,* pp. 375–382.

Heckel, P. (1991). *The Elements of Friendly Software Design: The New Edition.* San Francisco: SYBEX Publishing.

Hix, D., and R. Hartson. (1993). *Developing User Interfaces: Ensuring Usability Through Product and Process.* New York: John Wiley & Sons.

Kreitzberg, C. (1994). Managing for usability: The QUE design methodology. Unpublished manuscript, Cognetics Corporation, Princeton Junction, NJ.

Kumar, H. (1994). Cost estimate for expansion and operation of the Human-Computer Interaction Laboratory. Unpublished manuscript, University of Maryland.

Lewis, C., P. Polson, C. Wharton, and J. Rieman. (1990). Testing a walkthrough methodology for theory-based design of walk-up-and-use interfaces. In *Proceedings of the Conference on Human Factors in Computing Systems CHI '90,* pp. 235–241.

Marshall, C., B. McManus, and A. Prail. (1990). Usability of product X—lessons from a real product. *Behaviour & Information Technology, 9,* 3, 243–253.

McDaniel, S., G. Olson, and J. Olson. (1994). Methods in search of methodology—combining HCI and object orientation. *Proceedings of the Conference on Human Factors in Computing Systems CHI '94,* 145–151.

Myers, B. (1994). Challenges of HCI design and implementation. *interactions, 1,* 1, 73–83.

Myers, B., D. Giuse, R. Dannenberg, B. Vander Zanden, Brad, D. Kosbie, E. Pervin, A. Mickish, and P. Marchal. (1990). Garnet: Comprehensive support for graphical, highly-interactive user interfaces. *IEEE Computer, 23,* 11, 71–85.

Nielsen, J. (1993). *Usability Engineering.* New York: Academic Press.

Pausch, R. (1991). Simple user interface toolkit (SUIT): The Pascal of user interface toolkits. *Proceedings of ACM Symposium of User Interface Software and Technology, 4.*

Shneiderman, B. (1992). *Designing the User Interface: Strategies for Effective Human-Computer Interaction,* 2nd edition. Reading, MA: Addison-Wesley.

Telles, M. (1990). Updating an older interface. *Proceedings of the Conference on Human Factors in Computing Systems CHI '90,* pp. 243–247.

Weiser, M. (1991, September). The computer for the twenty-first century. *Scientific American,* 94–104.

CLASSIFIED BIBLIOGRAPHY

This bibliography is classified according to the following categories:

- New world order of business

- Introduction to object technology and business reengineering

- Learning to object think and program

- Business process reengineering

- Human cognition and work

- Object-oriented systems development

- Object-oriented programming

- The learning organization

NEW WORLD ORDER OF BUSINESS

Barker, Joel Arthur. *Future Edge: Discovering the New Paradigms of Success.* W. Morrow. 240 pp. 1992. Note: In 1993 HarperCollins reissued this book under the title *Paradigms: The Business of Discovering the Future.*

Bradley, Stephen P., Jerry A. Hausman, and Richard L. Nolan. *Globalization, Technology, and Competition: The Fusion of Computers and Telecommunications in the 1990s.* Harvard Business School Press. 400 pp. 1993.

Champy, James. *Reengineering Management: The Mandate for New Leadership.* HarperBusiness. 212 pp. 1995.

Davidow, William H., and Michael S. Malone. *The Virtual Corporation: Structuring and Revitalizing the Corporation for the 21st Century.* HarperCollins. 294 pp. 1992.

Gelernter, David. *Mirror Worlds or: The Day Software Puts the Universe in a Shoebox. How it Will Happen and What it Will Mean.* Oxford University Press. 237 pp. 1991.

Gerstein, Marc S. *The Technology Connection: Strategy and Change in the Information Age.* Addison-Wesley. 194 pp. 1987.

Goldman, S. L., R. N. Nagel, and K. Preiss. *Agile Competitors and Virtual Organizations: Strategies for Enriching the Customer.* Van Nostrand Reinhold. 400 pp. 1994.

Hamel, Gary, and C. K. Prahalad. *Competing for the Future: Breakthrough Strategies for Seizing Control of Your Industry and Creating the Markets of Tomorrow.* Harvard Business School Press. 336 pp. 1994.

Kelly, Kevin. *Out of Control: The Rise of Neo-Biological Civilization.* Addison-Wesley. 521 pp. 1994.

Keyes, Jessica. *Infotrends: The Competitive Use of Information.* McGraw-Hill. 221 pp. 1993.

Knights, David, and Fergus Murray. *Managers Divided: Organization Politics and Information Technology Management.* John Wiley. 271 pp. 1995.

Martin, James. *The Great Transition: Using the Seven Disciplines of Enterprise Engineering to Align People, Technology, and Strategy,* AMACOM, New York. 1995.

McKenney, James L. *Waves of Change: Business Evaluation Through Information Technology.* Harvard Business School Press. 240 pp. 1995.

Negroponte, Nicholas. *Being Digital.* Borzoi Books, Alfred A. Knopf. 243 pp. 1995.

Peters, Tom. *Liberation Management: Necessary Disorganization for the Nanosecond Nineties.* Macmillan. 834 pp. 1992.

Pinchot, Gifford and Elizabeth Pinchot. *The End of Bureaucracy and the Rise of the Intelligent Organization.* Berrett-Koehler Publishers. 399 pp. 1993.

Porter, Michael E. *Competitive Strategy: Techniques for Analyzing Industries and Competitors.* Free Press. 1980. *Competitive Advantage: Creating and Sustaining Superior Performance.* Free Press. 1985.

Rifkin, Jeremy. *The End of Work: The Decline of the Global Labor Force and the Dawn of the Post-Market Era.* G.P. Putnam's Sons. 350 pp. 1995.

Sakaiya, Taichi. *The Knowledge-Value Revolution, or A History of the Future.* Kodabsha International. 379 pp. 1991.

Senge, Peter M. *The Fifth Discipline: The Art and Practice of the Learning Organization.* Doubleday/Currency. 424 pp. 1990.

Stoll, Cliff. *Silicon Snake Oil: Second Thoughts on the Information Highway.* Doubleday. 247 pp. 1995.

Strassmann, Paul A. *Information Payoff: The Transformation of Work in the Electronic Age.* Collier Macmillan. 298 pp. 1985.

Strassmann, Paul A. *The Business Value of Computers*. Information Economics Press. 522 pp. 1990.

Tapscott, Don, and Art Caston. *Paradigm Shift: The New Promise of Information Technology*. McGraw-Hill. 337 pp. 1993.

Waldrop, Mitchell. *Complexity: The Emerging Science at the Edge of Order and Chaos*. Simon and Schuster. 380 pp. 1992.

Wang, Charles B. *Techno Vision: The Executive's Survival Guide to Understanding and Managing Information Technology*. McGraw-Hill. 198 pp. 1994.

INTRODUCTION TO OBJECT TECHNOLOGY AND BUSINESS ENGINEERING

Adiga, S. *Object-Oriented Software Systems in Manufacturing*. Chapman and Hall. 270 pp. 1992.

Baecker, Ronald M. *Readings in Groupware and Computer-Supported Cooperative Work: Assisting Human-Human Collaboration*. Morgan Kaufmann Publishers. 280 pp. 1994.

Champy, James. *Reengineering Management: The Mandate for New Leadership*. Harper Business. 212 pp. 1995.

Ciborra, Claudio. *Strategic Information Systems: A European Perspective*. Wiley. 242 pp. 1994.

Hammer, Michael, and J. Champy. *Reengineering the Corporation: A Manifesto for Business Revolution*. Harper Business. 1993, 1994 updated paperback edition.

Khoshafian, Setrag. *Object Orientation: Concepts, Languages, Databases, and User Interfaces*. Wiley. 434 pp. 1990.

Love, Tom. *Object Lessons: Lessons Learned in Object-Oriented Development Projects*. SIGS Books. 256 pp. 1993.

Mattison, Rob, and Michael J. Sipolt. *The Object-Oriented Enterprise: Making Corporate Information Systems Work.* McGraw-Hill. 400 pp. 1994.

Orfali, Robert, Dan Harkey, and Jeri Edwards. *Essential Client Server Survival Guide.* Wiley. 527 pp. 1994.

Orfali, Robert, Dan Harkey, and Jeri Edwards. (R) *The Essential Distributed Objects Survival Guide.* Wiley. 1995.

Simon, Alan R. *Enterprise Computing.* Bantam Books. 303 pp. 1992.

Strassmann, Paul A. *Information Payoff: The Transformation of Work in the Electronic Age.* Collier Macmillan. 298 pp. 1985.

Strassmann, Paul A. *The Business Value of Computers.* Information Economics Press. 522 pp. 1990.

Sutherland, Ewan, and Yves Morieux (Eds.). *Business Strategy and Information Technology.* Routledge. 243 pp. 1991.

Taylor, David. *Object-Oriented Technology: A Manager's Guide.* Addison-Wesley. 1991.

Wang, Charles B. *Techno Vision: The Executive's Survival Guide to Understanding and Managing Information Technology.* McGraw-Hill. 198 pp. 1994.

LEARNING TO OBJECT THINK AND PROGRAM

Ambler, Scott. *Objects Primer: The Application Developer's Guide to Object-Orientation.* SIGS Books. Forthcoming.

Baecker, Ronald M. *Readings in Groupware and Computer-Supported Cooperative Work: Assisting Human-Human Collaboration.* Morgan Kaufmann Publishers. 280 pp. 1994.

Budd, Timothy. *An Introduction to Object-Oriented Programming*. Addison-Wesley. 399 pp. 1991.

Coad, Peter, *The Object Game*. Object International. 1993. Board game that teaches "object think."

Coad, Peter, and J. Nicola. *Object-Oriented Programming*. Prentice Hall. 260 pp. 1993.

Coad, Peter, David North, and M. Mayfield. *Object Models: Strategies, Patterns, and Applications*. Prentice Hall. Book and disk. 450 pp. 1995.

Cogswell, Jeffery M. *Simple C++: Learn C++ While You Build the Incredible Robodog*. The Waite Group. 252 pp. 1994.

Computer Science Corporation/Object Management Group. *Object Technology Today*. Wiley. 1994.

Daniel, K. J., and G. Simpson. *Object-Oriented Technology: A Practical Guide to Programming, Design and Analysis, and Databases*. Addison-Wesley. 1992.

Entsminger, Gary. *The Tao of Objects*. M and T Books. 249 pp. 1990.

Firesmith, D. G., and E. M. Eykholt. *The Object Technology Dictionary*. SIGS Publications. 603 pp. 1995.

G6G Consulting Group. *The G6G Directory of Intelligent Software*, Volumes I-IV. G6G Consulting Group. 1994.

Gaumer, Dale J. *Directory of Object Technology*. SIGS Books. 1995.

Graham, Ian. *Migrating to Object Technology*. Addison-Wesley. 520 pp. 1995.

Hamilton, Margaret. *Object Thinking: Development Before the Fact*. McGraw-Hill. 320 pp. 1994.

Harmon, Paul. *Intelligent Software Systems Development: An IS Manager's Guide*. Prentice Hall. 512 pp. 1993.

Korienek, Gene, and Tom Wrench. *A Quick Trip to ObjectLand: Object-Oriented Programming with Smalltalk/V.* Prentice Hall. 192 pp. 1993.

Mattison, Rob, and Michael J. Sipolt. *The Object-Oriented Enterprise: Making Corporate Information Systems Work.* McGraw-Hill. 400 pp. 1994.

Meyer, B. *Object Success: A Manager's Guide to Object Technology.* Prentice Hall. 1995.

Orfali, Robert, Dan Harkey, and Jeri Edwards. *Essential Client/Server Survival Guide.* Wiley. 527 pp. 1994.

Orfali, Robert, Dan Harkey, and Jeri Edwards. (R) *The Essential Distributed Objects Survival Guide.* Wiley. 1995.

Taylor, David. *Object-Oriented Information Systems: Planning and Implementation.* Wiley. 357 pp. 1992.

Taylor, David A. *Business Engineering with Object Technology.* Wiley. 188 pp. 1995.

Winblad, A. L., S. D. Edwards, and D. R. King. *Implementing Object Technology*, 2nd Ed. Addison-Wesley. 1993.

Yourdon, E., K. Whitehead, J. Thumann, P. Nevermann, and K. Oppel. *Mainstream Objects.* Prentice Hall. 1995.

BUSINESS PROCESS REENGINEERING

Andrews, Dorine C., and Susan K. Stalick. *Business Reengineering: The Survival Guide.* Yourdon Press. 302 pp. 1994.

Argyris, Chris. *Knowledge for Action.* Jossey-Bass. 1993.

Arthur, L. J. *Improving Software Quality: An Insider's Guide to TQM.* Wiley. 1992.

Baba, Marietta, D. Falkenberg, and D. Hill. "The Cultural Dimensions of Technology Enabled Corporate Transformations," research paper, March 28, 1994. In

Technological Innovations and Cultural Processes: New Theoretical Perspectives. Edited by Santos, M. Josefa, and R. Diaz Cruz. National University of Mexico. 1995.

Bateson, Gregory. *Steps to an Ecology of Mind.* Ballantine. 1972.

Beer, Stafford. *Platform for Change.* Wiley. 1975.

Block, Peter. *Stewardship: Choosing Service Over Self-Interest.* Berrett-Koehler Publishers. 264 pp. 1993.

Block, Peter. *The Empowered Manager: Positive Political Skills at Work.* Jossey-Bass. 214 pp. 1991.

Boar, Bernard H. *Practical Steps for Aligning Information Technology with Business Strategies: How to Achieve a Competitive Advantage.* Wiley. 353 pp. 1994.

Boar, Bernard H. *The Art of Strategic Planning for Information Technology: Crafting Strategy for the 90s.* Wiley. 1994.

Bounds, Greg, et al. *Beyond Total Quality Management: Toward the Emerging Paradigm.* McGraw-Hill. 817 pp. 1994.

Braithwaite, Timothy. *Information Service Excellence Through TQM: Building Partnerships for Business Process Reengineering and Continuous Improvement.* ASQC Quality Press. 145 pp. 1994.

Champy, James. *Reengineering Management: The Mandate for New Leadership.* Harper-Collins. 1995.

Checkland, P. B. *Systems Thinking, Systems Practice.* Wiley. 330 pp. 1981.

Ciborra, Claudio. *Teams, Markets and Systems—Business Innovation and Information Technology.* Cambridge University Press. 250 pp. 1993.

Clegg, Stewart R. *Modern Organizations—Organization Studies in a Postmodern World.* Sage Publications. 1990.

Clemmer, Jim, Barry Sheehy, and Achieve International/Zengler Miller Associates. *Firing on All Cylinders: The Service/Quality System for High-Powered Corporate Performance.* Business One Irwin. 392 pp. 1992.

Conner, Daryl R. *Managing at the Speed of Change: How Resilient Managers Succeed and Prosper Where Others Fail.* Villard Books. 1992.

Cooksey, Clifton, Richard Beans, and Debra Eshelman. *Process Improvement: A Guide for Teams,* 2nd Ed. Coopers and Lybrand. 246 pp. 1993.

Covey, Stephen, R. A. Roger Merill and Rebecca R. Merrill. *First Things First.* Simon and Schuster. 1994.

Crawford, Anthony. *Advancing Business Concepts in a JAD Workshop Setting: Business Reengineering and Process Redesign Using Teamwork.* Prentice Hall. 208 pp. 1994.

Davenport, Thomas. *Process Innovation: Reengineering Work Through Information Technology.* Ernst and Young. Harvard Business School Press. 1993.

Davidow, William H., and Bro Uttal. *Total Customer Service: The Ultimate Weapon.* Harper Perennial. 227 pp. 1990.

Deming, W. Edwards. *Out of the Crisis.* Cambridge University Press. 507 pp. 1982.

Dimancescu, Dan. *The Seamless Enterprise: Making Cross Functional Management Work.* HarperBusiness. 249 pp. 1992.

Donovan, John J. *Business Re-engineering with Information Technology.* Prentice Hall. 224 pp. 1994.

Dunn, Robert H., and Richard S. Ullman. *TQM for Computer Software.* McGraw-Hill. 364 pp. 1994.

Fallon, Howard. *How to Implement Information Systems and Live to Tell About It.* Wiley. 1994.

Fisher, Kimball. *Leading Self-Directed Work Teams: A Guide to Developing New Team Leadership Skills.* McGraw-Hill. 263 pp. 1993.

Fisher, Kimball, and the Belgrad-Fisher-Rayner Team. *Tips for Teams: A Ready Reference for Solving Team Problems.* McGraw-Hill. 250 pp. 1995.

Fried, Louis. *Managing Information Technology in Turbulent Times.* Wiley. 1994.

Galbraith, Jar R., and Edward E. Lawler. *Organizing for the Future.* Jossey-Bass. 1993.

Gerstein, Marc S., David A. Nadler, Robert B. Shaw, and Associates. *Organizational Architecture: Designs for Changing Organizations.* Jossey-Bass. 284 pp. 1992.

Gunn, Thomas G. *In the Age of the Real-Time Enterprise: Managing for Sustained Performance with Enterprise Logistics Planning.* Oliver Wight Publications. 22 pp. 1994.

Hamel, Gary, and C. K. Prahalad. *Competing for the Future: Breakthrough Strategies for Seizing Control of Your Industry and Creating the Markets of Tomorrow.* Harvard Business School Press. 336 pp. 1994.

Handy, Charles B. *The Age of Paradox.* Harvard Business School Press. 303 pp. 1994.

Handy, Charles B. *The Age of Unreason.* Harvard Business School Press. 278 pp. 1989.

Harrington, H. J. *Business Process Improvement: The Breakthrough Strategy for Total Quality, Productivity, and Competitiveness.* McGraw-Hill. 274 pp. 1991.

Harrington, J. *Organizational Structure and Information Technology.* Prentice Hall. 1991.

Hastings, Colin. *The New Organization: Growing the Cultural of Organizational Networking.* McGraw-Hill. 178 pp. 1993.

Hofstede, Greet. *Cultures and Organizations: Software of the Mind.* McGraw-Hill. 1991.

Hunt, V. Daniel. *Reengineering: Leveraging the Power of Integrated Product Development.* Oliver Wight Publications. 300 pp. 1993.

Hunt, V. Daniel. *The Survival Factor: An Action Guide to Improving Your Business Today.* Oliver Wight Publications. 300 pp. 1994.

Institute of Industrial Engineers. *Beyond the Basics of Reengineering: Survival Tactics for the 90's.* Institute of Industrial Engineers. 250 pp. 1994.

Jacobson, Ivar, Maria Ericson, and Agneta Jacobson. *The Object Advantage: Business Process Engineering with Object Techology.* Addison-Wesley. 1994.

Jayachandra, Y. *Re-engineering the Networked Enterprise.* McGraw-Hill. 290 pp. 1994.

Johansson, Henry J., et al. *Business Process Reengineering: BreakPoint Strategies for Market Dominance.* John Wiley. 241 pp. 1993.

Katzenbach, Jon R., and Douglas K. Smith. *The Wisdom of Teams: Creating the High-Performance Organization.* Harvard Business School Press. 291 pp. 1993.

Keen, P .W. G. *Shaping the Future: Business Design Through Information Technology.* Harvard Business School Press. 264 pp. 1991.

Keen, Peter G. W., and J. Michael Cummins. *Networks in Action: Business Choices and Telecommunications Decisions.* Wadsworth Publishing Company. 742 pp. 1994.

Kelly, Kevin. *Out of Control: The Rise of Neo-Biological Civilization.* Addison-Wesley. 1994.

Keyes, Jessica. *Solving the Productivity Paradox: TQM for Computer Professionals.* McGraw-Hill. 300 pp. 1994.

Khoshafian, Setrag, B. Baker, R. Abnous, and K. Sheperd. *Intelligent Offices: Object-Oriented, Multi-Media Information Management in Client/Server Architectures.* Wiley. 1992.

Lilienfeld, Robert. *Rise of Systems Theory: An Ideological Analysis.* Wiley. 1978.

Lipnack, Jessica, and Jeffrey Stamps. *The Age of the Network: Organizing Principles for the 21st Century.* Oliver Wight Publications. 256 pp. 1994.

Lipnack, Jessica, and Jeffrey Stamps. *The TeamNet Factor: Bringing the Power of Boundary Crossing Into the Heart of Your Business.* Oliver Wight Publications. 414 pp. 1993.

Lowenthal, Jeffrey N. *Reengineering the Organization: A Step-By-Step Approach to Corporate Revitalization.* ASCQ Quality Press. 185 pp. 1994.

Martin, Andre J. *Infopartnering: The Ultimate Strategy for Achieving Efficient Consumer Response.* Oliver Wight Publications. 1994.

Martin, James. *Enterprise Engineering—The Key to Corporate Survival,* Vol. I-IV. Savant Institute. 1994. Also published as *The Great Transition: Using the Seven Disciplines of Enterprise Engineering to Align People, Technology, and Strategy.* AMACOM, New York. 1995.

Moody, Patricia E. *Breakthrough Partnering: Creating a Collective Enterprise Advantage.* Organizational Dynamics, Inc. 256 pp. 1993.

Morris, Daniel, and Joel Brandon. *Re-Engineering Your Business.* McGraw-Hill. 1993.

Neusch, Donna R., and Alan F. Siebenaler. *The High Performance Enterprise: Reinventing the People Side of Your Business.* Oliver Wight Publications. 380 pp. 1993.

Nolan, Richard L., and David C Croson. *Creative Destruction: A Six-Stage Process for Transforming the Organization.* Harvard Business School Press. 272 pp. 1995.

Organizational Dynamics, Inc. *Making Teams Work: A Guide to Creating and Managing Teams.* Organizational Dynamics, Inc. 146 pp. 1993.

Ouellette, L. Paul. *I/S at Your Service: Knowing and Keeping Your Clients.* Kendall/ Hunt. 206 pp. 1993.

Ouellette, L. Paul. *How to Market the I/S Department Internally.* AMACOM. 174 pp. 1992.

Peters, Tom. *The Pursuit of WOW!: Every Person's Guide to Topsy-Turvy Times.* Vintage Books. 1994.

Peters, Tom. *The Tom Peters Seminar: Crazy Times Call for Crazy Organizations* Vintage Books/Random House, 1994.

Petrozzo, Daniel P., and John C. Stepper. *Successful Reengineering: Now You Know What It Is—Here's How to Do It!* Van Nostrand Reinhold. 1994.

Pfeffer, Jeffrey. *Competitive Advantage Through People: Unleashing the Power of the Workforce.* Harvard Business School Press. 304 pp. 1994.

Postman, Neil. *Technopoly: The Surrender of Culture to Technology.* Random House. 1993.

Quinn, James B. *Intelligent Enterprises.* Free Press. 472 pp. 1992.

Raymond, Larry. *Reinventing Communication: Visual Language for Planning, Problem Solving and Reengineering.* ASQC Quality Press. 167 pp. 1994.

Rayner, Steven R. *Recreating the Workplace: The Pathway to High Performance Work Systems.* Oliver Wight Publications. 279 pp. 1993.

Roberts, Lon. *Process Reengineering: The Key to Achieving Breakthrough Success.* ASQC Quality Press. 1994.

Robson, George D. *Continuous Process Improvement: Simplifying Work Flow Systems.* Free Press. 1991.

Rodgers, T. J., WIlliam Taylor, and Rick Foreman. *No Excuses Management: Proven Systems for Starting Fast, Growing Quickly, and Surviving Hard Times.* Doubleday. 1992.

Rumelt, Richard P., and Dan E. Schendel. *Fundamental Issues in Strategy: A Research Agenda.* Harvard Business School Press. 656 pp. 1994.

Rummler, Geary, and Alan Brache. *Improving Performance: How to Manage the White Space on the Organization Chart*. Jossey-Bass. 1990.

Schmidt, Warren H., and Jerome P. Finnigan. *The Race Without a Finish Line: America's Quest for Total Quality*. Jossey-Bass Publishers. 402 pp. 1992.

Schmidt, Warren H., and Jerome P. Finnigan. *TQManager: A Practical Guide for Managing in a Total Quality Organization*. Jossey-Bass. 196 pp. 1993.

Scott-Morgan, Peter. *The Unwritten Rules of the Game*. McGraw-Hill. 200 pp. 1994.

Senge, Peter M. *The Fifth Discipline: The Art and Practice of the Learning Organization*. Doubleday/Currency. 424 pp. 1990.

Shekerjian, Denise. *Uncommon Genius—How Great Ideas Are Born*. Penguin Books. 1990.

Simon, Alan R. *The Computer Professional's Survival Guide*. McGraw-Hill. 176 pp. 1992.

Simon, Alan R. *Workgroup Computing: Workflow, Groupware, and Messaging*. McGraw-Hill. 350 pp. 1994.

Slater, Roger. *Integrated Process Management: A Quality Model*. McGraw-Hill, American Society for Quality Control. 278 pp. 1991.

Spurr, Kathy, P. Layzell, L. Jennison, and N. Richards (Eds.). *Software Assistance for Business Reengineering*. Wiley. 1994.

Stahl, Michael J., and Gregory M. Bounds, (Eds.). *Competing Globally Through Customer Value: The Management of Strategic Suprasystems*. Quorum. 822 pp. 1991.

Stalk, George, and Thomas M. Hout. *Competing Against Time: How Time-Based Competition is Reshaping Global Markets*. Collier Macmillan. 285 pp. 1990.

Strassmann, Paul A. *Information Warfare*. Information Economics Press. Forthcoming title.

Strassmann, Paul A. *The Alignment of Information Management With Business Planning.* Information Economics Press. Forthcoming title.

Strassmann, Paul A. *The Politics of Information Management.* Information Economics Press. 1994.

Taylor, David A. *Business Engineering with Object Technology.* Wiley. 188 pp. 1995.

Tomasko, Robert M. *Downsizing: Reshaping the Corporation for the Future.* AMACOM. 290 pp. 1987.

Tomasko, Robert M. *Rethinking the Corporation: The Architecture of Change.* AMACOM. 213 pp. 1993.

v Bertalanfy, Ludwig. *General Systems Theory.* George Braziller Publishers. 1968.

vanMeel, J. W. *The Dynamics of Business Engineering. Reflections on Two Case Studies Within the Amsterdam Municipal Police Force.* School of System Engineering, Policy Analysis, and Management. Delft University of Technology, Delft, the Netherlands. 1994.

Warnecke, Hans-Juergen. T*he_Fractal Company—A Revolution in Corporate Culture.* Springer. 1993.

Weinberg, Gerard M. *An Introduction to General Systems Thinking.* Wiley. 1988.

Weinberg, Gerard M. *General Principles of Systems Design.* Dorset House. 1988. (Note: Companion to *An Introduction to General Systems Thinking*).

Weinberg, Gerard M., and Gause, Donald C. *Are Your Lights On? How to Figure out What the Problem Really Is.* Winthrop Publishers. 156 pp. 1982.

Wellins, Richard S., William C. Byham, and Jeanne M. Wilson. *Empowered Teams.* Jossey-Bass. 1991.

Wheatley, Margaret. *Leadership and the New Science: Learning About Organization From an Orderly Universe.* Berrett-Koehler Publishers. 1992.

White, Thomas E., and Layna Fischer, Eds. *The Workflow Paradigm. The Impact of Information Technology on Business Process Reengineering.* Future Strategies Inc. 1994.

Whiteside, John, and Leatrice McLaughlin. T*he Phoenix Agenda: Power to Transform Your Workplace.* Oliver Wight Publications. 318 pp. 1993.

Yates, JoAnne. *Control through Communication: The Rise of System in American Management.* The John Hopkins University Press. 1989.

Zuboff, Shoshanah. *In the Age of the Smart Machine: The Future of Work and Power.* Basic Books. 468 pp. 1988.

Zuboff, Shoshanah. *Psychological and Organizational Implications of Computer-Mediated Work.* Center for Information Systems Research. Alfred P. Sloan School of Management, MIT. 26 pp. 1981.

HUMAN COGNITION AND WORK

Bass, Len, and Prasun Dewan, Eds. *User Interface Software.* Wiley. 1993.

Chisolm, John. *The art of software design. Unix Review.* March 1994. p. 11.

Collins, David. *Designing Object-Oriented User Interfaces.* Benjamin/Cummings. Adison-Wesley. 1995.

Constantine, Larry. *Constantine On Peopleware.* Prentice Hall. 1995.

Ehn, Pelle. *Work-Oriented Design of Computer Artifacts,* 2nd Ed. Arbetslivscebtrum. 1989.

Fowler, Susan. The GUI style guide. *AP Professional.* 407 pp. 1995.

Galitz, Wilbert. *It's Time to Clean Your Windows: Designing GUIs that Work.* Wiley. 477 pp. 1994.

Galitz, Wilbert. *User-Interface Screen Design,* 4th Ed. Wiley. 1992.

Go, Inc. *Penpoint User Interface Design Guidelines.* Addison-Wesley. 1992.

Hix, D., and R. Hartson. *Developing User Interfaces: Ensuring Usability Through Product and Process.* Wiley. 1993.

Jones, Mark K. (Mark Kirkland). *Human-Computer Interaction: A Design Guide.* Educational Technology Publications. 150 pp. 1989.

Kepple, L. GUI Testing. *M and T.* 1994.

Lakoff, George. *Women, Fire, and Dangerous Things: What Categories Reveal About the Mind.* The University of Chicago Press. 614 pp. 1987.

Lakoff, George, and M. Johnson. *Metaphors We Live By.* The University of Chicago Press. 614 pp. 1987.

Laurel, Brenda. *Computers as Theatre.* Addison-Wesley. 1993.

Laurel, Brenda. *The Art of Human-Computer Interface Design.* Addison-Wesley. 1990.

Lee, Geoff. *Object-Oriented GUI Application Development.* Prentice Hall. 250 pp. 1993.

Maddix, Frank. *Human-Computer Interaction: Theory and Practice.* Ellis Horwood. 306 pp. 1990.

Minsky, Marvin. *The Society of Mind.* Simon and Schuster. 1986.

Mulligan, Robert, Mark Altom, and David Simkin. *User Interface Design in the Trenches: Some Tips on Shooting From the Hip.* ACM Press, CHI '91, Conference/Proceeding.

Nadel, J. *How to Use Color Effectively in the Design of Usable GUIs.* Human Factors International. 1994.

Nielsen, Jakob, and Robert L. Mack, Eds. *Usability Inspection Methods.* Wiley. 1993.

Norman, Donald A. *Design of Everyday Things.* Doubleday. 1990.

Norman, Donald A. *Things That Make Us Smart.* Addison-Wesley. 1993.

Norman, Donald A. *Turn Signals are the Facial Expressions of Automobiles.* Addison-Wesley. 1992.

Norman, Donald A. *User Centered Systems Design.* Lawrence Erlbaum Assoc. 1986.

Preece, Jenny. *Human Computer Interaction.* Addison-Wesley. 640 pp. 1994.

Rubin, Jeffrey. *Handbook of Usability Testing: How to Plan, Design, and Conduct Effective Tests.* Wiley. 416 pp. 1993.

Sayles, Jonathan S., Peter Molchan, Steve Karlen, and Gary Bilodeau. *GUI-Based Design and Development For Client/Server Applications: Using PowerBuilder, SQLWindows, Visual Basic, PARTS Workbench.* Wiley. 310 pp. 1994.

Schaffer, E. *How to Design Usable GUIs* (video). Human Factors International. 1993.

Schrage, Michael. *Shared Minds: The New Technologies of Collaboration.* Random House. 227 pp. 1990.

Shneiderman, Ben. *Designing the User Interface: Strategies for Effective Human-Computer Interaction,* 2nd Ed. Addison-Wesley. 1992.

Shneiderman, Ben. *Sparks of Innovation in Human-Computer Interaction.* Addison-Wesley. 1993.

Suchman, Lucy. *Plans and Situated Actions: The Problem of Human-Machine Communications.* Cambridge University Press. 1987.

Sutcliffe, Alistair. *Human-Computer Interface Design.* Springer-Verlag, Macmillan Education. 205 pp. 1989.

Tognazini, Bruce. *Tog on Interface.* Addison-Wesley. 331 pp. 1992.

Wiener, Norbert. *The Human Use of Human Beings: Cybernetics and Society.* Da Capo Press. 1954. Avon Books. 1979.

Winograd, T., and C. F. Flores. *Understanding Computers and Cognition—A New Foundation for Design.* Addison-Wesley. 207 pp. 1987.

Winograd., Terry A., and Paul S. Adler, Eds. *Usability: Turning Technologies Into Tools.* Oxford University Press. 208 pp. 1992.

OBJECT-ORIENTED SYSTEMS DEVELOPMENT

Abdelguerfi, Mahdi, and Simon Lavington. *Emerging Trends in Database and Knowledge Base Machines.* IEEE Computer Society Press. 316 pp. 1995.

Agha, Gul, Peter Wegner, and Akinori Yonezawa. *Research Directions in Concurrent Object-Oriented Programming.* 544 pp. 1993.

Andleigh, Prabhatk, and Nichael R. Gretzinger. *Distributed Object-Oriented Analysis.* Prentice Hall. 260 pp. 1992.

Andriole, Stephen J. *Information Systems Design Principles for the 90s.* AFCEA Int. Press. 1990.

Babat, Subodh. *Object-Oriented Networks: Models for Network Architecture, Operations, and Management.* Prentice Hall. 475 pp. 1994.

Banchilhon, F., C. Delobel, and P. Kanellakis. *Building an Object-Oriented Database System: The Story of O2.* Morgan Kaufmann. 1992.

Barry and Associates. *DBMS Needs Assessment for Objects,* 3rd Ed. 1995.

Bassett, P.G. *Frame-Based Software Engineering.* Prentice Hall. 1994.

Beizer, Boris. *Black-Box Testing: Techniques for Functional Testing of Software and Systems*. John Wiley and Sons. 1995.

Berard, Edward. *A Comparison of Object-Oriented Development Methodologies*. Berard Software Engineering. 1992.

Berard, Edward. *A Project Management Handbook for Object-Oriented Software Development*. Berard Software Engineering. 1992. Prentice Hall. 600 pp. 1994.

Berard, Edward. *Essays on Object-Oriented Software Engineering*. Prentice Hall. 544 pp. 1993.

Berrisford, Graham, and Keith Robinson. *Object Oriented SSADM*. Prentice Hall. 524 pp. 1994.

Bertino, Elisa, and Lorengo Martino. *Object-Oriented Database Systems: Concepts and Architectures*. Addison-Wesley. 1994.

Biggerstaff, Ted J., and Perlis, Alan J. *Software Reusability I and II*. Addison-Wesley. 1989. 2 volumes.

Booch, Grady. *Object Solutions: A Source Book for Developers*, 2nd Ed. Addison-Wesley. 1994.

Booch, Grady. *Object-Oriented Analysis and Design With Applications*. 2nd Ed. Addison-Wesley. 1994. Includes an extensive classified bibliography that makes an excellent reference guide to OO development.

Brown, A. W. *Object-Oriented Databases and Their Applications to Software Engineering*. McGraw-Hill. 1991.

Bruce, Thomas. *Designing Quality Databases with IDEF1X Information Models*. Dorset House. 584 pp. 1992.

Burleson, Donald. *Practical Applications of Object-Oriented Techniques to Relational Databases*. Wiley. 1994.

Buschmann, Frank, Regine Meunier, Hans Rohnert, Peter Sommerlad, and Michael Stal. *Pattern-Oriented Software Architecture—A System of Patterns.* Wiley and Sons Ltd. February 1996.

Cardenas, Alfonso F., and Dennis McLeod. *Research Foundations in Semantic and Object-Oriented Databases.* Prentice Hall. 432 pp. 1990.

Carmichael, Andy. *Object Development Methods.* SIGS Books. 1994.

Carrol, John M. *Scenario-Based Design: Envisioning Work and Technology in System Development.* John Wiley and Sons. 1995.

Catell, R. G. G. *Object Data Management: Object-Oriented and Extended Relational Database Systems.* Addison-Wesley. 389 pp. 1994.

Checkland, Peter B. *Systems Thinking, Systems Practice.* Wiley. 330 pp. 1981.

Cherry, George W. *Software Construction by Object-Oriented Pictures.* Dorset House. 204 pp. 1990.

Chorafas, Dimitris N. *Intelligent Multimedia Databases.* Prentice Hall. 350 pp. 1994.

Chorafas, Dimitris N., and Heinrich Steinmann. *Object-Oriented Databases: An Introduction.* Prentice Hall. 375 pp. 1993.

Coad, Peter, and Edward Yourdin. *Object-Oriented Analysis,* 2nd Ed. Prentice Hall. 255 pp. 1991.

Coad, Peter, and Edward Yourdin. *Object-Oriented Design.* Prentice Hall. 244 pp. 1991.

Coleman, Derek, P. Arnold, S. Bodoff, C. Dollin, H. Gilcrist, F. Hayes, and P. Jeremaes. *Object-Oriented Development: The FUSION Method.* Prentice Hall. 400 pp. 1994.

Coleman, Derek, Ruth Malan, and Reed Letsinger. *Object-Oriented Development at Work: Fusion in the Real World.* Prentice Hall. 1996.

Collins, D. *Designing Object-Oriented User Interfaces.* Benjamin-Cummings. 1995.

Connell, John L., and Linda Shafer. *Object-Oriented Rapid Prototyping.* Prentice Hall. 250 pp. 1995.

Constantine, Larry. *Constantine on Peopleware.* Prentice Hall. 1995.

Cook, Steve, and John Daniels. *Designing Object Systems: Object-Oriented Modelling with Syntropy.* Prentice Hall. 317 pp. 1994.

Coulouris, George, Jean Dollimore, and Tim Kindberg. *Distributed Systems: Concepts and Design,* 2nd Ed. Addison-Wesley. 644 pp. 1994.

Cribbs, John, C. Roe, and S. Moon. *An Evaluation of Object-Oriented Analysis and Design Methodologies.* SIGS Books. 1994.

Curtis, Bill, William E. Hefley, Sally Miller, and Michael D. Konrad. *People Management Capability Maturity Model.* Draft Version 0.3. Software Engineering Institute. 1995.

Davis, Alan M. *Software Requirements: Objects, Functions, States, Revision.* Prentice Hall. 448 pp. 1993.

Davis, Alan M. *201 Principles of Software Development.* McGraw Hill. 256 pp. 1995.

DeBoever, Larry R. *Enabling Technologies for Client/Server: Implementation of Adaptive Systems.* McGraw-Hill. 400 pp. 1994.

deChampeaux, D. D. Lea, and P. Faure. *Object-Oriented Systems Development.* Addison-Wesley. 532 pp. 1993.

Desfray, Philippe. *Object Engineering: The Fourth Dimension.* Addison-Wesley. 352 pp. 1994.

Devlin, Keith. *Logic and Information.* Cambridge University Press. 307 pp. 1991.

Dewire, Dawna Travis. *Application Development for Distributed Environments.* McGraw-Hill. 296 pp. 1994.

Dillon, Tharam S., and Poh Lee Tan. *Object-Oriented Conceptual Modeling.* Prentice Hall. 328 pp. 1993.

Due, Richard. *Object Engineering: Managing Object Technology.* Addison-Wesley. 256 pp. 1996.

Eliens, A. *Principles of Object-Oriented Software Development.* Addision-Wesley. 1995.

Ellis, John. *Objectifying Real-Time Systems.* SIGS Books. 1994.

Ellison, Karen. *Developing Real-Time Embedded Software in a Market-Drive Company.* Wiley. 1994.

Embley, David W., Barry D. Kurtz, and Scott N. Woodfield. *Object-Oriented Systems Analysis: A Model-Driven Approach.* Prentice Hall. 256 pp. 1991.

Eppinger, Jeffrey L. *Camelot and Avalon: A Distributed Transaction Facility.* (The Morgan Kaufmann Series in Data Management Systems). Morgan Kaufmann Publishers. 505 pp. 1991.

Finkelstein, Anthony, Jeff Kramer, Bashar Nuseibeh. *Software Process Modeling and Technology.* Research Studies Advanced Software Development Series, Research Studies Press. 362 pp. 1994.

Firesmith, Donald G. *Object-Oriented Requirements Analysis and Logical Design.* Wiley. 1993.

Firesmith, Donald G. *Testing Object-Oriented Software.* SIGS Books. Forthcoming title.

Fishwick, Paul. *Simulation Model Design and Execution: Building Digital Worlds.* Prentice Hall. 432 pp. 1995.

Franz, M. *Object-Oriented Programming Featuring Actor.* Scott, Foresman. 1990.

Gamma, E., R. Helm, R. Johnson, and J. Vlissides. *A Catalog of Object-Oriented Design Patterns.* Taligent. 1993.

Gamma, E., R. Helm, R. Johnson, and J. Vlissides. *Design Patterns: Elements of Resuable Object-Oriented Software.* Addison-Wesley. 416 pp. 1995.

Goldberg, Adele, and Kenneth S. Rubin. *Succeeding with Objects: Decision Frameworks for Project Management.* Addison-Wesley. 608 pp. 1995.

Gorman, Michael. *Enterprise Database in a Client/Server Environment.* Wiley-QED Publications. 375 pp. 1993.

Graham, Ian. *Object-Oriented Methods.* 2nd Ed. Addison-Wesley. 1994.

Graham, Ian. *Migrating to Object Technology.* Addison-Wesley. 520 pp. 1995.

Gray, Peter, K. G. Krishnarao, and N. W. Patton, Eds. *Object-Oriented Databases: A Semantic Data Model Approach.* Prentice Hall. 300 pp. 1992.

Grey, Jim, and Andreas Reuter. *Transaction Processing: Concepts and Techniques,* (The Morgan Kaufmann Series in Data Management Systems). Morgan Kaufmann Publishers. 1070 pp. 1993.

Grey, Jim, Nancy A. Lynch, Michael Meritt, William E. Weihl, Alan Fekete, *Atomic Transactions: In Concurrent and Distributed Systems.* The Morgan Kaufmann Series in Data Management Systems. Morgan Kaufmann Publishers. 476 pp. 1993.

Gupta, R., and E. Horowitz. *Object-Oriented Databases with Applications to CASE, Networks, and VLSI CAD.* Prentice Hall. 1991.

Hall, Carl L. *Technical Foundations of Client/Server Systems.* Wiley. 1994.

Halliday, Steve, and Mike Wiebel. *Object-Oriented Software Engineering.* Prentice Hall. 320 pp. 1993.

Hamilton, M. *Object Thinking: Development Before the Fact*. McGraw-Hill. 1994.

Hares, John. *SSADM Version 4: The Advanced Practitioner's Guide*. Wiley. 1994.

Harland, D. M. *REKURSIV: Object-Oriented Computer Architecture*. Ellis Horwood/ E. Halstead Press. 1988.

Henderson-Sellers, B. *A Book of Object-Oriented Knowledge: Object-Oriented Anaylsis, Design, and Implementation: A New Approach to Software Engineering*. Prentice Hall. 240 pp. 1991.

Henderson-Sellers, B., and J. M. Edwards. *Book Two of Object-Oriented Knowledge: The Working Object*. (Moses Method). Prentice Hall. 1994.

Hollowell, G. *Handbook of Object-Oriented Standards: The Object Model*. Addison-Wesley. 1993.

Humphrey, Watts S. *Managing the Software Process*. Addison-Wesley. 1990.

Humphrey, Watts S. *A Discipline for Software Engineering*. Addison-Wesley. 1995.

Hutt, Andrew T. F., Ed. *Object Analysis and Design: Description of Methods*. Wiley. 216 pp. 1994.

Hutt, T. F., Ed. *Object Analysis and Design: Comparisons of Methods*. Wiley. 224 pp. 1994.

IBM. *VisualAge: Guide to the Smalltalk Development Environment*. IBM. 1995.

Jacobson, Ivar, Maria Ericson, and Agneta Jacobson. *The Object Advantage: Business Process Engineering with Object Technology*. Addison-Wesley. 1994.

Jacobson, Ivar, P. Jonsson, and G. Overgaard. *Object-Oriented Software Engineering*. Addison-Wesley. 1992.

Johnson, James R. *The Software Factory: Managing Software Development and Maintenance*, 2nd Ed. Wiley-QED Publications. 277 pp. 1991.

Jones, Caper. *Applied Software Measurement: Assuring Productivity and Quality.* McGraw-Hill. 1991.

Khoshafian, Setrag. *Object-Oriented Databases.* Wiley. 1993.

Khoshafian, Setrag, B. Baker, R. Abnous, and K. Sheperd. *Intelligent Offices: Object-Oriented, Multi-Media Information Management in Client/Server Architectures.* Wiley. 1992.

Kiczales, G., J. des Rivieres, and D. Bobrow. *The Art of the Metaobject Protocol.* MIT. 1991.

Kilov, Haim and J. Ross. *Information Modeling: An Object-Oriented Approach.* Prentice Hall. 320 pp. 1994.

Kim, J., and J. Lerch. *Towards a Model of Cognitive Process in Logical Design: Comparing Object-Oriented and Traditional Functional Decomposition Software Methodologies.* Carnegie Mellon University. 1992.

Kim, Won, Ed. *Modern Database Management: Object-Oriented and Extended Relational Database Systems.* Addison-Wesley. 1995.

Kim, Won. *Introduction to Object-Oriented Databases.* MIT. 1990.

Kim, Won. *Modern Database Systems: The Object Model, Interoperability, and Beyond,* Addison-Wesley. 1995.

Knudsen, J. L., O. L. Madsen, B. Magnusson, and M. Lofgren. *Object-Oriented Environments: The Mjolner Approach.* Prentice Hall. 500 pp. 1992.

Koelmel, Robert L. *Implementing Application Solutions in a Client/Server Environment.* Wiley. 1994.

Kristen, G. *Object Orientation, The KISS-Method.* Addison-Wesley. 1994.

Kurtz, B., S. Woodfield, and D. Embley. *Object-Oriented System Analysis and Specification: A Model Driven Approach.* Prentice Hall. 1992.

Lano, Kevin, and Howard Haughton. *Object-Oriented Specification Case Studies.* Prentice Hall. 300 pp. 1994.

Larson, James A. *Database Directions: From Relational to Distributed, Multimedia and Object-Oriented Database Systems.* Prentice Hall. 304 pp. 1995.

Lee, G. *Object-Oriented GUI Application Development.* Prentice Hall. 1993.

Lenzerini, Maurizio, Daniele Nardi, and Maria Simi. *Inheritance Hierarchies in Knowledge Representation and Programming Languages.* Wiley. 310 pp. 1991.

Lewis, Ted G., Glenn Andert, Paul Calder, Erich Gamma, Wolfgang Pree, Larry Rosenstein, Kurt Schmucker, Andre Weigand, and John Vlissides. *Object-Oriented Application Frameworks.* 352 pp. 1995.

Loomis, Mary E. S. *Object Databases: The Essentials.* Adison-Wesley. 256 pp. 1995.

Lorenze, Mark. *Object-Oriented Software Development: A Practical Approach.* Prentice Hall. 227 pp. 1993.

Lorenze, Mark, and Jeff Kidd. *Object-Oriented Software Metrics.* Prentice Hall. 200 pp. 1994.

Loucopoulos, Pericles. *Conceptual Modeling, Databases, and CASE: An Integrated View of Information Systems Development.* Wiley. 553 pp. 1992.

Love, Tom. *Choosing OO Methods.* Video. SIGS Books. 1993.

Love, Tom. *Design Masters.* Video. SIGS Books. 1993.

MacLean, Roy, and David Gradwell. *Analyzing Systems: Determining Requirements for Object-Oriented Development.* Prentice Hall. 312 pp. 1994.

Marick, Brian. *Craft of Software Testing: Subsystems Testing Including Object-Based and Object-Oriented Testing.* Prentice Hall. 200 pp. 1994.

Martin, James. *Principles of Object-Oriented Analysis and Design*. Prentice Hall. 448 pp. 1993.

Martin, James. *Enterprise Engineering: The Key to Corporate Survival*. Vol. I-IV. Savant Institute. 1994.

Martin and Co. *White Paper: Extending Information Engineering With Rules and Objects*. James Martin and Co. 30 pp. 1993.

Martin, James, and James Odell. *Object-Oriented Analysis and Design*. Prentice Hall. 400 pp. 1992.

Martin, James, and James Odell. *Object-Oriented Methods: A Foundation*. Prentice Hall. 1995.

Martin, James, and James Odell. *Object-Oriented Methods: The Pragmatics*. Prentice Hall. Forthcoming.

McCarthy, Jim. *Dynamics of Software Development*. Microsoft Press. 1995.

McDermid, J. *Software Engineer's Reference Book*. CRC. 1993.

McGregor, John D., and David A. Sykes. *Object-Oriented Software Development: Engineering Software for Reuse*. Van Nostrand Reinhold. 352 pp. 1992.

Meyer, Bertrand. *An Object-Oriented Environment: Principles and Applications*. Prentice Hall. 231 pp. 1994.

Meyer, Bertrand. *Object Success: A Manager's Guide to Object Orientation, Its Impact on the Corporation and Its Use for Reengineering the Software Process*. Prentice Hall. 1995.

Meyer, Bertrand. *Object-Oriented Software Construction*. Prentice Hall. 534 pp. 1988.

Meyer, Bertrand. *Reusable Software: The Base Object-Oriented Component Libraries*. Prentice Hall. 536 pp. 1994.

Meyer, Bertrand. *An Object-Oriented Environment: Principles and Applications.* Prentice Hall. 260 pp. 1994.

Montgomery, Stephen L. *Object-Oriented Information Engineering: Analysis, Design, and Implementation.* Academic Press. 324 pp. 1994.

Morrison, J. Paul. *Flow-Based Programming: A New Approach to Application Development.* Van Nostrand Reinhold. 1994.

Mowbray, Thomas J., and Ron Zahavi. *The Essential CORBA: System Integration Using Distributed Objects.* John Wiley and Sons. 316 pp. 1995.

Object Management Group. *Object Management Architecture Guide,* 2nd Ed. Wiley. 1993.

Object Management Group. *Common Object Services Specification.* Vol. 1. Wiley. 1994.

Object Management Group and X/Open Co., Ltd. *The Common Object Request Broker: Architecture and Specification.* Wiley. 1993.

Olson, Dave. *Exploiting Chaos: Cashing In on the Realities of Software Development.* Van Nostrand Reinhold. 1993.

Ozsu, M. Tamer, Umeshwar Dayal, and Patrick Valduriez Inria. *Distributed Object Management.* Morgan Kaufmann Publishers. 441 pp. 1993.

Page-Jones, Meilir. *What Every Programmer Should Know About Object-Oriented Design.* Dorset House. 370 pp. 1995.

Palsberg, Jens, and Michael I. Schwartzbach. *Object-Oriented Type Systems.* Wiley. 180 pp. 1994.

Parsaye, K., and M. Chignell. *Intelligent Database Tools and Applications: Object-Oriented Hypermedia, Visualization, and Automatic Discovery.* Wiley. 1993.

Parsaye, K., et al. *Intelligent Databases: Object-Oriented, Deductive Hypermedia Technologies*. Wiley. 479 pp. 1989.

Paulk, Mark C., Charles V. Weber, Bill Curtis, and Mary Beth Chrissis. *The Capability Maturity Model: Guidelines for Improving the Software Process*. Addison-Wesley. 1995.

Petroski, Henry. *Design Paradigms: Case Histories of Error and Judgement in Engineering*. Cambridge University Press. 209 pp. 1994.

Potter, C. *Object Databases: An Evaluation and Comparison*. ButlerBloor. 1994.

Pree, Wolfgang. *Design Patterns for Object-Oriented Software Development*. Addison Wesley. 300 pp. 1995.

Rajlich, V., and J. Silva. *Two Object-Oriented Decomposition Methods*. Wayne State University. 1987.

Rao, Bindu Rama. *Object-Oriented Databases: Technology, Applications, and Products*. McGraw-Hill. 1994.

Robertson, James, and Suzanne Robertson. *Complete Systems Analysis: The Workbook, The Textbook, The Answers*. Dorset House. 592 pp. 1994.

Robinson, P. *Hierarchical Object-Oriented Design*. Prentice Hall. 1993.

Rumbaugh, James, M. Blaha, W. Premerlani, F. Eddy, and W. Lorensen. *Object-Oriented Modelling and Design*. Prentice Hall. 528 pp. 1991.

Sayles, J. S., and P. Molchan. *Using the MicroFocus Workbench Development Tools: DB/DC, Client/Server, Object COBOL and More*. Includes disk. Wiley. 1993.

Schur, Stephen. *The Database Factory: Active Database for Enterprise Computing*. Wiley. 286 pp. 1994.

Selic, Bran, G. Gullekson, and P. Ward. *Real-Time Object-Oriented Modeling*. Wiley. 525 pp. 1994.

Sessions, Roger. *Object Persistence: Beyond Object-Oriented Databases*. Prentice Hall. 250 pp. 1995.

Shaw, Mary, and David Garlan. *Software Architecture: Perspectives on an Emerging Discipline*. Prentice Hall. 300 pp. 1996.

Shelton, Robert. *Understanding Business Objects*. Addison-Wesley. Forthcoming title.

Shelton, Robert. *OOBE: The Modeler's Handbook*. Addison-Wesley. Forthcoming title.

Shirazi, Behrooz A., Ali R. Hurson, and Krishna M. Kavi. *Scheduling and Load Balancing in Parallel and Distributed Systems*. IEEE Computer Society Press. 448 pp. March 1995.

Shlaer, S., and S. Mellor. *Object Lifecycles: Modeling the World in States*. Prentice Hall. 200 pp. 1992.

Shlaer, S., and S. Mellor. *Object-Oriented Systems Analysis: Modeling the World in Data*. Prentice Hall. 192 pp. 1988.

SIGS Publications. *Focus on ODBMS*. SIGS Publications.

Simon, Alan, and Tom Wheeler. *Open Client/Server Computing and Middleware*. AP Professional. 272 pp. 1995.

Sims, Oliver. *Business Objects: Delivering Cooperative Objects for Client/Server*. McGraw-Hill. 224 pp. 1994.

Sowa, J. *Principles of Semantic Networks*. Morgan Kaufman Publishers. 1991.

Spurr, Kathy, Paul Layzell, Leslie Jennison, and Neil Richards. *Business Objects: Software Solutions*. Wiley. 233 pp. 1994.

Spurr, Kathy, Paul Layzell, Leslie Jennison, Neil Richards. *Computer Support for Co-operative Work*. Wiley. 246 pp. 1994.

Stark, L., and K. Bowyer. *Generic Object Recognition Using Form and Function.* World Scientific Publishing. 1994.

Starr, Leon. *Practical Guide of Shlaer/Mellor OOA.* Prentice Hall. 300 pp. 1994.

Strauss, Susan H., and Robert G. Ebenau. *Software Inspection Process.* McGraw-Hill. 362 pp. 1994.

Sullo, Gary C. *Object Engineering: Designing Large-Scale Object-Oriented Systems.* Wiley. 325 pp. 1994.

Sully, Philip. *Modelling the World With Objects.* Prentice Hall. 200 pp. 1993.

Takeuchi, Akikazu. *Parallel Logic Programming.* Wiley Series in Parallel Computing. 256 pp. 1993.

Taligent, Inc., and Sean Cotter. *Inside Taligent Technology.* Addison-Wesley. 448 pp. 1995.

Taligent, Inc., and Sean Cotter. *The Power of Frameworks for Windows and OS/2 Developers.* Addison-Wesley. 176 pp. 1995.

Taylor, A., and D. Shafer. *Cooperation: An Object-Oriented Enterprise by NCR.* Prentice Hall. 1993.

Tello, E. R. *Object-Oriented Programming for Artificial Intelligence: A Guide to Tools and System Design.* Addison-Wesley. 1989.

Tichy, Walter F. *Configuration Management.* Trends in Software. 158 pp. 1995.

Tkach, Daniel, and Richard Puttick. *Object Technology in Applications Development.* Benjamin/Cummings. 225 pp. 1994.

Tkach, Daniel, Walter Fang, and Andrew So. *Visual Modeling Technique: Object Technology Using Visual Programming.* Addison-Wesley. 400 pp. 1996.

Tozer, J. *Object-Oriented Enterprise Modeling.* Prentice Hall. 1992.

Treleaven, P. C. *Parallel Computers: Object-Oriented, Functional, Logic.* Wiley Series in Parallel Computing. 297 pp. 1990.

Tsai, Jeffrey J. P., and Steve J. H. Yang. *Monitoring and Debugging of Distributed Real-Time Systems.* 440 pp. January 1995.

Walden, Kim, and Jean-Marc Nerson. *Seamless Object-Oriented Software Architecture.* Prentice Hall. 302 pp. 1994.

Ward, P. T. *Principles of Object-Oriented Development for Real-Time and Information Systems Developers.* Dorset House.

Wayner. *Agents Unleashed: Public Domain Look w/DS.* Academic Press. April 1995.

Weinberg, G. *Rethinking Systems Analysis and Design.* Dorset House. 1988.

Weinberg, Gerard M., and Donald C. Gause. *Exploring Requirements: Quality Before Design.* Dorset House. 320 pp. 1989.

Weinberg, Gerard M. *Quality Software Management.* Vol. 1. *Systems Thinking.* Vol. 2. *First-Order Measurement.* Vol. 3. *Congruent Action.* Dorset House. 1991.

Whitaker, Ken. *Managing Software Maniacs: Finding, Managing, and Rewarding a Winning Development Team.* Wiley. 1994.

White, Iseult. *Using the Booch Method: A Rational Approach.* Benjamin/Cummings. 250 pp. 1994.

White, I. *Rational Rose Essentials: Using the Booch Method.* Benjamin/Cummings. 1995.

Wilkie, George. *Object-OrientedSoftware Engineering: The Professional Developer's Guide.* Institute of Software Engineering. Addison-Wesley. 399 pp. 1993.

Wilkinson, Nancy. *Using CRC Cards: An Informal Approach to Object-Oriented Development.* SIGS Books. 230 pp. 1995.

Winblad, A. L., S. D. Edwards, and D. R. King. *Object-Oriented Software*. Addison Wesley. 291 pp. 1990.

Wirfs-Brock, Rebecca, B. Wilkerson, and Lauren Wiener. *Designing Object-Oriented Software*. Prentice Hall. 368 pp. 1990.

Wong, W. Plug and Play: An Object-Oriented Construction Kit. *M and T*.

Yourdin, Edward. *Object-Oriented Systems Design: An Integrated Approach*. Prentice Hall. 350 pp. 1994.

Yourdin, Edward, and Carl Argila. *Case Studies in Object-Oriented Analysis and Design*. Prentice Hall. 300 pp. 1995.

Yourdin, Edward, Katherine Whitehead, Jim Thurmann, Peter Nevermann, and Karin Oppel. *Mainstream Objects*. Prentice Hall. 300 pp. 1995.

Zeigler, Bernard P. *Object-Oriented Simulation with Hierarchical, Modular Models: Intelligent Agents and Endomorphic Systems*. Academic Press. 395 pp. 1990.

OBJECT-ORIENTED PROGRAMMING

Alger, Jeff. Secrets of the C++ Masters. *AP Professional*. 388 pp. 1995.

Anderson, Arthur E., Jr., and William J. Heinze. *C++ Programming and Fundamental Concepts*. Prentice Hall. 480 pp. 1992.

Anderson, Arthur E., Jr., and William J. Heinze. *Object-Oriented Programming and Design Using C++*. Prentice Hall. 480 pp. 1992.

Ayer, Steve. *Object-Oriented Client/Server Application Development: Using ObjectPal and C++*. McGraw-Hill. 276 pp. 1994.

Bar-David, Tsvi. *Object-Oriented Design for C++*. Prentice Hall. 350 pp. 1993.

Barclay, Kenneth, and Brian Jordan. *C++: Problem Solving and Programming*. Prentice Hall. 500 pp. 1993.

Barkataki, Naba. *Object-Oriented Programming in C++*. SAMS Books. 666 pp. 1993.

Bernstein, Daniel J. *Using Motif With C++*. Prentice Hall. 300 pp. 1995.

Berry, John Thomas. *C++ Programming*. The Waite Group. 408 pp. 1992.

Blaschek, Gunther. *Object-Oriented Programming With Prototypes*. Springer-Verlag. 335 pp. 1994.

Blum, Adam. *Neural Network in C++: An Object-Oriented Framework for Building Connectionist Systems*. Wiley. 214 pp. 1994.

Bourne, J. R. *Object-Oriented Engineering: Building Engineering Systems Using Smalltalk*. Irwin. 1992.

Budd, Timothy. *An Introduction to Object-Oriented Programming*, 2nd Ed. Addison-Wesley. 448 pp. 1996.

Budd, Timothy. *Classic Data Structures in C++*. Addison-Wesley. 576 pp. 1994.

Bugg, Keith E., and Jack Tackett, Jr. *The Visual C++ Construction Kit: A Programmer's Resource*. Wiley. 323 pp. 1994.

Burnett, Margaret, Ed., Adele Goldberg, and Ted Lewqis. *Visual Object-Oriented Programming*. Prentice Hall. 300 pp. 1995.

Burns, A., and A.J. Wellings. *Real-Time Systems and Their Programming Languages*. Addison Wesley. 1990.

Cargill, Tom. *C++ Programming Style*. Addison-Wesley. 233 pp. 1992.

Carroll, Martin D., and Margaret A. Ellis. *Designing and Coding Reuseable C++*. Addison-Wesley. 350 pp. 1995.

Christian, Kaare. *Borland C++: Techniques and Utilities.* Ziff-Davis Press. 568 pp. 1993.

Cline, Marshall P., and Greg A. Lomow. *C++ FAQs: Frequently Asked Questions.* Addison-Wesley. 1995.

Coad, Peter, J. Nicola. *Object-Oriented Programming.* Prentice Hall. 260 pp. 1993.

Cogswell, Jeffery M. *Simple C++: Learn C++ While You Build the Incredible Robodog.* The Waite Group. 252 pp. 1994. (have fun!)

Coplien, J. *Advanced C++ Programming Styles and Idioms.* Addison-Wesley. 1992.

Coplien, James O., and Schmidt, Douglas C., Eds. *Pattern Languages of Program Design.* Addison-Wesley. 1995.

Cox, Brad. A. J. Novobilski. *Object-Oriented Programming: An Evolutionary Approach.* 2nd Ed. Addison-Wesley. 1991.

Cunningham, S. et al. *Computer Graphics Using Object-Oriented Programming.* Wiley. 1992.

Deitel, Harvey M., and Paul J. Deitel. *C++: How to Program.* Prentice Hall. 1008 pp. 1994.

Dewhurst, Stephen C., and Kathy Stark. *Programming in C++.* 2nd Ed. Prentice Hall. 320 pp. 1995.

Eckel, Bruce. *Thinking C++.* Prentice Hall. 500 pp. 1995.

Ege, Raimund. *Programming in an Object-Oriented Environment.* Academic Press. 300 pp. 1992.

Ege, Raimund. *Object-Oriented Programming With C++,* 2nd Ed. AP Professional. 358 pp. 1994.

Ellis, Margaret, and Bjarne Stroustrup. *The Annotated C++ Reference Manual.* Addison-Wesley. 447 pp. 1990.

Flamig, Bryan. *Practical Algorithms in C++*. Book/disk pak. 442 pp. 1995.

Franz, M. *Object-Oriented Programming Featuring Actor*. Scott, Foresman. 1990.

Friedman, F. L., and E. B. Koffman. *Problem Solving, Abstraction, and Design Using C++*. Addison-Wesley. 1994.

Garnfinkel, S., and M. Mahoney. *NeXTSTEP Programming: Step One—Object-Oriented Applications*. Springer-Verlag. 1993.

Goldberg, Adele. *Smalltalk-80: The Interactive Programming Environment*. Addison-Wesley. 516 pp. 1984.

Goldberg, Adele, and D. Robson. *Smalltalk-80: The Language and Its Implementation*. Addison-Wesley. 715 pp. 1983.

Goodwin, M. *Graphical User Interfaces in C++ and Object-Oriented Programming*. MIS. 1991.

Gore, Jacob. *Object Structures: Building Object-Oriented Components with Eiffel*. Addison-Wesley. 352 pp. 1996.

Gorlen, K. E., Sm M. Orlow, and P. S. Plexico. *Data Abstraction and Object-Oriented Programming in C++*. Wiley. 403 pp. 1990.

Gunter, Carl A., and John C. Mitchell. *Theoretical Aspects of Object-Oriented Programming Types, Semantics, and Language Design*. MIT Press. Foundations of Computing Series. 548 pp. 1994.

Gurganus, Keith, and Danny Alexander. *Microsoft Visual C++ Windows Primer*. Horizons Technology. 400 pp. May 1994.

Heinze, William J. *Object-Oriented Programming and Design Using C++*. Prentice Hall. 500 pp. 1995.

Hekmatpour, Sharam. *C++: A Guide for Programmers*. Prentice Hall. 250 pp. 1991.

Henderson, Peter. *Object-Oriented Specification and Design with C++*. McGraw-Hill. 263 pp. 1993.

Henricson, Mats, and Erik Nyquist. *Industrial Strength C++: Rules and Recommendations*. Prentice Hall. 250 pp. 1995.

Holub, Allen I. *C + C++: Programming with Objects in C and C++*. McGraw-Hill. 427 pp. 1992.

Holub, Allen I. *Enough Rope to Shoot Yourself in the Foot: 40 Rules for C++ and C Programming*. McGraw-Hill. 200 pp. 1994.

Horstmann, Cay S. *Mastering Object-Oriented Design in C++*. Wiley. 454 pp. 1995.

IBM. *Introduction to Object-Oriented Programming with IBM Smalltalk*. IBM.

Jamsu, Ku. *Success with C++*. Jamsu Press. 443 pp. 1994.

Jewell, Dave. *Instant Delphi 95 Programming*. WROX Press. 450 pp. February 1995.

Johnsonbaugh, Richard, and Martin Kalin. *Object-Oriented Programming in C++*. Prentice Hall. 600 pp. 1995.

Knolle, N. *Advanced NeXTSTEP Programming: Distributed Objects, OODBMS, Hypermedia, Groupware*. Wiley. 1995.

Korienek, Gene. *An Excursion to ObjectLand*. ObjectLand, Inc. 1994.

Korienek, Gene, and Tom Wrench. *A Quick Trip to ObjectLand: Object-Oriented Programming with Smalltalk/V*. Prentice Hall. 192 pp. 1993.

Krasner, Glenn, Ed. *Smalltalk-80: Bits of History, Words of Advice*. Addison-Wesley. 336 pp. 1983.

Lafore, Robert. *Object-Oriented Programming With Turbo C++*. The Waite Group. 741 pp. 1991.

Lakos, John S. *Large-Scale Software Development in C++*. Addison Wesley. 203 pp. 1995.

Lalonde, Wilf. *Discovering Smalltalk*. Addison-Wesley. 1994.

Lalonde, W., and J. Pugh. *Smalltalk in Action*. Prentice Hall. 1994.

Lalonde, W., and J. Pugh. *Smalltalk V: Practice and Experience*. Prentice Hall. 1993.

Lalonde, W., and J. Pugh. *Inside Smalltalk*. Vols. 1 and 2. Prentice Hall. 1990, 1991.

Lammers, S. *Programmers at Work*. Microsoft Press. 1980.

Lee, Geoff. *Object-Oriented GUI Application Development*. Prentice Hall. 250 pp. 1993.

Lewis, Simon. *The Art and Science of Smalltalk*. Prentice Hall. 250 pp. 1995.

Liberty, Jesse. *Teach Yourself C++*. SAMS Books. 815 pp. 1994.

Lippman, Stanley B. *C++ Primer*. Addison-Wesley. 614 pp. 1992. (not a business oriented primer).

Lippman, Stanley B. *Inside the C++ Object Model*. Addison-Wesley. 250 pp. 1996.

Lorenz, M. *Rapid Software Development with Smalltalk*. Prentice Hall. 1995.

Marchesi, M. *Object-Oriented Programming in Smalltalk/V*. Prentice Hall. 400 pp. 1992.

Mark, Dave. *Learn C++ on the PC. With Semantec Thin C++*. Addison-Wesley. 425 pp. 1994. (a first book).

Mark, Dave. *Learn C++ on the Macintosh. With Semantec Thin C++*. Addison-Wesley. 425 pp. 1994. (a first book).

Martin, Robert C. *Designing Object-Oriented C++ Applications Using the Booch Method*. Prentice Hall. 500 pp. 1995.

Meyer, Bertrand. *EIFFEL: The Language.* Prentice Hall. 300 pp. 1992.

Meyer, B. *Reusable Software: The Base Object-Oriented Component Libraries (OOS).* Prentice Hall. 1994.

Meyers, Scott. *Effective C++: 50 Specific Ways to Improve Your Programs and Designs.* Addison-Wesley. 206 pp. 1992.

Meyers, Scott. *More Effective C++: 35 New Ways to Improve Your Programs and Designs.* Addison-Wesley. 320 pp. 1996.

Microsoft. *Microsoft Windows Guide to Programming, and Microsoft C++ Tutorial.* Microsoft Corp. 1992.

Mitchell, Ed. *Object-Oriented Programming from Square One.* Que. 654 pp. 1993.

Moosenbock, H. *Object-Oriented Programming in Oberon-2.* Springer-Verlag. 1993.

Moss, C. *Prolog ++: The Power of Object-Oriented and Logic Programming.* Addison-Wesley. 1994.

Mullin, M. *Object-Oriented Program Design with Examples in C++.* Addison-Wesley. 303 pp. 1989.

Mullin, M. *Rapid Prototyping for Object-Oriented Systems.* Addison-Wesley. 226 pp. 1990.

Murray, Robert. *C++ Strategies and Tactics.* Addison-Wesley. 282 pp. 1993.

Musser, David R. *STL Tutorial and Reference Guide: C++ Programming with the Standard Template Library.* Addison-Wesley. 496 pp. 1996.

Nghiem, Alex D. *NeXTSTEP Programming: Concepts and Applications.* Prentice Hall. 350 pp. 1993.

Obin, R. *Object Orientation: An Introduction for COBOL Programmers.* Micro Focus Publishing. 1994.

Pappas, Chris H., and William H. Murray. *The Visual C++ Handbook*. McGraw-Hill. 982 pp. 1994.

Papurt, David M. *Inside the Object Model: The Sensible Use of C++*. SIGS Books. 320 pp. 1995.

Parker, Richard O. *Easy Object Programming for Windows Using Microsoft Visual C++*. Prentice Hall. 592 pp. 1995.

Pinson, L., and R. Weiner. *An Introduction to Object-Oriented Programming and Smalltalk*. Addison-Wesley. 273 pp. 1988.

Pinson, L., and R. Weiner, Eds. *Applications of Object-Oriented Programming*. Addison-Wesley. 1990.

Pinson, L., and R. Weiner. *An Introduction to Object-Oriented Programming and C++*. Addison-Wesley. 273 pp. 1988.

Pinson, L., and R. Weiner. *The C++ Workbook*. Addison-Wesley. 349 pp. 1990.

Plauger, P. J. *The Draft Standard C++ Library*. Prentice Hall. 608 pp. 1995.

Pohl, Ira. *Object Oriented Programming Using C++*. Benjamin/Cummings. 496 pp. 1993.

Rao, Bindu Rama. *C++ and the OOP Paradigm*. McGraw-Hill. 188 pp. 1993.

Rudd, Anthony. *C++ Complete: A Reference and Tutorial to the Proposed C++ Standard*. Wiley. 1994.

Saks, Dan. *C++ In Detail*. Prentice Hall/RandD Publications. 300 pp. 1994.

Salde, Stephen. *Object-Oriented LISP*. Prentice Hall. 320 pp. 1995.

Saumyendra, S., and C. P. Korobkin. *C++: Object-Oriented Data Structures*. Springer-Verlag, 1994.

Savic, Dusko. *Object-Oriented Programming with Smalltalk/V*. Ellis Horwood. 1990.

Sayles, J. S., and P. Molochan. *Using the Microfocus Workbench Development Tools: DB/DC, Client/Server, Object COBOL and More*. Wiley. 1993.

Schildt, Herbert. *Mastering C++ and Instructor's Manual*. Glencoe/McMillan/McGraw-Hill. 316 pp. 1994.

Schildt, Herbert. *C++: The Complete Reference*. Glencoe/Macmillan/McGraw-Hill. 784 pp. 1994.

Schildt, Herbert. *C++ From the Ground Up*. Glencoe/Macmillan/McGraw-Hill. 512 pp. 1994.

Sedgewick, Robert. *Algorithms in C++*. Addison-Wesley. 660 pp. 1992.

Sessions, Roger. *Class Construction in C and C++: Object-Oriented Programming*. Prentice Hall. 477 pp. 1992.

Shafer, D., and D. Ritz. *Practical Smalltalk*. Springer-Verlag. 1991.

Shafer, D. *Smalltalk Programming with Windows*. Prima Pubs.

Shammas, Namir Clement. *Secrets of the Visual C++ Masters*. SAMS Publishing. 824 pp. 1993.

Shapiro, J. *A C++ Toolkit*. Prentice Hall. 1991.

Skublics, Suzanne, E. Klimas, D. Thomas, and A. Bradley. *Smalltalk With Style*. Prentice Hall. 160 pp. 1995.

Smith, David N. *Concepts of Object-Oriented Programming:With Examples in SmallTalk*, 2nd Ed. McGraw-Hill. 187 pp. 1991. 320 pp. 1994.

Smith, David. *IBM Smalltalk: The Language*. Benjamin/Cummings. Addison-Wesley. 1994.

Soukup, Jiri. *Taming C++: Pattern Classes and Persistence for Large Projects.* Addison-Wesley. 416 pp. 1995.

Springer, G., and D. P. Friedman. *Scheme and the Art of Programming.* MIT Press/McGraw-Hill. 1989.

Spuler, David. *C++ and C Efficiency.* Prentice Hall. 220 pp. 1993.

Spuler, David. *C and C++ Debugging.* Book and disk. Prentice Hall. 200 pp. 1994.

Sridhar, M. A. *Building Portable C++ Applications with ACL.* Addison-Wesley. 600 pp. 1996.

Staugaard, Andrew C., Jr. *Structuring Techniques: An Introduction to C++.* Prentice Hall. 768 pp. 1994.

Stevens, A. *C++ Database Development.* MIS Press. 1992.

Stroustrup, B. *The C++ Programming Language.* 2nd Ed. Addison-Wesley. 669 pp. 1991.

Stroustrup, B. *The Design and Evolution of C++.* Addison-Wesley. 352 pp. 1994.

Switzer, Robert. *EIFFEL: An Introduction.* Prentice Hall. 176 pp. 1993.

Teale, Steve. *C++ IO Streams Handbook.* Addison-Wesley. 448 pp. 1993.

Thomas, Peter, and Ray Weedon. *Object-Oriented Programming in Eiffel.* Addison-Wesley. 536 pp. 1995.

Tucker, Allen B., et al. *Fundamentals of Computing. I: C++ Edition: Logic, Problem-Solving, Programs.* 2nd Ed. McGraw-Hill. 512 pp. 1994.

Tucker, Allen B., et al. *Fundamentals of Computing. II: C++ Edition: Abstraction, Data Structures, and Large Software Systems.* McGraw-Hill. 512 pp. 1994.

Voss, Greg. *Object-Oriented Programming: An Introduction*. McGraw-Hill. 1994. (not a first book).

Wang, Paul S. *C++ with Object-Oriented Programming*. PWS Publishing Company. 457 pp. 1994.

Watson, Mark. *C++ Power Paradigm*. McGraw-Hill. 218 pp. 1995.

Weiss, Mark Allen. *Data Structures and Algorithm Analysis in C++*. Benjamin/ Cummings. 475 pp. 1994.

Welch, Brent B. *Practical Programming in TCL and TK*. Book/disk. Prentice Hall. 400 pp. 1995.

Welstead, Stephen T. *Neural Network and Fuzzy Logic Applications in C/C++*. Wiley. 493 pp. 1994.

Wernecke, J. *OpenInventor C++ Reference Manual: The Official Reference Document for OpenInventor*. Release 2. Addison-Wesley. 1993.

Wernecke, J. *The Inventor Mentor: Programming Object-Oriented 3D Graphics with OpenInventor*. Release 2. Addison-Wesley. 1993.

Wernecke, J. *The Inventor Toolmaker: Extending OpenInventor*. Release 2. Addison-Wesley. 1993.

Wiener, Richard. *Software Development Using Eiffel: There May Be Life After C++*. Prentice Hall. 350 pp. 1995.

Winder, R. *Developing C++ Software*. Wiley. 400 pp. 1991. (Intro)

Winston, Patrick. *On to C++*. Addison-Wesley. 288 pp. 1994.

Woollard, Rex, Robert Lafore, and Harry Henderson. *Master C++: Let the PC Teach You Object-Oriented Programming*. The Waite Group. 391 pp. 1992.

Young, Douglas A. *Object-Oriented Programming with C++ and OSF/Motif.* Prentice Hall. 434 pp. 1992.

THE LEARNING ORGANIZATION

Bloom, Benjamin. *Taxonomy of Educational Objectives. Handbook I: Cognitive Domain.* David McKay Pubs. 1956.

Bloom, Benjamin, David R. Krathwohl, and Dertram B. Masia. *Taxonomy of Educational Objectives. Handbook II: Affective Domain.* David McKay Pubs. 196 pp. 1964.

Bouldin, Barbara M. *Agents of Change: Managing the Introduction of Automated Tools.* Yourdon Press. 198 pp. 1989.

Capper, P. *Organizational Learning: A Review of Current Theory and Practice in the USA.* Christchurch. NZISRD. 1994.

Constantine, Larry. *Constantine On Peopleware.* Prentice Hall. 1995.

Crum, Thomas F. *The Magic of Conflict: Turning a Lot of Work into a Work of Art.* Simon and Schuster. 1987

Davis, Stanley M. *Future Perfect.* Addison-Wesley. 243 pp. 1987.

Davis, Stanley M., and Jim Botkin. *The Monster Under the Bed: How Business is Mastering the Opportunity of Knowledge for Profit.* Simon and Schuster. 1994.

Davis, Stanley M., and Bill Davidson. *20/20 Vision.* Simon and Schuster. 223 pp. 1991.

Gagne, Robert M. *The Conditions of Learning.* Holt, Rinehart, and Winston. 308 pp. 1965.

Garfield, Charles A.,and Hal Sina Bennett. *Peak Performance: Mental Training Techniques of the World's Greatest Athletes.* Jeremy P. Tarcher, Inc. 1984.

Gross, Ronald. *Peak Learning: A Master Course in Learning How to Learn.* Jeremy P. Tarcher, Inc. 1991.

Houston, Jean. *The Possible Human: A Course in Enhancing Your Physical, Mental, and Creative Abilities.* Jeremy Tarcher, Inc. 1982.

Kelly, Leslie. *The ASTD Technical and Skills Training Handbook.* McGraw-Hill. 512 pp. 1994.

Kline, Peter. *The Everyday Genius: Restoring Children's Natural Joy of Learning—and Yours Too!* Great Ocean Publishers. 1988.

Mager, Robert F. *Preparing Instructional Objectives,* 2nd Ed. Pittman Learning. 136 pp. 1984.

Markova, Dawna. *The Art of the Possible: A Compassionate Approach to Understanding the Way People Think, Learn, and Communicate.* Conari Press. 1991.

Masie, Elliott. *The Computer Training Handbook,* 2nd Ed. Lakewood Publications. 1995.

Ostrander, Shiela, Lynn Schroeder, and Nancy Ostrander. *Superlearning.* Dell Publishing. 1979.

Pedler, Mike, John Burgoyne, and Tom Boydell. T*he Learning Company: A Strategy for Sustainable Development.* McGraw-Hill. 213 pp. 1991.

Pike, Robert W. *Creative Training Techniques Handbook.* Lakewood Books. 1989.

Quinn, James B. *Intelligent Enterprises.* Free Press. 472 pp. 1992.

Reynolds, Angus, and Roberto Araya. *Building Multimedia Performance Support Systems.* McGraw-Hill. 250 pp. 1994.

Rose, Colin. *Accelerated Learning.* Dell Publishing Company. 1985.

Russell, Peter. *The Brain Book.* E. P. Dutton. 1979.

Senge, Peter M. *The Fifth Discipline: The Art and Practice of the Learning Organization.* Doubleday/Currency. 424 pp. 1990.

Senge, Peter M., et al. *The Fifth Discipline Fieldbook: Strategies and Tools for Building a Learning Organization.* Doubleday/Currency. 593 pp. 1994.

Shekerjian, Denise. *Uncommon Genius—How Great Ideas Are Born.* Penguin Books. 1990.

Shuster, D. H., and C. E. Gritton. *Suggestive Accelerative Learning Techniques.* Gordon and Breach Science Publishers. 1985.

Tobin, Daniel R. *Re-educating the Corporation: Foundations for the Learning Organization.* Oliver Wight Publications. 289 pp. 1993.

Van Oeech, Roger. *A Kick in the Seat of the Pants: Using Your Explorer, Artist, Judge, and Warrior to Be More Creative.* Perennial Library. 153 pp. 1986.

Van Oeech, Roger. *A Whack on the Side of the Head: How You Can Be More Creative.* Warner Books. 196 pp. 1990.

Van Oeech, Roger. *Creative Whack Pack: A Pack of Cards Which is a Creative Thinking Workshop in a Box.* Available from Resources for Organizations, Inc.

vos Savant, Marilyn, and Leonore Fleischer. *Brain Building: Exercising Yourself Smarter.* Bantam Books. 1990.

Weinberg, Gerard M., and Gause, Donald C. *Are Your Lights On? How to Figure Out What the Problem Really Is.* Winthrop Publishers. 156 pp. 1982.

Wick, Calhoun W., and Lu Stanton Leon. *The Learning Edge: How Smart Managers and Smart Companies Stay Ahead.* McGraw-Hill. 232 pp. 1993.

Williams, Linda Verlee. *Teaching for the Two-Sided Mind: A Guide to Right Brain/Left Brain Education.* Simon and Schuster. 1983.

Wonder, Jacquelyn, and Priscilla Donovan. *Whole-Brain Thinking: Working from Both Sides of the Brain to Achieve Peak Job Performance.* Ballantine Books. 1984.

INDEX

SIGS BOOKShelf

 SIGS BOOKS

Applying OMT
Kurt W. Derr

Applying OMT is a how-to guide on implementation processes and practical approaches for the popular Object Modeling Technique (OMT) created by James Rumbaugh et al. The book begins by providing a thorough overview of such fundamental concepts as modeling and prototyping and then moves into specific implementation strategies using C++ and Smalltalk. By using a typical business application as a case study, the author illustrates the complete modeling process from start to finish.

1995/557 pages/softcover/ISBN 1-884842-10-0/Order# 2100/$44/£ 34

Dictionary of Object Technology
The Definitive Desk Reference
Donald G. Firesmith and Edward M. Eykholt

Dictionary of Object Technology is the only reference of its kind dedicated to the terminology used in the object technology field. With over 3,000 main entries and over 600 pages, this long-awaited and much needed dictionary is cross-referenced by major components and includes complete appendices specific to industry standards, programming languages, and more.

1995/628 pages/hardcover/ISBN 1-884842-09-7/Order# 2097/$55/£ 42

The Directory of Object Technology
Edited by Dale J. Gaumer

Find exactly what you're looking for, the moment you need it. This is the only complete guide devoted to OO information worldwide.

This book puts the entire OO industry at your fingertips. With over 900 entries, it is the most comprehensive object technology resource guide available. This book will help you define and then identify the products and services you need. Divided into five separate sections, the Directory provides a complete listing of vendors, products, services, and consultants.

1995/softcover/385 pages/ISBN 1-884842-08-9/Order# 6A07-2089/ $69/£ 46

The Object Primer
The Application Developer's Guide to Object-Orientation
Scott W. Ambler

The Object Primer is the ultimate introductory text on object-oriented technology. By reading this book, you'll gain a solid understanding of object-oriented concepts and object oriented analysis techniques.

This book provides all a developer needs to know to get started using object-oriented technology immediately.

November 1995/250 pages/softcover/ISBN 1-884842-17-8/Order# 6A07-2178/$35/£ 28

What Every Software Manager Must Know to Succeed with Object Technology
John Williams

The two biggest causes of failure of object-based projects are the software managers' lack of understanding of the technology and their inability to recognize that OT projects must be managed differently from other projects.

The author shows managers what object technology is and how to manage it effectively. This is the only book that truly addresses the substantive issues that managers must deal with when implementing object technology.

1995/294 pages/softcover/ISBN 1-884842-14-3/Order# 6A07-2143/$35/£ 29

Managing Your Move to Object Technology
Barry McGibbon

Written for software managers, **Managing Your Move to Object Technology** clearly defines and illustrates the management implications associated with the transition to object technology. Although other books may cover the technological benefits of OT, this is one of the few to address the business management issues associated with new technology and the corporate environment. It covers what OT will do to the corporate culture, not simply what it will do for it.

1995/288 pages/softcover/ISBN 1-884842-15-1/Order# 6A07-2151/$35/£ 29

Getting Results with the Object-Oriented Enterprise Model
Thornton Gale and James Eldred

Enterprise modeling is the primary tool used in business reengineering. Historically, the number one problem with enterprise modeling has been the lack of formalism. **Getting Results with the Object-Oriented Enterprise Model** tackles this dilemma head-on and prescribes a formal methodology based on object technology.

1996/650 pages/softcover/ISBN 1-884842-16-X/Order# 216X/$45/£ 30

Reliable Object-Oriented Software Applying Analysis and Design
Ed Seidewitz and Mike Stark

Reliable Object-Oriented Software presents the underlying principles associated with object-orientation and its practical application. More than just another text on methodology, Reliable Object-Oriented Software focuses on the fundamental concepts related to the process of software development and architectural design in order to lay the basis necessary for the development of robust, maintainable, and evolvable software.

November 1995/425 pages/softcover/ISBN 1-884842-18-6 /Order# 2186/$45/£ 30

Using CRC Cards
An Informal Approach to Object-Oriented Development
Nancy M. Wilkinson

Using CRC Cards is a comprehensive introduction to CRC (Class, Responsibility, Collaborator) cards. It includes a description of the cards and how they can be used in interactive sessions to develop an object-oriented model of an application.

In this book, the author draws on her years of project experience to describe how CRC cards can contribute at all stages of the software lifecycle. It includes practical examples of how to utilize CRC cards in projects using either formal or informal development techniques.

1995/243 pages/softcover/ISBN 1-884842-07-0/Order# 2070/$29/£ 19

The Blueprint for Business Objects
Peter Fingar

The Blueprint for Business Objects provides a clear and concise guide to making informed decisions about emerging object technology and to mastering the skills you need to make effective use of the technology in business.

Based on the workplace experiences of several major corporations, The Blueprint for Business Objects presents a framework designed for business and information systems professionals. It provides the reader with a roadmap, starting at the level of initial concepts and moving up to the mastery level.

1996/300 pages/softcover/ISBN 1-884842-20-8/Order# 2208/$39/£ 26

Inside the Object Model
David M. Papurt
Foreword by James J. Odell

Inside the Object Model serves two key functions: it teaches object-oriented analysis and design from first principles and clearly explains C++ mechanisms that implement object-oriented concepts.

Drawing on nearly 10 years of programming and teaching experience, David M. Papurt thoroughly describes the relationship between the basic principles and concerns of object modeling and the C++ programming language. Each chapter uses independent examples to illustrate key concepts described in the text.

1995/540 pages/softcover/ISBN 0-884842-05-4/Order# 2054/$39/£ 26

Object Lessons
Tom Love

In this usable guide to developing and managing OO software projects, well-respected consultant and OOP pioneer Tom Love reveals the absolute do's and don'ts in adopting and managing object-oriented technology. Object Lessons is filled with applicable advice and practical suggestions for large-scale commercial software projects.

If you are an Applications Programmer, Project Leader or Technical Manager making decisions concerning design and management of large-scale commercial object-oriented software, this book is for you.

1994/275 pages/softcover/ISBN 1-9627477-3-4/Order# 7734/$29/£ 19

Using Motif with C++
Daniel J. Bernstein

As more software industry professionals gain experience in both object-oriented development and the graphical user interface (GUI), it is clear that GUI libraries offer several advantages over other kinds of libraries and that they are fun to use.

This book provides step-by-step instructions on how to create a library for programming GUIs in the C++ language. Written for both beginning and experienced Motif programmers, this book is both a tutorial for writing a portable Motif-based interface library in C++ and a reference for enhancing and maintaining such software.

1995/392 pages/softcover/ISBN 0-884842-06-2/Order #2062/$39/£ 26

A Unified Object Modeling Approach
Written and Narrated by Doug Rosenberg

A Unified Object Modeling Approach is the first CD-ROM to present all aspects of a Unified Object Modeling Approach: what it is, how to use it, what role it will play in your future.

On these two interactive, multimedia CDs, renowned trainer and author Doug Rosenberg walks you through the Unified Modeling Approach. Using words and diagrammatic illustrations, he explains the Model's strengths and weaknesses, and how to get the most out of it.

The following examples are resident on both CDs: Video on Demand, Portfolio Management, Onboard Navigation System, and Hospital Information System.

1996/2 Disks/ISBN 1-884842-31-3/Order# 2313/$995/£ 792

Next Generation Computing
The Fast Track to Distributed Business Objects
Peter Fingar, Dennis Read and Jim Stikeleather

The unique format of this white-paper anthology is the fastest and easiest way to learn about the next generation of computing. This book covers major topic areas in succinct yet complete chapters.

Written in a clear and compact style, each of these crisp 30-minute business briefs will be invaluable to your staff, developers, and managers.

1996/300 pages/softcover/ISBN 1-884842-29-1/Order #2291/$50/£ 33

Object-Oriented COBOL
Edmund C. Arranga and Frank P. Coyle

This is the only book that walks COBOL users through the next phase of the COBOL language: Object-Oriented COBOL.

Written by experts in the field of COBOL programming, **Object-Oriented COBOL** teaches you how to integrate OOCOBOL with object-oriented methodologies. It provides explanations and roadmaps that will help you understand, navigate, and successfully integrate analysis and design concepts with enabling OOCOBOL constructs.

May 1996/400 pages/softcover/ISBN 1-884842-43-8/Order# 2348/$39/£ 26

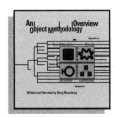

An Object Methodology Overview
Written and Narrated by Doug Rosenberg

An Object Methodology Overview is a CD-ROM designed to help users select the proper methodology for their specific project. This state-of-the-art training tool offers an in-depth comparative overview of various popular OOA and OOD methods and highlights the best application of each methodology. It includes information on seven methodologies: OMT (Rumbaugh), Objectory (Jacobson), The Booch Method, Coad/Yourdon, CRC Responsibility Driven Development (Wirfs-Brock), Martin/Odell, and Shlaer/Mellor.

1995/1 Disk/ISBN 1-884842-30-5/Order# 2305/$995/£ 792

Developing Visual Programming Applications Using Smalltalk
Michael Linderman

Developing Visual Programming Applications Using Smalltalk uses object-oriented visual programming environments to illustrate the concepts of object-oriented software construction. It introduces blueprints as a method to record visual programming applications and includes sample applications using VisualAge, VisualSmalltalk, and VisualWorks.

March 1996/Approx. 300 pages/ISBN 0-884842-28-3/Order # 2283/$39/£ 26

The Smalltalk Developer's Guide to VisualWorks
Tim Howard
Foreword by Adele Goldberg

The Smalltalk Developer's Guide to VisualWorks provides an in-depth analysis of the popular application development tool produced by ParcPlac-Digitalk. Designed to enhance development acumen, this book serves as a guide to using VisualWorks to its full potential.

1995/645 pages/softcover/ISBN 1-884842-11-9/Order# 2119/$45/£ 31

Deploying Distributed Business Software
Ted Lewis

Written in a clear and concise style, this is a must-have guide for technical managers and leaders who want the latest information on distributed computing and client/server computing. Comprehensive yet readable, the book analyzes software technology and standards in database, visual programming, groupware, middleware, remote access, and programming technology.

1996/Approx. 250 pages/softcover/ISBN 1-884842-19-4/Order# 2194/$35/£ 23

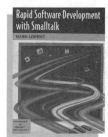

Rapid Software Development with Smalltalk
Mark Lorenz

Rapid Software Development with Smalltalk will help professional software developers write Smalltalk code faster without sacrificing software quality. The book covers the spectrum of OO analysis, design, and implementation techniques and provides a proven process for architecting large software systems.

1995/237 pages/softcover/ISBN 1-884842-12-7/Order# 2127/$29/£ 19

ORDER FORM

❏ **YES!** Please send me the following books:

Title   *Author*

_____

_____

_____

Subtotal: _____
Shipping: $5
Total: _____

❏ Enclosed is my check (payable to SIGS Books).
Please charge my
  ❏ Amex ❏ Visa ❏ Mastercard

Card # _____

Exp. _____

Signature_____

Please add $5 shipping and handling in U.S. ($10 shipping in Canada, $15 everywhere else). NY State residents add appropriate sales tax.
Prices subject to change without notice.

Name _____

Address _____

_____

City/State/Zip_____

Phone *(in case we have trouble with your order)*

_____

SIGS Guarantee: If you are not 100% satisfied with your SIGS book, return it within 15 days for a full refund (less S+H).

Return this form to:

U.S.A. **SIGS Books,71 West 23rd Street**
      New York, NY 10010

U.K. **SIGS Books**
     Brocus House, Parkgate Road,
     Newdigate, Surrey RHS 5AH, England

Germany **SIGS Conferences GmbH**
        Odenthaler Str. 47
        D-51465 Bergisch Gladbach, Germany